AQA

PE

cirencester
co lec

Symond Burrows
Ross Howitt
Sue Young

Editor: Mike Murray

cirencester
college
a beacon college

AQA

PE

Carl Atherton
Symond Burrows
Ross Howitt
Sue Young

Editor: Mike Murray

Approval message from AQA

This textbook has been approved by AQA for use with our qualification. This means that we have checked that it broadly covers the specification and we are satisfied with the overall quality. Full details of our approval process can be found on our website.

We approve textbooks because we know how important it is for teachers and students to have the right resources to support their teaching and learning. However, the publisher is ultimately responsible for the editorial control and quality of this book.

Please note that when teaching the **AQA PE** course, you must refer to AQA's specification as your definitive source of information. While this book has been written to match the specification, it cannot provide complete coverage of every aspect of the course.

A wide range of other useful resources can be found on the relevant subject pages of our website: www.aqa.org.uk.

AN HACHETTE UK COMPANY

The Publishers would like to thank the following for permission to reproduce copyright material.

Photo credits

p.1 © Valentin Casarsa/Digital Vision/Getty Images; **p.16** © ALLSTAR Picture Library/Alamy Stock Photo; **p.17** *t* © Juice Images / Alamy Stock Photo, *b* © epa european pressphoto agency b.v./Alamy Stock Photo; **p.18** © Photographee.eu/Shutterstock; **p.19** © Pete Saloutos/Shutterstock; **p.20** © Back Page Images/REX/Shutterstock; **p.21** *l* © Dean Drobot/Shutterstock, *r* © Valentin Casarsa/Digital Vision/Getty Images; **p.23** *l* © ddp USA/REX/Shutterstock, *r* © Hagen Hopkins/Getty Images; **p.24** © Carmo Correia/Alamy Stock Photo; **p.25** © Friday/Fotolia; **p.26** © avevizavi_com/Shutterstock; **p.27** *tr* © David Cannon/Getty Images, *br* © Carl Atherton; **p.32** *l* © JEKESAI NJIKIZANA/AFP/Getty Images, *r* © Nick Stubbs/Shutterstock; **p.33** © karelnoppe – Shutterstock; **p.34** © Cultura RM/Alamy Stock Photo; **p.36** *r* © Larry C. Lawson/CSM/REX/Shutterstock, *l* © ben radford/Corbis via Getty Images; **p.39** © Sarah Ansell/Alamy Stock Photo; **p.40** © ddp USA/REX/Shutterstock; **p.42** © Jed Leicester/BPI/REX/Shutterstock; **p.43** © wavebreakmedia/Shutterstock; **p.45** © sportpoint/Alamy Stock Photo; **p.46** © Matt McNulty/JMP/REX/Shutterstock; **p.50** *t* © Undrey/Shutterstock, *c* © Martin Novak – 123RF, *b* © Digital Vision/Getty Images; **p.51** *tr* © Julian Finney/Getty Images, *l* © Halfpoint/Shutterstock, *br* © Elenathewise/Fotolia; **p.52** *t* © Jale Ibrak/Fotolia, *ct* © wavebreakmedia/Shutterstock, *cb* © lunamarina/Fotolia, *b* © Yiorgos GR/Shutterstock; **p.53** © aabejon/Getty Images; **p.54** *t* © sportpoint/Alamy Stock Photo, *b* © miljko/Getty Images; **p.55** © Ian Walton/Getty Images; **p.57** © Larry C. Lawson/CSM/REX/Shutterstock; **p.59** © Larry C. Lawson/CSM/REX/Shutterstock; **p.64** © Miguel Tovar/LatinContent/Getty Images; **p.65** *tr* © Miguel Tovar/LatinContent/Getty Images, *cr* © Andy Lyons/Getty Images, *br* © THOMAS LOHNES/AFP/Getty Images; *l* © PCN Photography/Alamy Stock Photo; **p.67** © PeopleImages.com via Getty Images; **p.68** *tl* © IBL/REX/Shutterstock, *tr* © MARTIN BUREAU/AFP/Getty Images, *b* © FRANCISCO LEONG/AFP/Getty Images; **p.72** *l* © GREG BAKER/AFP/Getty Images, *c* © Clive Brunskill/Getty Images, *br* © wavebreakmedia/Shutterstock, *tr* © Xinhua News Agency/REX/Shutterstock; **p.73** *l* © Brian McEntire/iStock/Thinkstock, *c* © ostill/Shutterstock, *r* © Wally Skalij/Los Angeles Times via Getty Images; **p.75** *t* © Michael Steele/Getty Images, *b* © Gilbert Iundt; Jean-Yves Ruszniewski/TempSport/Corbis/VCG via Getty Images; **p.76** © Gilbert Iundt; Jean-Yves Ruszniewski/TempSport/Corbis/VCG via Getty Images); **p.77** *tl* © Steve Russell/Toronto Star via Getty Images, *tr* © Adam Pretty/Getty Images, *b* © GREG BAKER/AFP/Getty Images; **p.80** *l* © GUSTOIMAGES/Science Photo Library/Getty Images, *r* © Tom Jenkins/Getty Images; **p.81** © GUSTOIMAGES/Science Photo Library/Getty Images; **p.85** © karelnoppe – Shutterstock; **p.86** © Popperfoto/Getty Images; **p.87** *l* © Bryn Lennon/Getty Images, *r* © DOMINIC FAVRE/AFP/Getty Images; **p.88** © Jaroslav Uher/Fotolia; **p.89** Photo by DAVID ILIFF. License: CC-BY-SA 3.0/Wikimedia; **p.90** © ZUMA Press, Inc./Alamy Stock Photo; **p.91** © Laszlo Szirtesi/Alamy Stock Photo; **p.93** © Imagestate Media (John Foxx)/F1rst V3071; **p.94** © Nicholas Piccillo/Getty Images; **p.95** © Eoin Mundow/REX/Shutterstock; **p.96** © Kieran Galvin/REX/Shutterstock; **p.97** *t* © Andy Hooper/Daily Mail/REX/Shutterstock, *b* © Image Source/Alamy Stock Photo; **p.98** *t* © Sasha Samardzija/Shutterstock, *b* © Monkey Business Images/Shutterstock; **p.99** © Canadian Press/REX/Shutterstock; **p.101** © Andy Hooper/Andy Hooper Daily Mail/REX/Shutterstock; **p.102** *t* © Sandra Mailer/REX/Shutterstock, *cl* © MANUEL QUEIMADELOS/Alamy Stock Photo, *bl* © Aflo Co. Ltd./Alamy Stock Photo, *br* © TGSPhoto/REX/Shutterstock; **p.105** *t* © aleksey ipatov/Fotolia, *b* © Pixathlon/REX/Shutterstock; **p.107** © Joggie Botma/Fotolia; **p.108** *t* © Detail Nottingham/Alamy Stock Photo, *b* © Colin Underhill/Alamy Stock Photo; **p.109** © Action Plus via Topfoto; **p.111** © ZUMA Press, Inc./Alamy Stock Photo; **p.112** © Pablo Gonzalez Cebrian/Alamy Stock Photo; **p.113** © Bagu Blanco/BPI/REX/Shutterstock; **p.117** © Monkey Business – Fotolia; **p.125** © Xinhua/Alamy Stock Photo; **p.127** © Chris McGrath/Getty Images; **p.128** © Xinhua/Alamy Stock Photo; **p.129** *t* © Glyn Thomas Photography/Alamy Stock Photo, *b* © Sports Field Times/Alamy Stock Photo; **p.130** © INS News Agency Ltd./REX/Shutterstock; **p.131** © David Lichtneker/Alamy Stock Photo; **p.132** © Christopher Ison/Alamy Stock Photo; **p.133** © Getty Images for UK Sport/Getty Images; **p.135** © Roger Sedres/Alamy Stock Photo; **p.136** © BSIP SA/Alamy Stock Photo; **p.138** © Bob Thomas/Getty Images; **p.139** *t* © Classic Image/Alamy Stock Photo, *b* © Bob Thomas/Getty Images; **p.141** © Neil Tingle/Alamy Stock Photo; **p.144** *l* © Daniel Padavona – Shutterstock, *r* © Cultura RM/Alamy Stock Photo; **p.146** © James Marsh/BPI/REX/Shutterstock; **p.147** © Mark Large/Daily Mail/REX/Shutterstock; **p.148** © Man Utd via Getty Images; **p.150** © steevy84 – Fotolia; **p.151** © Tim de Waele/Corbis via Getty Images; **p.152** © Gunnar Berning/Bongarts/Getty Images; **p.154** © John Gichigi/Getty Images; **p.156** *l* © Simon Price/Alamy Stock Photo, *r* © Gary M Prior/Allsport/Getty Images; **p.157** © Manuel Blondeau/Icon Sport via Getty Images; **p.158** © Clive Thompson UK/Alamy Stock Photo; **p.160** © Simon Price/Alamy Stock Photo; **p.162** © Dan Mullan/Getty Images; **p.166** © Startraks Photo/REX/Shutterstock; **p.167** © Chris Condon/PGA TOUR/Getty Images; **p.173** © blas – Fotolia; **p.174** © BSIP, LAURENT/B. HOP AME/SCIENCE PHOTO LIBRARY; **p.176** © JAMES KING-HOLMES/SCIENCE PHOTO LIBRARY; **p.179** Courtesy of Cosmed via Wikipeida Commons (https://creativecommons.org/licenses/by-sa/3.0/deed.en); **p.180** © Iain Masterton/Alamy Stock Photo; **p.181** © phoelixDE/Shutterstock; **p.184** © David Caudery/MacFormat Magazine via Getty Images; **p.185** © Daboost/Shutterstock; **p.186** © John Gaffen 2/Alamy Stock Photo; **p.188** © Maridav/Shutterstock; **p.190** © Alamy Stock Photo; **p.192** © Cultura RM/Alamy Stock Photo; **p.198** © xalanx – 123RF; **p.200** © xalanx – 123RF; **p.201** *t* © Jasper Juinen/Getty Images, *c* © PHILIPPE HUGUEN/AFP/Getty Images, *b* © IAN KINGTON/AFP/Getty Images; **p.202** *t*, *c* & *b* © Cathy Yeulet – 123RF; **p.206** © Fairfax Media/Fairfax Media via Getty Images; **p.222** *tl* © Juriah Mosin – Shutterstock, *tr* © iofoto – Shutterstock, *bl* © Dragon Images – Shutterstock, *br* © Maridav – Shutterstock; **p.223** *l* © IBL/REX/Shutterstock, *c* © MARTIN BUREAU/AFP/Getty Images, *r* © FRANCISCO LEONG/AFP/Getty Images; **p.236** © Nicholas Piccillo/Shutterstock.

Acknowledgements

Every effort has been made to trace all copyright holders, but if any have been inadvertently overlooked, the Publishers will be pleased to make the necessary arrangements at the first opportunity.

Although every effort has been made to ensure that website addresses are correct at time of going to press, Hodder Education cannot be held responsible for the content of any website mentioned in this book. It is sometimes possible to find a relocated web page by typing in the address of the home page for a website in the URL window of your browser.

Hachette UK's policy is to use papers that are natural, renewable and recyclable products and made from wood grown in sustainable forests. The logging and manufacturing processes are expected to conform to the environmental regulations of the country of origin.

Orders: please contact Bookpoint Ltd, 130 Milton Park, Abingdon, Oxon OX14 4SE. Telephone: +44 (0)1235 827720. Fax: +44 (0)1235 400454. Email education@bookpoint.co.uk Lines are open from 9 a.m. to 5 p.m., Monday to Saturday, with a 24-hour message answering service. You can also order through our website: www.hoddereducation.co.uk

ISBN: 978 1 4718 5959 5

Cover photo © Pali Rao/Getty Images

Illustrations by Integra Software Services Pvt. Ltd., Pondicherry, India

Typeset in 11/13pt ITC Berkeley Oldstyle Std Book by Integra Software Services Pvt. Ltd., Pondicherry, India

Printed in Slovenia

A catalogue record for this title is available from the British Library.

Contents

Introduction

This book has been written and designed for the new AQA Physical Education specifications introduced for first teaching in September 2016.

AQA A-level Physical Education 2 covers the content required for **year 2** of AQA A-level Physical Education (7582) for first examination in 2018.

A separate book – **AQA A-level Physical Education 1** – covers the content for **year 1** and AQA AS Physical Education (7581) for first examination in 2017.

To view the full specifications, and examples of assessment material, for AQA AS or AQA A-level Physical Education, please visit AQA's website: www.aqa.org.uk. The content of this book, as well as AQA A-level Physical Education 1, covers the topics in the new specification.

How to use this book

Each chapter has a range of features that have been designed to present the course content in a clear and accessible way, to give you confidence and to support you in your revision and assessment preparation.

Chapter objectives

- Each chapter starts with a clear list of what is to be studied.

CHECK YOUR UNDERSTANDING

These questions have been designed specifically to help check that you have understood different topics.

STUDY HINTS

These are suggestions to help clarify what you should aim to learn.

ACTIVITIES

Activities appear throughout the book and have been designed to help you develop your understanding of various topics.

KEY TERMS

Key terms, in bold in the text, are defined.

PRACTICE QUESTIONS

These are questions to help you get used to the type of questions you may encounter in the exam.

SUMMARY

- These boxes contain summaries of what you have learned in each section.

Book coverage of specification content

A-level content		Covered in
	3.1.1 Applied Anatomy and Physiology	
3.1.1.2	Cardiovascular system	Book 1, chapter 1.1
3.1.1.3	Respiratory system	Book 1, chapter 1.2
3.1.1.4	Neuromuscular system	Book 1, chapter 1.3
3.1.1.5	The musculo-skeletal system and analysis of movement in physical activities	Book 1, chapter 1.4
3.1.1.6	Energy systems	Book 2, chapter 1.1
	3.1.2 Skill Acquisition	
3.1.2.1	Skill, skill continuums and transfer of skills	Book 1, chapter 2.1
3.1.2.2	Impact of skill classification on structure of practice for learning	Book 1, chapter 2.1
3.1.2.3	Principles and theories of learning and performance	Book 1, chapter 2.2
3.1.2.4	Use of guidance and feedback	Book 1, chapter 2.2
3.1.2.5.1	General information processing model	Book 2, chapter 2.1
3.1.2.5.2	Efficiency of information processing	Book 2, chapter 2.1
	3.1.3 Sport and Society	
3.1.3.1.1	Pre-industrial (pre-1780)	Book 1, chapter
3.1.3.1.2	Industrial and post-industrial (1780–1900)	Book 1, chapter
3.1.3.1.3	Post World War II (1950 to present)	Book 1, chapter
3.1.3.2.1	Sociological theory applied to equal opportunities	Book 1, chapter
	3.2.1 Exercise Physiology	
3.2.1.1	Diet and nutrition and their effect on physical activity and performance	Book 1, chapter 4.1
3.2.1.2	Preparation and training methods in relation to maintaining physical activity and performance	Book 1, chapter 4.2
3.2.1.3	Injury prevention and the rehabilitation of injury	Book 2, chapter 3.1
	3.2.2 Biomechanical Movement	
3.2.2.1	Biomechanical principles	Book 1, chapter 5.1
3.2.2.2	Levers	Book 1, chapter 5.1
3.2.2.3	Linear motion	Book 2, chapter 4.1
3.2.2.4	Angular motion	Book 2, chapter 4.2
3.2.2.5	Projectile motion	Book 2, chapter 4.3
3.2.2.6	Fluid mechanics	Book 2, chapter 4.4

A-level content		Covered in
	3.2.3 Sport Psychology	
3.2.3.1.1	Aspects of personality	Book 1, chapter 6.1
3.2.3.1.2	Attitudes	Book 1, chapter 6.1
3.2.3.1.3	Arousal	Book 1, chapter 6.1
3.2.3.1.4	Anxiety	Book 1, chapter 6.2
3.2.3.1.5	Aggression	Book 1, chapter 6.2
3.2.3.1.6	Motivation	Book 1, chapter 6.2
3.2.3.1.7	Achievement motivation theory	Book 2, chapter 5.1
3.2.3.1.8	Social facilitation	Book 1, chapter 6.3
3.2.3.1.9	Group dynamics	Book 1, chapter 6.3
3.2.3.1.10	Importance of goal setting	Book 1, chapter 6.3
3.2.3.1.11	Attribution theory	Book 2, chapter 5.1
3.2.3.1.12	Self-efficacy and confidence	Book 2, chapter 5.1
3.2.3.1.13	Leadership	Book 2, chapter 5.1
3.2.3.1.14	Stress management	Book 2, chapter 5.1
	3.2.4 Sport and society and the role of technology in physical activity and sport	
3.2.4.1	Concepts of physical activity and sport	Book 2, chapter 6.1
3.2.4.2	Development of elite performers in sport	Book 2, chapter 6.2
3.2.4.3	Ethics in sport	Book 2, chapter 6.3
3.2.4.4	Violence in sport	Book 2, chapter 6.4
3.2.4.5	Drugs in sport	Book 2, chapter 6.5
3.2.4.6	Sport and the law	Book 2, chapter 6.6
3.2.4.7	Impact of commercialisation on physical activity and sport and the relationship between sport and the media	Book 2, chapter 6.7
3.2.4.8	The role of technology in physical activity and sport	Book 1, chapter 7.1; Book 2, chapter 6.8

Chapter 1.1
Energy systems

Chapter objectives

After reading this chapter you should be able to:

- Understand the energy continuum to explain which energy system is the main energy provider according to the intensity and duration of exercise.
- Identify the difference in ATP production depending on the fibre type used.
- Identify that during short duration/high intensity exercise the anaerobic glycolytic and ATP–PC systems are used.
- Understand the effects of using the anaerobic glycolytic energy system through an explanation of lactate accumulation, lactate threshold and OBLA.
- Explain oxygen consumption during exercise and recovery through oxygen deficit and EPOC.
- Identify VO_2 max and explain the factors that affect it and how it is measured.
- Explain the measurements of energy expenditure to include indirect calorimetry, lactate sampling, and respiratory exchange ratio.
- Understand the impact of altitude training, high intensity interval training, plyometrics and speed agility quickness on energy systems.

Energy transfer in the body

We need a constant supply of energy so that we can perform everyday tasks such as tissue repair and body growth. The more exercise we do, the more energy is required. When we exercise, the body converts energy from food into energy for muscle contractions in order to produce movements such as running, jumping, catching and throwing. This chapter looks at how this energy is provided in a wide range of physical activities from the 100 metres where energy is required very quickly, to the marathon where energy needs to be provided for a long period of time. The *intensity* and *duration* of an activity play an important role in the way in which energy is provided.

In the body the energy we use for muscle contractions comes from **adenosine triphosphate (ATP)**. It is the only usable form of chemical energy in the body. The energy we derive from the foods that we eat, such as carbohydrates, is broken down to release energy that is used to form ATP. ATP consists of one molecule of adenosine and three (tri) phosphates (Figure 1).

The energy that is stored in ATP is released by breaking down the bonds that hold this compound together (Figure 2).

KEY TERM

Adenosine triphosphate (ATP): The only usable form of energy in the body.

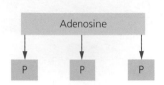

Figure 1 An ATP molecule

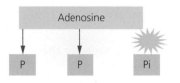

Figure 2 Energy is released when the compound is broken down

STUDY HINT

Intensity and duration of exercise play a key role in deciding which system is used to provide the energy so apply this knowledge and choose the correct system!

KEY TERMS

Glycolysis: A process in which glucose is converted to pyruvate to produce energy.

Sarcoplasm: The fluid that surrounds the nucleus of a muscle fibre and is the site where anaerobic respiration takes place.

Krebs cycle: A series of cyclical chemical reactions that take place using oxygen in the matrix of the mitochondrion.

Enzymes are used to break down compounds and in this instance ATPase is the enzyme used to break down ATP leaving adenosine di-phosphate (ADP) and an inorganic phosphate (Pi) (Figure 3).

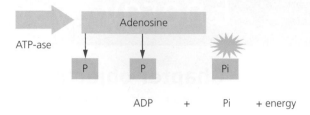

Figure 3 ATP-ase breaks down ATP to produce ADP and Pi

The body has to constantly rebuild ATP by converting the ADP and Pi back into ATP. We can re-synthesise ATP from three different types of chemical reactions in the muscle cells. These chemical reactions are fuelled by either food or a chemical called phosphocreatine which is found in the muscles. The conversion of these fuels into energy takes place through one of three energy systems:

1 The aerobic system
2 The ATP–PC system
3 The anaerobic glycolytic system

Each energy system is suited to a particular type of exercise depending on its intensity and duration, and whether oxygen is present. The higher the intensity of the activity, the more the individual will rely on anaerobic energy production from either the ATP–PC or the anaerobic glycolytic systems. The lower the intensity and the longer the duration of the activity, the more the individual will use the aerobic system.

The aerobic system

When exercise intensity is low and oxygen supply is high, e.g. jogging, the aerobic system is the preferred energy pathway. This system breaks down glucose into carbon dioxide and water which, in the presence of oxygen, is much more efficient. The complete oxidation of glucose can produce up to 38 molecules of ATP. Fats in the form of fatty acids and proteins in the form of amino acids can also be broken down. The products of fat and protein metabolism are reduced to the molecule acetyl coenzyme A that enters the Krebs cycle (stage two of the aerobic system).

How it works to provide energy

The aerobic system has three stages:

1 *Glycolysis.* This first stage is anaerobic so it takes place in the **sarcoplasm** of the muscle cell. Glycolysis is the breakdown of glucose to pyruvic acid and is discussed in more detail later in this chapter. For every molecule of glucose undergoing glycolysis, a net of two molecules of ATP is formed.

Before the pyruvic acid produced in glycolysis can enter the next stage (Krebs cycle) it is oxidised into two acetyl groups and is then carried into Krebs cycle by coenzyme A.

2 *Krebs cycle.* The two acetyl groups diffuse into the matrix of the mitochondria (see Figure 5) and a complex cycle of reactions occurs in a process known as

the Krebs cycle. Here the acetyl groups combine with oxaloacetic acid, forming citric acid. Hydrogen is removed from the citric acid and the rearranged form of citric acid undergoes 'oxidative carboxylation' which simply means that carbon and hydrogen are given off. The carbon forms carbon dioxide which is transported to the lungs and breathed out and the hydrogen is taken to the electron transport chain. The reactions that occur result in the production of two molecules of ATP.

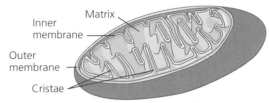

Figure 4 A cross-section through a mitochondrion

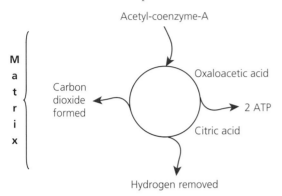

Figure 5 The Krebs cycle

3 *Electron transport chain.* Hydrogen is carried to the electron transport chain by hydrogen carriers. This occurs in the cristae of the mitochondria and the hydrogen splits into hydrogen ions and electrons and they are charged with potential energy. The hydrogen ions are oxidised to form water while the hydrogen electrons provide the energy to re-synthesise ATP. Throughout this process 34 ATP are formed.

Memory tools

Remember **GKE** (**G**et **K**inetic **E**nergy) for the three stages of the aerobic system: **G** stands for glycolysis, **K** stands for Krebs cycle and **E** stands for electron transport chain.

It is important to remember that so far we have only discussed glucose with regards to the aerobic system, but fats in the form of fatty acids and proteins in the form of amino acids are two other energy sources that can be broken down under aerobic conditions to provide energy for us to exercise. (Protein metabolism is not in the specification as its breakdown is very complex and it is not a significant source during exercise but it is important to realise that it can produce some energy.) These can both enter the Krebs cycle and eventually the electron transport chain to produce ATP.

Beta oxidation

Stored fat is broken down into glycerol and free fatty acids for transportation by the blood. These fatty acids then undergo a process called beta oxidation whereby they are converted into acetyl coenzyme A, which is the entry molecule for the Krebs cycle. From this point on, fat metabolism follows the same path as glycogen metabolism. More ATP can be made from one molecule of fatty acids than one molecule of glucose, which is why in long duration, low-intensity exercise, fatty acids will be the predominant energy source but this does depend on the fitness of the performer.

KEY TERM

Electron transport chain: Involves a series of chemical reactions in the cristae of the mitochondria where hydrogen is oxidised to water and 34 ATP are produced.

STUDY HINT

Make sure you have a basic overview of each energy system and can identify when they are used.

Advantages of the aerobic system	Disadvantages of the aerobic system
● More ATP can be produced: 36 ATP. ● There are no fatiguing by-products (carbon dioxide and water). ● Lots of glycogen and triglyceride stores so exercise can last for a long time.	● This is a complicated system so cannot be used straight away. It takes a while for enough oxygen to become available to meet the demands of the activity and ensure glycogen and fatty acids are completely broken down. ● Fatty acid transportation to muscles is low and also requires 15% more oxygen to be broken down than glycogen.

CHECK YOUR UNDERSTANDING

The aerobic system has three stages, one of which is the 'Krebs cycle'. Describe how energy is produced during the 'Krebs cycle'.

ACTIVITY

Test your knowledge and try to draw your own diagram, starting with glucose in the top left-hand corner and ending with the electron transport chain in the bottom right-hand corner. Then add the stages to summarise aerobic energy metabolism.

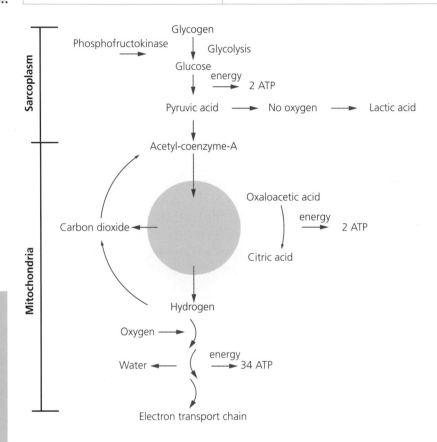

Figure 6 Summary of the aerobic system

The ATP–PC system

This is an energy system using **phosphocreatine (PC)** as its fuel. PC is an energy-rich phosphate compound found in the sarcoplasm of the muscles and can be broken down quickly and easily to release energy to re-synthesise ATP. Its rapid availability is important for a single maximal movement such as the long jump take-off or shot putt. However, the disadvantage of this system is that the stores are limited, as there is only enough PC to last for 5–8 seconds and it can only be replenished during low-intensity work when oxygen is available. Think of Usain Bolt running the 100 m. He does not run the whole 100 m with PC as his only energy source. He slows down in the last 20 m as his stores of PC run out and he has to use a slower method of producing energy.

KEY TERM

Phosphocreatine (PC): An energy-rich phosphate compound found in the sarcoplasm of the muscles.

ACTIVITY

Can you think of four different sporting examples when the ATP–PC system would be the predominant method of re-synthesising ATP?

How it works to provide energy

The ATP–PC system is an **anaerobic** process and re-synthesises ATP when the enzyme creatine kinase detects high levels of ADP. It breaks down the phosphocreatine in the muscles to phosphate and creatine, releasing energy:

Phosphocreatine (PC) $\rightarrow$ phosphate (Pi) + creatine (C) + energy

This energy is then used to convert ADP to ATP in a **coupled reaction**:

Energy $\rightarrow$ + Pi + ADP $\rightarrow$ ATP

For every molecule of PC broken down, there is enough energy released to create one molecule of ATP. This means the system is not very efficient but it does have the advantage of not producing fatiguing by-products and its use is important in delaying the onset of the anaerobic glycolytic system (see later). However, the fact it runs out quickly means that if there is a need to work at a high level of intensity for longer, then we need to find another source of energy to re-synthesise ATP. We can do this using carbohydrates in the anaerobic glycolytic system.

Advantages of the ATP–PC system	Disadvantages of the ATP–PC system
• ATP can be re-synthesised rapidly using the ATP–PC system. • Phosphocreatine stores can be re-synthesised quickly – (30 s = 50% replenishment and 3 mins = 100%). • There are no fatiguing by-products. • It is possible to extend the time the ATP–PC system can be utilised through use of creatine supplementation.	• There is only a limited supply of phosphocreatine in the muscle cell, i.e. it can only last for 10 seconds. • Only one mole of ATP can be re-synthesised for every mole of PC. • PC re-synthesis can only take place in the presence of oxygen (i.e. when the intensity of the exercise is reduced).

The short-term lactate anaerobic system/ anaerobic glycolytic system

The ATP–PC system is an immediate anaerobic system but as already discussed can only supply energy for a short amount of time. The **short-term lactate anaerobic system**, also called the anaerobic glycolytic system, provides energy for high-intensity activity for longer than the ATP–PC system. However, how long this system last depends on the fitness of the individual and how high the exercise intensity is. Working flat out to exhaustion will mean the system will last a much shorter time (hence short-term). This is because the demand for energy is extremely high. In practice an elite athlete who has just run the 400 m in under 45 seconds will not be able to run it again immediately at the same pace! However reduce the intensity a little and the system can last up to 2–3 minutes because the demand for energy is slightly less. The anaerobic glycolytic system re-synthesises ATP from the breakdown of the fuel glucose. This is supplied from the digestion of carbohydrates and is stored in the muscles and liver as glycogen, where it is readily available.

How it works to provide energy

When the PC stores are low, the enzyme glycogen phosphorylase is activated to break down the glycogen into glucose, which is then further broken down to pyruvic acid by the enzyme phosphofructokinase. This process is called anaerobic glycolysis and takes place in the sarcoplasm of the muscle cell where oxygen is not available. Since this is an anaerobic process, the pyruvic acid is then further broken down into lactic acid by the enzyme lactate dehydrogenase (LDH).

During anaerobic glycolysis, energy is released to allow ATP re-synthesis. The net result is two molecules of ATP are produced for one molecule of glucose broken down. (There are actually four moles of ATP produced but two are used to provide energy for glycolysis itself.)

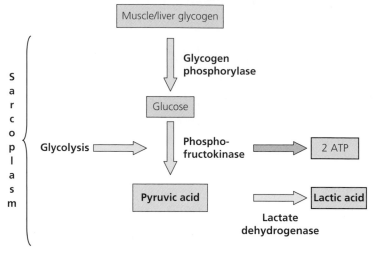

Figure 7 The lactate anaerobic system

STUDY HINT

The key points about glycolysis are:
- Breakdown of glucose to pyruvic acid.
- Produces two molecules of ATP.
- During intense exercise, pyruvic acid converted into lactic acid.

STUDY HINT

The anaerobic glycolytic system is the predominant energy system for high-intensity activity lasting up to 3 minutes.

CHECK YOUR UNDERSTANDING

Name the **main** energy system being used in the 400 m **and** explain how this system provides energy for the working muscles.

KEY TERM

Energy continuum: A term which describes the type of respiration used by physical activities. Whether it is aerobic or anaerobic respiration depends on the intensity and duration of the exercise.

The **anaerobic glycolytic system** provides energy for high-intensity activities lasting up to 3 minutes but can peak at 45 seconds, for example, 400 m.

Advantages of the anaerobic glycolytic system	Disadvantages of the anaerobic glycolytic system
• ATP can be re-synthesised quite quickly due to very few chemical reactions and lasts for longer than the ATP–PC system. • In the presence of oxygen, lactic acid can be converted back into liver glycogen or used as a fuel through oxidation into carbon dioxide and water. • It can be used for a sprint finish (i.e. to produce an extra burst of energy).	• Lactic acid as the by-product! The accumulation of acid in the body denatures enzymes and prevents them increasing the rate at which chemical reactions take place. • Only a small amount of energy can be released from glycogen under anaerobic conditions (5% as opposed to 95% under aerobic conditions).

The energy continuum of physical activity

When we start any exercise, the demand for energy will rise rapidly. The **energy continuum** is a term used to describe which energy system is used for different types of physical activity. It refers to the contribution that the different energy systems make to the production of energy, depending on the intensity and duration of exercise. The three energy systems do not work independently of one another. They all contribute during all types of activities, but one of them will be the predominant energy provider. The *intensity* and *duration* of the activity are the factors that decide which will be the main energy system in use. For some activities it is easy to identify which is the predominant energy system. The 100 m, for example, is a highly explosive, short duration activity which takes an elite performer approximately 10 seconds to complete so the ATP–PC system will be the predominant energy system. In contrast, the marathon is a long duration, lower intensity activity so the aerobic system will be the predominant energy system.

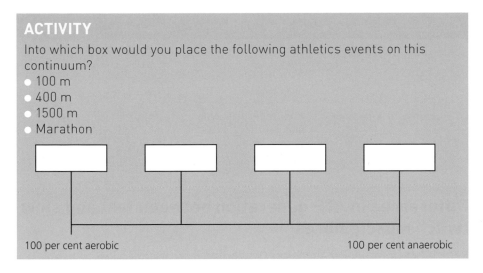

However, in a game where the level of intensity is constantly changing, there will be a mix of all three energy systems as the main energy provider.

ACTIVITY

Copy and complete the table below by giving examples from a game of your choice to show when each of the three energy systems will be used.

NAME OF GAME	ATP–PC SYSTEM	ANAEROBIC GLYCOLYTIC SYSTEM	AEROBIC SYSTEM

The energy continuum is often explained in terms of thresholds. The ATP–PC/anaerobic glycolytic threshold is the point at which the ATP–PC energy system is exhausted and the anaerobic glycolytic system takes over. This is shown in Figure 8 at 10 seconds. The anaerobic glycolytic/ aerobic threshold shown in Figure 8 at 3 minutes is the point at which the anaerobic glycolytic system is exhausted and the aerobic system takes over.

CHECK YOUR UNDERSTANDING

Analyse the relative contributions of different energy systems in a game of basketball compared to a game of football.

Figure 8 The energy continuum related to exercise duration

Duration of performance	Energy supplied by	Example
Less than 10 seconds	ATP–PC	100 m, long jump
8–90 seconds	ATP–PC and anaerobic glycolytic	200 m, 400 m, gymnastic floor routine
90 seconds to 3 minutes	Anaerobic glycolytic and aerobic	1500 m, a round of boxing
3+ minutes	Aerobic	Marathon, cross-country skiing

Differences in ATP generation between fast and slow twitch muscle fibres

Remember from Book 1 that slow twitch fibres are used for low to medium intensity activity so therefore use aerobic respiration as their main method of receiving fuel. Fast twitch fibres are recruited for high intensity activities such as sprinting so anaerobic respiration is their main energy pathway. Anaerobic respiration is much quicker than aerobic respiration but it is an inefficient process, producing only two ATP per glucose molecule, and muscles fatigue much quicker due to the build-up of lactic acid.

The table below summarises the differences in ATP generation between fast and slow twitch fibres:

Slow twitch (Type 1)	Fast twitch (Type 2x)
• The main pathway for ATP production is in the aerobic system. • It produces the maximum amount of ATP available from each glucose molecule (up to 36 ATP). • Production is slow but these fibres are more endurance based so less likely to fatigue.	• The main pathway for ATP production is via the lactate anaerobic energy system (during glycolysis). • ATP production in the absence of oxygen is not efficient – only two ATP produced per glucose molecule. • Production of ATP this way is fast but cannot last for long as these fibres have least resistance to muscle fatigue.

STUDY HINT
Slow twitch fibres are aerobic and fast twitch fibres are anaerobic.

Energy transfer during long duration/ lower intensity exercise

As already mentioned on page 2, exercising for long periods of time at low intensity uses the *aerobic system* as the preferred method for producing energy. This is because at low intensity exercise, the demand for oxygen can easily be met and glucose can be broken down much more efficiently when oxygen is present. Fats are used for energy at low intensity, but as intensity increases, their usage becomes limited because they require more oxygen than glucose in their breakdown. As soon as oxygen supplies become limited, fat use for energy drops.

Oxygen consumption during exercise (maximal and submaximal oxygen deficit)

When we exercise, the body uses oxygen to produce energy (re-synthesise ATP). **Oxygen consumption** is the amount of oxygen we use to produce ATP and is usually referred to as VO_2. At rest we consume oxygen at a

KEY TERMS

Oxygen consumption: The amount of oxygen we use to produce ATP.

VO$_2$ max: The maximum volume of oxygen that can be taken up by the muscles per minute.

Sub-maximal oxygen deficit: When there is not enough oxygen available at the start of exercise to provide all the energy (ATP) aerobically.

rate of approximately 0.3 to 0.4 litres per minute. At the start of exercise we use more oxygen to provide more ATP so our oxygen consumption increases. As the intensity of the exercise increases, so does the amount of oxygen consumed until a performer reaches maximal oxygen consumption which can be 3–6 litres per minute. This is our **VO$_2$ max** which is the maximum volume of oxygen that can be taken up and used by the muscles per minute.

When we start to exercise, insufficient oxygen is distributed to the tissues for all the energy to be provided aerobically. This is because it takes time for the circulatory system to respond to the increase in demand for oxygen and it also takes time for the mitochondria to adjust to the rate of aerobic respiration needed. As a result, energy is provided anaerobically to satisfy the increase in demand for energy until the circulatory system and mitochondria can cope! This is referred to as **sub-maximal oxygen deficit**.

Maximum oxygen deficit is usually referred to as maximal accumulated oxygen deficit or MAOD. It gives an indication for anaerobic capacity. Figure 10 shows the difference between maximal and sub-maximal oxygen deficit. As you can see from the graph, oxygen deficit is bigger during maximal exercise as the performer is short of more oxygen at the start as they have to work more anaerobically. Hence the idea of maximal (accumulated) oxygen deficit.

STUDY HINT

You should aim to be able to label oxygen deficit on a graph.

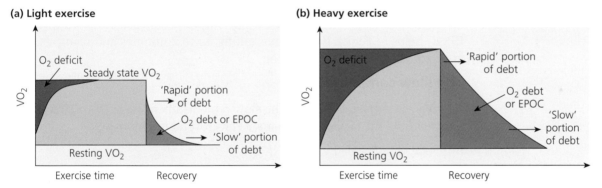

Figure 9 The difference between maximal and sub-maximal oxygen deficit

Oxygen consumption during recovery (excess post-exercise oxygen consumption EPOC)

Recovery involves returning the body to its pre-exercise state. When a performer finishes exercise, oxygen consumption still remains quite high in comparison with oxygen consumption at rest. This is because extra oxygen needs to be taken in and used to try to help the performer recover. This breathlessness after exercise is often referred to as **excess post-exercise oxygen consumption (EPOC)**.

There are two main components to EPOC.

The fast component

The fast replenishment stage uses the extra oxygen that is taken in during recovery to restore ATP and phosphocreatine and to re-saturate myoglobin with oxygen. Complete restoration of phosphocreatine takes up to 3 minutes but 50 per cent of stores can be replenished after only 30 seconds, during which time approximately 3 litres of oxygen are consumed.

KEY TERM

EPOC: The amount of oxygen consumed during recovery above that which would have been consumed at rest during the same time.

STUDY HINT

Questions have often asked why a performer is breathless after exercise. Remember this breathlessness is EPOC!

KEY TERM

Fast component: The restoration of ATP and phosphocreatine stores and the re-saturation of myoglobin with oxygen.

ACTIVITY

This knowledge of recovery times for the replenishment of ATP and phosphocreatine is useful for a coach or performer who will want to prevent the use of the lactic acid system with its fatiguing by-product. Can you think of an example in a team game where it is possible to delay play for up to a minute to allow for significant restoration of PC stores?

CHECK YOUR UNDERSTANDING

Use the graph below to work out how much PC has been restored at 1 minute.

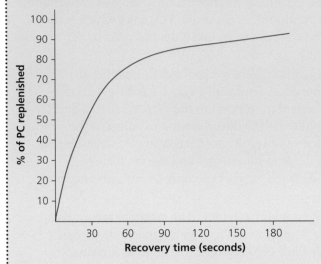

The graph above shows the relationship between recovery time and the replenishment of muscle phosphagens after exercise.

Myoglobin has a high affinity for oxygen. It stores oxygen in the sarcoplasm that has diffused from the haemoglobin in the blood. After exercise, oxygen stores in the myoglobin are limited. The surplus of oxygen supplied through EPOC helps replenish these stores, taking up to 2 minutes and using approximately 0.5 litres of oxygen.

The slow component

The oxygen consumed during the slow replenishment stage (sometimes referred to as the lactacid component) has several functions:

Removal of lactic acid

Lactic acid accumulates during exercise, and during recovery it needs to be removed. Full recovery may take up to an hour or longer, depending on the intensity and duration of the exercise. Lactic acid can be removed in the following ways:

- When oxygen is present, lactic acid can be converted back into pyruvate and oxidised into carbon dioxide and water in the inactive muscles and organs. This can then be used by the muscles as an energy source.
- Transported in the blood to the liver where it is converted to blood glucose and glycogen (**the Cori cycle**).
- Converted into protein.
- Removed in sweat and urine.

The majority of lactic acid can be oxidised in mitochondria so performing a cool-down can accelerate its removal. This is because exercise keeps the metabolic rate of muscles high and keeps capillaries dilated, which means oxygen can be flushed through, removing the accumulated lactic acid. The slow replenishment stage of recovery begins as soon as lactic acid appears in the muscle cell, and will continue using breathed oxygen until recovery is complete. This can take up to 5–6 litres of oxygen in the first half hour of recovery, removing up to 50 per cent of the lactic acid.

KEY TERM

The Cori cycle: The process where lactic acid is transported in the blood to the liver where it is converted to blood glucose and glycogen.

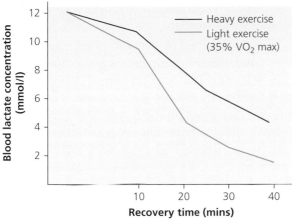

Figure 10 Blood lactate removal for different intensities of exercise

ACTIVITY

Can you put the following labels in the correct position?
- Oxygen consumption during exercise
- Oxygen deficit
- Fast replenishment stage
- Slow replenishment stage

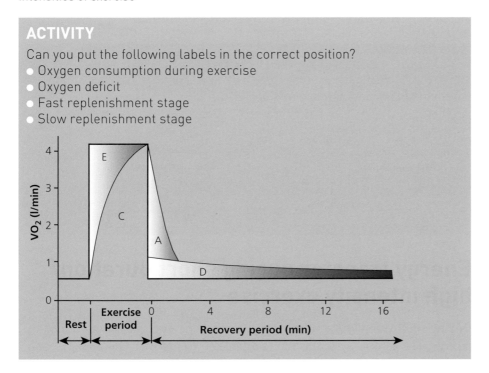

Maintenance of breathing and heart rates

Maintaining breathing and heart rates requires extra oxygen to provide the energy needed for the respiratory and heart muscles. This assists recovery as the extra oxygen is used to replenish ATP and phosphocreatine stores, re-saturate the myoglobin and remove lactic acid, therefore returning the body back to its pre-exercise state.

Glycogen replenishment

Glycogen is the main energy provider and, as it is the fuel for both the aerobic system and anaerobic glycolytic system, it will be depleted during exercise. The replacement of glycogen stores depends on the type of exercise undertaken and when and how much carbohydrate is consumed following exercise. It may take several days to complete the restoration of glycogen after a marathon, but in less than an hour after high duration, short intensity exercise, a significant amount of glycogen can be restored as lactic acid and is converted back to blood glucose and glycogen in the liver via the Cori cycle. Eating a high carbohydrate meal will accelerate glycogen restoration, as will eating within one hour following exercise.

There are two nutritional windows for optimal recovery after exercise. The first is 30 minutes after exercise where both carbohydrates and proteins should be consumed in a 3:1 or 4:1 ratio. The combination of carbohydrates and protein helps the body to re-synthesise muscle glycogen much more efficiently than just consuming carbohydrates on their own. Many elite athletes drink chocolate milkshake after exercise. The second nutritional window is 1–3 hours after exercise and a meal high in protein, carbohydrate and healthy fat should be consumed.

Increase in body temperature

When temperature remains high, respiratory rates will also remain high and this will help the performer take in more oxygen during recovery. However, extra oxygen (from the slow component of EPOC) is needed to fuel this increase in temperature until the body returns to normal.

CHECK YOUR UNDERSTANDING

At the end of an 800 m swim, the swimmer will be out of breath and will continue to breathe heavily even though they have come to a complete rest. Explain why this breathlessness occurs.

ACTIVITY

Copy the following diagram and see if you can summarise the functions of the fast and slow components of EPOC:

EPOC

Fast component:
•
•

Slow component:
•
•
•

Energy transfer during short duration/high intensity exercise

During short duration/high intensity exercise, energy has to be produced rapidly. The aerobic system is too complicated to produce energy rapidly so the body needs to rely on anaerobic respiration, using the ATP–PC system and the anaerobic glycolytic system. However, these systems cannot produce energy for long periods of time. As we have already discussed, the ATP–PC system can only produce energy for high intensity activities lasting up to 10 seconds. The anaerobic glycolytic energy system can last for longer (up to 3 minutes) but it depends on what intensity the performer is working at for how long it lasts. Think of a 400-metre runner – they will complete their event in 45–60 seconds using mainly the anaerobic glycolytic system. At the end of their race, they will be exhausted because of the build-up of lactic acid and certainly unable to run another race without a long period of recovery. Compare this with an 800-metre runner – they will not be running as fast, but will still be mainly using their anaerobic glycolytic energy system, but because the demand for energy is less, they can run using that system for longer.

Lactate accumulation

Lactate and lactic acid are not the same thing but the terms are often used interchangeably. Using the anaerobic glycolytic system produces the by-product lactic acid as a result of glycolysis. The higher the intensity of exercise, the more lactic acid is produced. This lactic acid quickly breaks down, releasing hydrogen ions (H+). The remaining compound then combines with sodium ions (Na+) or potassium ions (K+) to form the salt lactate. As lactate accumulates in the muscles, more hydrogen ions are present and it is actually the presence of hydrogen ions that increases acidity. This slows down enzyme activity which affects the breakdown of glycogen causing muscle fatigue. The lactate produced in the muscles diffuses into the blood and blood lactate can be measured.

The lactate threshold and onset blood lactate accumulation (OBLA)

As exercise intensity increases, the body moves from working aerobically to anaerobically. This crossing of the aerobic/anaerobic threshold is also known as the **lactate threshold** and is the point at which lactic acid rapidly accumulates in the blood (increase by 2 millimoles per litre of blood above resting levels). We are constantly producing small amounts of lactate due to red blood cell activity when working at low intensity but the levels are low and the body deals with these effectively. However, as the intensity of the exercise increases and the body is unable to produce enough oxygen to break down lactate, the levels of lactate build up/accumulate and this is known as **OBLA** (onset blood lactate accumulation).

OBLA and lactate threshold are simply different ways of measuring the same thing. OBLA is the older term and lactate threshold is a more recent American term. At rest, approximately 1–2 millimoles per litre of lactate can be found in the blood. However, during intense exercise, levels of lactate will rise dramatically and as it starts to accumulate, OBLA occurs. This is usually when the concentration of lactate is around 4mmol per litre. Measuring OBLA gives an indication of endurance capacity. Some individuals can work at higher levels of intensity than others before OBLA and can delay when the threshold occurs.

Lactate threshold is expressed as a percentage of VO_2 max. As fitness increases, the lactate threshold becomes delayed. Average performers may have a lactate threshold that is 50–60 per cent of their VO_2 max, whereas elite performers may have a lactate threshold that is 70, 80 or even 90 per cent of their VO_2 max. Training has a limited effect on VO_2 max because VO_2 max is largely genetically determined. The big difference in performance comes from the delayed lactate threshold. When we exercise we tend to work at or just below our lactate threshold – in other words, at a level where fatigue (caused by lactate) is not going to cause our performance to deteriorate. The fitter we are, the higher our lactate threshold as a percentage of our VO_2 max and hence the harder we can work.

STUDY HINT

Lactic acid or lactate?
Lactic acid is $C_3H_6O_3$. When lactic acid releases H^+, the remaining bit of the acid joins with Na^+ to form a salt – lactate. These terms are often used interchangeably because glycolysis produces lactic acid which immediately dissociates and lactate is formed.

KEY TERMS

Lactate threshold: The point during exercise at which lactic acid quickly accumulates in the blood.

OBLA: The point when lactate levels go above 4 millimoles per litre.

The graphs show changes in oxygen uptake (VO$_2$) and lactate levels of an average performer and an elite performer. There are noticeable differences between the two graphs. Can you find them and explain why?

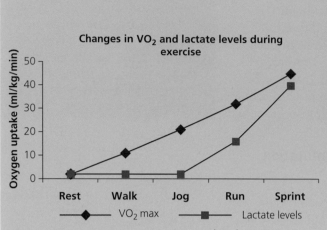

Figure 11a Changes in oxygen uptake (VO$_2$) and lactate levels of an average performer

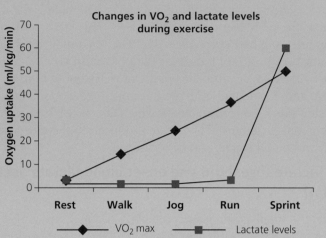

Figure 11b Changes in oxygen uptake (VO$_2$) and lactate levels of an elite performer

The multi-stage fitness test is a good practical example to illustrate OBLA. As the test becomes more and more demanding because of the reduced time to complete each shuttle, the performer eventually reaches a point where energy cannot be provided aerobically. This means the performer has to use the anaerobic systems to re-synthesise ATP. Levels of lactate produced in the muscles increase until eventually muscle fatigue occurs and the performer slows down or is no longer able to keep up with the bleep.

CHECK YOUR UNDERSTANDING

As part of their training programme, an elite 400 m runner uses interval training. The table below shows their time for six 400 m sprints, where each sprint was followed by a 60-second recovery period:

First run	Second run	Third run	Fourth run	Fifth run	Sixth run
52.4 s	52.8 s	53.1 s	53.4 s	53.6 s	54.2 s

During this training session, the athlete would have reached their lactate threshold. What do you understand by the term lactate threshold and how would the majority of the athlete's energy be supplied during the periods of activity?

Factors affecting the rate of lactate accumulation

Exercise intensity

The higher the exercise intensity, the greater the demand for energy (ATP) and the faster OBLA occurs. Fast twitch fibres are used for high intensity exercise and can only maintain their workload with the use of glycogen as a fuel. When glycogen is broken down in the absence of oxygen into pyruvic acid, lactic acid is formed.

Muscle fibre type

Slow twitch fibres produce less lactate than fast twitch fibres. When slow twitch fibres use glycogen as a fuel, due to the presence of oxygen, the glycogen can be broken down much more effectively and with little lactate production.

Rate of blood lactate removal

If the rate of lactate removal is equivalent to the rate of lactate production, then the concentration of blood lactate remains constant. If lactate production increases, then lactate will start to accumulate in the blood until OBLA is reached. (How lactate is removed will be discussed later in this chapter.)

The respiratory exchange ratio

This is described in more detail later on in this chapter. It is the ratio of carbon dioxide produced compared to oxygen consumed. As this ratio has a value close to 1:0, glycogen becomes the preferred fuel and there is a greater chance of the accumulation of lactate.

Fitness of the performer

A person who trains regularly will be in a better position to delay OBLA as adaptations occur to trained muscles. Increased numbers of mitochondria and myoglobin, together with an increase in capillary density, improve the capacity for aerobic respiration and therefore avoid the use of the lactate anaerobic system.

Lactate-producing capacity and sprint/power performance

Elite sprinters and power athletes will have a much better anaerobic endurance than non-elite sprinters. This is because their body has adapted to cope with higher levels of lactate. In addition, through a process called **buffering**, they will be able to increase the rate of lactate removal and consequently have lower lactate levels. Buffering works rather like a sponge mopping up water but instead the sponge soaks up the lactate. This means the athletes will be able to work at higher intensities for longer before fatigue sets in. As well as being able to tolerate higher levels of lactate, the trained status of their working muscles will lead to adaptive responses. There will be a greater number and size of mitochondria and the associated oxidative enzymes, increased capillary density and more myoglobin.

KEY TERM

Buffering: A process which aids the removal of lactate and maintains acidity levels in the blood and muscle.

Factors affecting VO$_2$ max/aerobic power

VO$_2$ max is the maximum volume of oxygen that can be taken up and used by the muscles per minute. An individual's VO$_2$ max will determine endurance performance in sport. Average VO$_2$ max for an A-level student is around 45–55 ml/kg/min for males and 35–44 ml/kg/min for females. Three-time Tour de France winner Greg LeMond has a VO$_2$ max of 92.5 ml/kg/min. This means he has more oxygen going to the muscles and can utilise this oxygen to provide energy to enable a high rate of exercise. One of the reasons why this is possible is that his body has adapted as a result of his training to take up and use more oxygen. These are physiological factors that have increased his VO$_2$ max but there also other more general factors that can affect VO$_2$ max.

CHECK YOUR UNDERSTANDING
State and explain three structural/physiological characteristics that can lead to an improvement in VO$_2$ max.

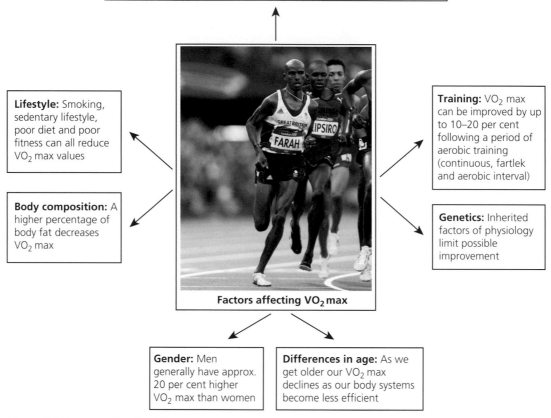

Physiological
- Increased maximum cardiac output
- Increased stroke volume/ejection fraction/cardiac hypertrophy
- Greater heart rate range
- Less oxygen being used for heart muscle so more available to muscles
- Increased levels of haemoglobin and red blood cell count
- Increased stores of glycogen and triglycerides
- Increased myoglobin content
- Increased capillarisation around the muscles
- Increased number and size of mitochondria
- Increased surface area of alveoli
- Increased lactate tolerance

Lifestyle: Smoking, sedentary lifestyle, poor diet and poor fitness can all reduce VO_2 max values

Body composition: A higher percentage of body fat decreases VO_2 max

Training: VO_2 max can be improved by up to 10–20 per cent following a period of aerobic training (continuous, fartlek and aerobic interval)

Genetics: Inherited factors of physiology limit possible improvement

Factors affecting VO_2 max

Gender: Men generally have approx. 20 per cent higher VO_2 max than women

Differences in age: As we get older our VO_2 max declines as our body systems become less efficient

Figure 12 Factors affecting VO_2 max

Measurements of energy expenditure

Measuring how much energy an athlete uses gives an indication of the intensity of the exercise that is being performed and can be used to identify levels of fitness. It will highlight the dietary requirements needed for the performer to recover and replace the energy they have used, as well as providing feedback on the effectiveness of a training programme. The following measurements are all used by elite performers to gauge energy expenditure.

Indirect calorimetry

Indirect calorimetry is discussed in Chapter 6.8 The role of technology in physical activity and sport, but the emphasis is on testing and recording. You also need to know how indirect calorimetry works as a method of measuring energy expenditure. It is a technique that provides an accurate estimate of energy expenditure through gas exchange. It measures how much carbon dioxide is produced and how much oxygen is consumed at both rest and during aerobic exercise. Calculating the gas volumes also

KEY TERMS

Calorimetry: The calculation of heat in physical changes and chemical reactions.

Indirect calorimetry: Measures the production of CO_2 and/or the consumption of O_2.

enables us to find out the main substrate being used (fat or carbohydrate). The accuracy of this test is very reliable as it gives a precise calculation of VO_2 (oxygen consumption) and VO_2 max.

Figure 13 Indirect calorimetry

Lactate sampling

Blood lactate measurements are used amongst elite performers in sports such as running, swimming and rowing to monitor training and predict performance. Lactate sampling involves taking a tiny blood sample and a handheld device analyses the blood and indicates how much lactate is present. This is an accurate and objective measure of the level of lactate in the blood. It can also be used as a means of measuring exercise intensity. The higher the exercise intensity at which the lactate threshold occurs, the fitter the athlete is considered to be. Lactate testing can give an idea of level of fitness. It will allow the performer to select relevant training zones, whether they are expressed in terms of heart rate (beats per minute) or power (watts), in order to get the desired training effect. Regular lactate testing provides a comparison from which the coach and performer can see whether improvement has occurred. If test results show a lower lactate level at the same intensity of exercise, this should indicate that the performer has an increase in peak speed/power, increased time to exhaustion, improved recovery heart rate and finally a higher lactate threshold.

Figure 14 Measuring blood lactate levels

VO$_2$ max test

There are many tests that can evaluate VO$_2$ max and you probably tried a few when you studied for your PE GCSE. The most common one is the multi-stage fitness test or more commonly called the 'bleep' test. Here the individual performs a 20-metre progressive shuttle run to a bleep, until they reach complete exhaustion. The level that is reached can be compared with a standard results table. Other tests include the Harvard step test and Cooper's 12-minute run, but all of these only give an indication or prediction of VO$_2$ max. A sports science laboratory can produce much more valid and reliable results using **direct gas analysis**.

Tests using this method involve increasing intensities on a treadmill, **cycle ergometer** or rowing machine. Tests on a treadmill are accurate methods carried out under laboratory conditions. An individual runs on a treadmill to exhaustion while the air that is expired is calculated by computer software. The volume and concentration of oxygen in the expired air is then measured and compared with the percentage of oxygen that is in atmospheric air to see how much oxygen has been used during the task.

Respiratory exchange ratio (RER)

The **respiratory exchange ratio (RER)** is the ratio of carbon dioxide produced *compared* to oxygen consumed and is used as a measure of exercise intensity. It provides information about fuel usage during exercise. Energy sources such as carbohydrates, fat and protein can all be oxidised to produce energy. For a certain volume of oxygen, the energy released will depend upon the energy source. Calculating the respiratory exchange ratio (RER) will determine which of these energy sources is being oxidised and hence whether the performer is working aerobically or anaerobically. The RER ratio is calculated using the following equation:

$$RER = \frac{\text{Carbon dioxide expired per minute (VCO}_2)}{\text{Oxygen consumed per minute (VO}_2)}$$

- A RER value close to 1 = performer using carbohydrates
- A RER value of approx. 0.7 = performer using fats
- A RER value greater than 1 = anaerobic respiration so more CO$_2$ being produced than O$_2$ consumed

Here is a table to show the percentage of fats and carbohydrates used from the RER:

Ratio	Percentage fat
0.70	100
0.75	83
0.80	67
0.85	50
0.90	33
0.95	17
1.00	0

Measuring the respiratory exchange ratio requires an athlete to be attached to a gas analyser while on a treadmill or cycle ergometer so that accurate

KEY TERMS

Direct gas analysis: Measures the concentration of oxygen that is inspired and the concentration of carbon dioxide that is expired.

Cycle ergometer: A stationary bike that measures how much work is being performed.

Figure 15 A treadmill test

KEY TERM

The respiratory exchange ratio (RER): The ratio of carbon dioxide produced compared to oxygen consumed.

readings can be taken on the amount of carbon dioxide produced compared to oxygen consumed.

Impact of specialist training methods on energy systems

Altitude training

At both sea level and altitude the percentage of oxygen within air remains the same. However, the partial pressure of O_2 drops as altitude increases, usually by up to 50 per cent at an altitude of 5000 m. Therefore there is a reduction in the diffusion gradient of oxygen between the air and the lungs and between the alveoli and blood. This means that not as much oxygen diffuses into the blood so haemoglobin is not as fully saturated with oxygen, which results in the lower O_2 carrying capacity of the blood. As less O_2 is therefore delivered to the working muscles, there is a reduction in aerobic performance and VO_2 max and a quicker onset of anaerobic respiration.

However, elite endurance athletes choose to train at altitude (preferably over 2500 m above sea level) for several weeks as there are lots of benefits to performance. Altitude training is also done to acclimatise players to the lower level of oxygen available in the atmosphere. The England squad flew out to Austria in May 2010 to train at two altitude camps before they headed to South Africa for the World Cup even though two of their opening three Group C matches were played at sea level.

However, altitude training does have its disadvantages. When the athlete first experiences altitude, it is very difficult to train at the same intensity due to the reduction in the partial pressure of oxygen so there can be a loss of fitness or detraining. In addition altitude sickness is a possibility, which can have a detrimental effect on a training programme. The benefits gained from altitude training can be lost very quickly on return to sea level and the body can only produce a limited amount of EPO. Living away from home can also result in psychological problems such as homesickness.

Figure 16 Altitude training

CHECK YOUR UNDERSTANDING
The results from the respiratory exchange ratio (RER) can be used to check that training is effective. Can you explain the term respiratory exchange ratio?

KEY TERM

Altitude training: Usually done at 2500 m+ above sea level where the partial pressure of oxygen is lower.

High intensity interval training (HIIT)

Interval training can be used for both aerobic and anaerobic training. It is a form of training in which periods of work are interspersed with recovery periods. Four main variables are used to ensure the training is specific:

- The duration of the work interval.
- The intensity or speed of the work interval.
- The duration of the recovery interval.
- The number of work intervals and recovery intervals.

High intensity interval training (HIIT) involves short intervals of maximum intensity exercise followed by a recovery interval of low to moderate intensity exercise, for example 4 minutes of intense exercise made up of 8 × 20 seconds maximum effort work intervals, each followed by a 10-second recovery interval. The work interval is anaerobic and the recovery aerobic. Pushing your body to the max during the work interval increases the amount of calories you burn as it takes longer to recover from each work session. HIIT therefore improves fat burning potential, glucose metabolism and both aerobic and anaerobic endurance. There are many variations of HIIT that involve:

- different numbers of high intensity work intervals and low intensity recovery intervals
- different lengths of time for the work and recovery intervals
- different exercise intensity for the recovery interval (low or medium intensity).

Plyometrics

If a greater anaerobic capacity is crucial to successful performance, for example, speed for the 100 m and power for the long jump or rebounding in basketball, then **plyometrics** is one method of strength training that improves these fitness components. Plyometrics training involves high intensity explosive activities such as hopping, bounding, depth jumping and medicine ball work and uses fast twitch fibres. It works on the concept that muscles can generate more force if they have previously been stretched. Think of an elastic band – the more it can be stretched, the greater the force that follows. So, if an eccentric contraction occurs first (which stretches the muscle) followed by a concentric contraction, the force generated can be increased dramatically. This is frequently called the stretch shortening cycle and consists of three phases:

- Eccentric phase or pre-loading/pre-stretching phase. On landing, the muscle performs an eccentric contraction where it lengthens under tension.
- Amortisation phase is next and is the time between the eccentric and concentric muscle contractions. This time needs to be as short as possible so the energy stored from the eccentric contraction is not lost. When an eccentric contraction occurs, a lot of the energy required to stretch or lengthen the muscle is lost as heat but some of the energy can be stored and is then available for the subsequent concentric contraction.
- Concentric or muscle contraction phase uses the stored energy to increase the force of the contraction.

Plyometrics: Involves repeated rapid stretching and contracting of muscles to increase muscle power.

Figure 17 Plyometric training

Memory tools

Remember **PAM** for the three phases: **P** for pre-loading/or pre-stretching, **A** for amortisation and **M** for muscle contraction!

An example of plyometric exercises to develop leg strength involves a line of benches, boxes and hurdles where the performer has to jump, hop and leap from one to the other. Recovery occurs as you walk back to the start line and repeat the exercise.

To develop arm strength, press-ups could be performed with mid-air claps or through throwing and catching a medicine ball. In these exercises, the triceps muscle experiences a quick stretch on the landing for the press-up and on catching the heavy medicine ball. This is followed by a concentric muscle action as the triceps extends the arms in the upward phase of the press-up or the execution of the throw.

Speed, agility, quickness (SAQ)

Speed refers to how fast a person can move over a specified distance or how quickly a body part can be put into motion. It is important in all sports but even more effective in games when combined with agility, which is the ability to move and position the body quickly and effectively while under control. Good agility requires a combination of speed, co-ordination, balance and flexibility. These are all important fitness components for a games player and can be developed through SAQ training. This is a type of training that aims to improve multi-directional movement through developing the neuromuscular system. Drills include zig zag runs and foot ladders and often a ball is introduced so passing occurs throughout the drill, making it more sport-specific. As SAQ training uses activities performed with maximum force at high speed, energy is provided anaerobically.

Figure 18 Arm plyometrics

Figure 19 SAQ training

SUMMARY

In this chapter you have studied lots of different topics. You need to be able to link specialist training methods with energy systems and look at the impact these training methods have on energy production and recovery. Make sure you can explain how each of the three energy systems produces energy and identify when they are used. Ensure you understand energy transfer during long duration/lower intensity exercise and short duration/high intensity exercise. A knowledge of the recovery process (EPOC) is essential and you need to be aware of the importance of oxygen consumption, both during exercise and then recovery. You also need to learn measurements of energy expenditure as they provide the athlete with information on how hard they are working and which energy system is producing the energy.

PRACTICE QUESTIONS

1   Elite athletes may use the results from lactate sampling to ensure that their training is effective. Explain the term lactate sampling.   (2 marks)

2   Wayde Van Niekerk holds the world record for the 400 m with a time of 43.03 seconds. Explain how the majority of energy was provided during the race.   (4 marks)

3   At the end of a team game, players may experience EPOC. Define EPOC and give the functions of the fast component of EPOC and explain how these functions are achieved.   (4 marks)

4   Explain the factors that can affect lactate threshold.   (3 marks)

5   Elite athletes spend considerable time developing their fitness, using a variety of methods, in order to produce peak performance.

   a) Explain why some athletes, such as marathon runners, may choose to spend time training at altitude.   (3 marks)

   b) What are the potential problems associated with altitude training?   (3 marks)

6   The triathlon is an athletic event that involves performers undertaking a long distance swim, immediately followed by a cycle race and then finally a run of several kilometres. Name the main energy system being used throughout the race and explain how this system provides energy for the working muscles. At the end of the race, the triathlete will be out of breath and will continue to breathe heavily even though they have come to a complete rest. Explain why this breathlessness occurs.   (15 marks)

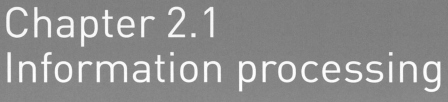

Chapter 2.1
Information processing

Chapter objectives

In the chapter on skill characteristics in Book 1 (Chapter 2.1), it was suggested that skill has a cognitive (thinking) aspect and a motor (moving) aspect. This chapter looks at those two parts in much more detail, looking at the processes by which information is first collected from the environment, interpreted and then acted upon.

After reading this chapter you should be able to:

● Understand how sports performers use information from the environment to facilitate movement by using various senses to collect information such as hearing, vision, touch, balance and kinesthesis.

● Explain how sporting information is stored and used in the memory by looking at memory models and how these can be interpreted.

● Understand the influences that determine how decisions are made when information is collected by the senses and how this is responded to by a study of Whiting's information processing model.

● Look at what happens after decisions are made when sports performers react to stimuli and to assess the factors that can affect those reactions, including the psychological concepts of Hick's law, the psychological refractory period and the single channel hypothesis.

● Assess how a sports performer might adapt information to help control movement by using a schema.

Information processing and memory

In sporting situations, a good player will often take a look at their surroundings before they attempt to utilise some of the skills you have discussed in Book 1, Chapter 2.1. You may often witness the team playmaker such as the fly half in rugby or the netball centre take a quick look at the position of the defenders before they receive the ball in order to decide the best option available to them. This process of taking account of the sporting environment and then making decisions prior to the execution of a skill is referred to as **information processing**.

Figure 1 When playing netball the player in possession has to make decisions!

KEY TERMS

Information processing: The methods by which data from the environment are collected and utilised.

Input stage: Information picked up by the senses.

Display: The sporting environment.

KEY TERM

Receptor systems: The senses that pick up information from the display.

Initially, information processing can be divided into three parts: input, decision making and output. Each part follows the other in a specific order. These sequential parts are shown below, indicating the processes as a flow chart.

Input → Decision making → Output

Input

The first process is the **input stage**. During this initial stage, the performer uses the senses to pick up information from the sporting environment. The sporting environment can be called the **display** and while the sporting display does include aspects such as the condition of the pitch, it also refers to sports-specific items such as the opposition, the court, the crowd, the ball, the officials and of course your team mates! There are quite a lot of things to think about in a split second before receiving a ball, a consideration that will become important later.

Figure 2 The display is everything in the sporting environment that can be processed by the performer

Senses

Information is picked up from the display using the senses and there are five senses that are very important in sport. These senses used to collect information are collectively known as the **receptor systems**:

● Sight (or vision)
● Auditory sense (hearing)
● Touch
● Balance
● Kinesthesis.

The first sense used in sport is sight or vision. The performer can pick up the flight of the ball or the position of an opponent using their sight. Picking up such information early can be useful and may mean that the information on the flight of the ball is processed quickly, allowing the performer a fraction of a second more to make their decision. That split second advantage can make the difference at the top level.

The second of the senses used in sport is the auditory sense, otherwise known as hearing. A player may hear the call of a team mate or the sound of the referee's whistle, for example. A cricketer may hear the sound of the ball catching the edge of the bat before attempting to make a catch.

These two senses, hearing and sight, can be classed as external senses as information is collected from the environment. There are more senses used in sport that can be classed as internal since they are used from within. The internal senses are collectively called the **proprioceptors**. These senses provide intrinsic information about touch, balance and kinesthesis.

The sense of touch is important in sport and can be used to feel for the grip on the ball or the feel of the springboard used by a diver through the feet. The sense of balance is also important in sport. The basketball player who must set their feet before taking a free throw needs to be balanced to ensure the accuracy of the shot. A more obvious example is the gymnast who needs an acute sense of balance when competing on the beam or during a floor routine.

The gymnast referred to in the above example may also make use of another sense that details important information about the position and orientation of the body. This sense is called **kinesthesis** and it is a sense from within the performer, using sensors within the muscle receptors that relay information about muscle tension and therefore body position. The swimmer will use the sense of kinesthesis to help them be aware of body position during a tumble turn. The sense of kinesthesis is sometimes unnoticed by the performer but its use is important and can be relied upon as skills are practised and developed.

Figure 3 The gymnast uses the sense of balance when competing on the beam

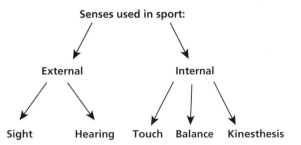

Senses used in sport:

External — Sight, Hearing
Internal — Touch, Balance, Kinesthesis

Figure 4 Senses used in sport

Decision making

The second stage of information processing is the decision-making stage. At this point the performer must make a decision based on all the information collected by the senses. In order to make such decisions, the process of selective attention and the use of the memory system are really important at this stage.

The difficulty in this part of the process lies in the fact that the performer can receive a host of information from the five senses and yet needs to make their decision based only on the important aspects of that information. Perception might be used to determine not just the attackers who are free to receive a pass, but to identify the attacker who is most likely to get the ball. The ball and the position of opponents in a game might be information that is vital but the crowd might be something that the performer wishes to ignore. Significantly, there is a process that helps the sports performer to separate the relevant information from the irrelevant information. This process is called **selective attention**.

Selective attention

Selective attention is essentially a filtering process that identifies the information needed by the performer and disregards the less important parts. It would help the badminton player focus on the position of the opponent and the flight of the shuttlecock while ignoring the crowd and the things in the display that are outside the court.

Figure 5 The badminton player needs to focus on the flight of the shuttlecock

Developing selective attention

In top-class performers the process of selective attention is almost automatic. Experience builds the effectiveness of the process and selective attention can be developed by both coaches and performers. Sports performers can enhance the process of selective attention by learning to focus and concentrate on the important information, getting used to the idea of a **stimulus**. If this stimulus is made more intense, loud or bright when the performer is training, it will help to develop the art of concentration. For example, in football training the use of a brightly coloured ball may help the player to develop the instinct to pick up the pace on the incoming pass early. In an opposite sense, the performer may also learn to ignore the irrelevant information by training with distractions in a realistic environment. In 2014 as preparation for the Six Nations international championship game against Wales, the England Rugby Union team prepared for the game by training to the accompaniment of the Welsh national anthem, and other sounds associated with a passionate crowd, played over the loud-speaker system, in anticipation of the atmosphere expected at the game. The players were told to concentrate on their calls and communication and to ignore the crowd noise.

Figure 6 Wales vs England Rugby Union: the players learned to ignore the crowd

Improved motivation helps the process of selective attention. Coach and player could enhance motivation by using rewards such as positive comments, and once motivation is increased, the performer becomes more alert to the important information. The application of mental practice can help the process of selective attention when the performer runs through the upcoming task in the mind before movement starts.

For example, a climber would plan their moves and the types of holds and grips they intend to use before they commence the next phase of the intended route! Before starting, the climber would mentally rehearse their moves in the order of occurrence, saving time and energy on the actual climb, as it allows them to choose their next move quickly and not have to look around while hanging about on the rock face.

The benefits of selective attention

As you can imagine, by reference to the examples above, the process of selective attention is useful to the sports performer. Selective attention can improve reaction time significantly. If a tennis player picks up the flight of the ball early, they can begin their movements towards the ball that fraction of a second sooner and get into position to make the return a little earlier. Focusing on the relevant information improves the chances of making a correct decision. By ignoring the irrelevant information, a player may be able to concentrate on more detailed aspects of the task, as a more accomplished performer would do when selecting the precise part of the court they want to land the tennis return. By limiting the amount of information that is noted in sport, selective attention helps the decision-making process since, as will be revealed later in this chapter, the working memory has a limited capacity and too much information could affect memory function. Once the relevant information regarding the task has been identified, the performer can begin the second stage of information processing and start to make some decisions.

STUDY HINT

Experienced players learn to develop their ability to use selective attention.

Figure 7 A climber on the rock face

STUDY HINT

Selective attention helps the performer to make faster decisions.

ACTIVITY

Consider a game or event that you recently took part in. Think of some of the decisions you made during that game or event. What information did you use to make those decisions and what information was not needed? Try to list the relevant and irrelevant information.

KEY TERMS

Perception: The process of coding and interpreting sensory information.

Translatory mechanisms: Adapting and comparing coded information to memory so that decisions can be made.

Effector mechanism: The network of nerves that sends coded impulses to the muscles.

STUDY HINT

DCR = Detection, Comparison and Recognition.

STUDY HINT

The translatory mechanism adapts information, compares past experiences with the memory system and helps to make decisions so that the correct motor programme is used.

ACTIVITY

Make a list of the types of feedback and describe each type.

DCR

The perceptual stage of information processing involves three aspects of activity called **detection**, **comparison** and **recognition**. Detection means that the performer has picked up the relevant information and identified that information as important, using the senses and the process of selective attention as discussed. In a sense then, detection belongs in the input or identification stage of the process. The comparison aspect of information processing involves trying to match the information identified as important to information already in the memory of the performer, and hence the importance of the memory system becomes important to the performer.

Recognition means that the performer has used information from the memory to identify an appropriate response. This response can then be put into action.

Translatory mechanisms

The **translatory mechanism** helps to convert information so that decisions can be made. If you translate a language you would convert an unfamiliar language into one that you know. The same applies here, but in sporting terms the information from the senses, once it has been filtered, is then adapted into an image that can be sent to the memory for comparison. The translatory mechanism uses past experiences so that information received can be linked with these past experiences and sent to the memory system. Similar actions which have been stored in the memory can be recognised and then used. Actions are stored in the memory in the form of motor programmes. The translatory mechanism uses coded information from the perceptual process to pick out an appropriate motor programme. In the example of the tennis return, the information about the flight of the ball and the position of the opponent are compared to an appropriate image of a backhand return.

Output

The effector mechanism and the muscular output

The **effector mechanism** is the network of nerves that is responsible for delivering the decisions made during the perceptual process to the muscles so that those muscles can perform the action. The muscles will receive the information in the form of coded impulses and once this impulse is received, then the muscles will contract and the response can begin.

Feedback

Feedback is information used during or after the response to aid movement correction. Types of feedback have been discussed in Book 1, Chapter 2.2. Try the Activity on the left to remind you!

ACTIVITY

Information-processing models

The features of information processing occur in a specific order. Look again at the main points of each of the processes involved in information processing and see if you can place them in the order you think they would occur. List each process in order from first to last.

Here's a clue: the environment is the starting point since it contains all the information needed to perform. We begin by selecting information from the sporting environment that we can sense, the display. But what happens next? And after that?

Here are the terms to place in order:

- Environment
- Effector mechanism
- Translatory mechanism
- Feedback data
- Display
- Muscular system output data
- The sensory organs
- Perceptual mechanism (includes selective attention).

The order you came up with may also have looked like the one in the model below, in the sense that the order you came up with matches the sequence in the Whiting model. The Whiting model begins with the display and ends with some feedback – did you get a similar order? Yours may have been a simple linear model rather than circular, but if you got a similar order, well done!

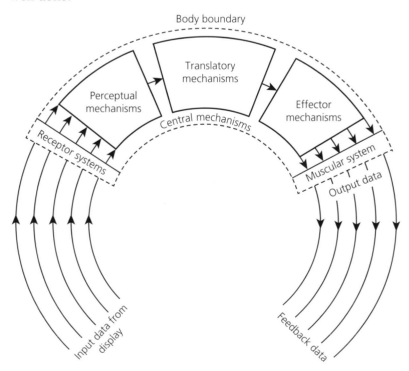

Figure 8 Whiting's information-processing model; Whiting 1969, *Acquiring Ball Skill*

The model is a similar illustration to the one that you should have composed in the previous Activity. It uses the parts of information processing we have discussed and puts them in an order. If we relate the model to the action of returning a serve in tennis then the following order should occur:

1 The environment – contains the information needed to perform.

2 The display – information is available to the tennis player from the environment – the court, the crowd, the opponent and the initial flight of the ball.

3 Receptor systems – the player uses five senses to collect information from the display:
- vision to see the flight of the ball
- sound to hear the ball being struck by the opponent
- balance to adjust the feet ready for the return
- touch to feel the grip on the racket
- kinesthesis to recognise limb position as the player begins to prepare to strike the ball.

4 In the perceptual mechanism, the player detects the host of information picked up by the receptors and ensures it is filtered into relevant and irrelevant information by the process of selective attention. Therefore the flight of the ball is focused on and the crowd is ignored.

5 During the translatory mechanisms, the tennis player will compare the relevant information picked up from perception to an action, perhaps an appropriate return shot that is stored in the memory. The comparison and recognition parts of the process begin to operate.

6 The effector mechanism now sends the coded impulse to the muscles.

7 The muscles pick up this impulse and begin to contract.

8 Output – the response begins and the return is hit!

9 During and after this response, feedback is available in various forms to the player.

ACTIVITY

Look at the diagram of the Whiting model. Where do you think selective attention might occur?

ACTIVITY

Some questions to think about from the Whiting model are given below. Consider and discuss with your fellow students.

Why are there numerous arrows going from the effector mechanisms into the muscular system?

Why are there numerous arrows going into the perceptual mechanisms but only one arrow going out?

Why do you think the central mechanisms are included in the model?

CHECK YOUR UNDERSTANDING

1 What is information processing?

2 What do you understand by the term 'Display'?

3 Name two external senses used in sport and give an example of how each might be used.

4 Name three internal senses, or proprioceptors, used in information processing and give examples of how each might be used.

5 What is selective attention?

6 Name three advantages to a sports performer of using selective attention.

7 What does DCR mean?

The memory system

The memory system forms an integral part of the processing of sporting information. The memory system contains a series of memory stores and some methods by which information is transferred and held in these stores. Figure 9 outlines the memory system as compiled by the sports scientists Baddeley and Hitch in 1978.

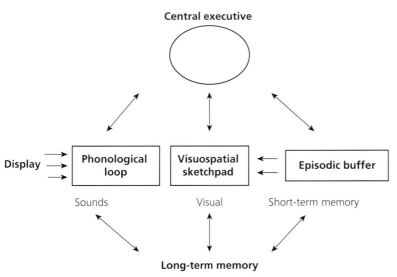

Figure 9 The memory system: 'The working memory'

The working memory

The **working memory** consists of a central control centre, known as the **central executive**. The central executive has overall control over all the information entering and leaving the working memory. It quickly identifies which information should be sent to one of its sub-memory systems. These sub-divisions of the working memory are known as 'sub-systems' and they perform different functions. These three sub-systems are:

1 **The phonological loop:** In sport, information such as the coach's instructions, the call of a team mate or the sound of a ball hitting a racket can be processed in the phonological loop. The function of the phonological loop is to deal with the auditory information presented from the senses. It has a phonological store and an articulatory system that helps it to produce a memory trace. This memory trace, which is an initial mental idea of the skill, can be sent to the long-term memory where it can trigger a motor programme, or images that contain components of a skill, so that this motor programme can then be used to produce movement.

2 **The visuospatial sketchpad**: This relates to some important sporting aspects. It concerns visual (sight) and spatial (where) information. It also helps to process information about the feel of the movement such as the flight of a gymnast during a vault. It holds information about what we see and is further divided into two sections: the visual cache, which holds information about form and colour, and the inner scribe, which deals with spatial and movement information. This latter component is of significance to sports performers and it suggests that information about sporting actions can be recognised and acted upon.

KEY TERMS

Working memory: So named since it performs a number of functions.

Central executive: The control centre of the working memory model, it uses three other 'systems' to control all the information moving in and out of the memory system.

Phonological loop: Deals with auditory information from the senses and helps produce the memory trace.

Visuospatial sketchpad: Used to temporarily store visual and spatial information.

Figure 10 The player has a fraction of a second to filter information about the flight of the ball when this information is picked up

3 **The episodic buffer:** This is responsible for co-ordinating the work of the phonological loop and the visuospatial sketchpad into sequences. It produces integrated sequences of sight, sound and movements which can be sent to the long-term memory. These sequences produce patterns of skilled actions that are put in order and sent to the long-term memory. These sequences are the starting point for the initiation of motor programmes, which are patterns of the whole skill, and can be used to produce movement. The information about the path of the ball, the sound of the ball on the stick and the position of the limbs may help the skill of receiving the ball before making a dribble in hockey.

Working memory and long-term memory

The first job of the working memory is to pick up the relevant information from the sporting environment and once this information is received, the memory goes to work. Selective attention (see above) is used to filter out irrelevant information. The working memory has links with long-term memory, sending coded information for future storage and use.

Having collected the relevant information, the working memory produces a memory trace, a mental snapshot of the skill being used, and it then works with its partner, the **long-term memory (LTM)** by sending this memory trace to it so that the trace can be compared to information already contained in the storage area of the LTM. The LTM can then send information back to the working memory for use in the current sporting situation.

It is therefore apparent that the memories work together in a two-way process to help the sports performer compare information and make decisions. In an example from tennis, the working memory would send an image or trace of the position of the opponent and the flight of the ball to the long-term memory so that the scenario can be immediately compared to information already stored there and an appropriate return shot can then be decided upon. This two-way process can be undertaken very quickly!

Figure 11 The position of the opponent in tennis can determine the type of return shot used

Features and functions of the memory system

The characteristics and actions of the memory system are:
- The working memory initiates the action by sending the memory trace.

- However, the working memory has a limited capacity. It can only deal with around seven items of information at any one time and too much information, or information overload, could mean that important information is lost or disregarded by the performer. It is therefore useful that selective attention limits the amount of information sent to the working memory.

- In addition to a limited capacity, the working memory has a limited time scale – it lasts for around 30 seconds until the information within it is either lost or used.

- Important information can be stored in the long-term memory in the form of a motor programme, a more permanent trace of a skill consisting of all the components that make up that skill.

- The long-term memory has a large capacity and it can store information for a lifetime if needed. You can probably recall those early swimming lessons you had as a child when you perhaps learned to swim and gained some certificates as a reward. Once those early lessons were over, you may not have continued to go swimming and may now limit your activity in the pool to holiday times only. Even so, the swimming action is still there in the memory and although you may not be as good, you can still manage to swim safely!

Figure 12 You don't forget how to swim, even if you learned a long time ago

Storing information

The key to effective use of the memory system in sport is to ensure that useful information and motor programmes are stored in the long-term memory so that learned skills can be moved back to the working memory, for use at the current time. To ensure items are stored in the LTM, the coach and player could use a number of strategies:

- **Rewards:** Extrinsic and intrinsic rewards help to motivate the performer to want to remember correct actions.

- **Association** of actions you wish to learn with appropriate actions or emotions already stored in the memory. If we consider swimming again, the feeling of satisfaction and pride generated from getting the reward of a certificate can be linked with the actual swimming actions used to earn that reward and so those actions are remembered.

- The use of **mental practice:** When the parts or sub-routines of a skill are imagined over and over again in the mind without physical movement, this can help to store information in the memory. Mental practice is particularly useful for helping to remember the correct sequence of a serial skill such as a trampoline routine, since the components of that sequence can be rehearsed in the correct order, making it less likely for the performer to forget their routine.

- **Breaking the task down** into parts, especially when the skill is complicated, can help to prevent information overload. Therefore the performer can learn one aspect of the task before going on to learn the next part of the skill. In team games, such as netball, a set move or pre-planned tactic, e.g., a passing sequence used to move the ball up the court, may be learned in parts until it is finally secured in the LTM. A team may begin with practising the early pass from the goal defence, then work on the subsequent passes up to the moment the ball is received by the goal shooter. The technique of breaking the task into parts so that it is more easily recalled is known as **chunking**.

Figure 13 A sequence or move in netball can be broken into parts to help remember the actions

KEY TERMS

Association: Linking the stored actions of a skill to a stored emotion or other action.

Mental practice: Going over the action in the mind without physical movement.

Chunking: Breaking the skilled action into parts or sub-routines.

- Information can also be stored in the long-term memory by getting the performer to **focus** and concentrate on the task in hand. If you think about it, focusing on the task and ignoring distractions helps the process of selective attention which in turn will ensure that correct information goes to short-term and then long-term memory.

- The obvious and perhaps most important method of storing information in the long-term memory is by **repetition of an action**. Repeated practice to the stimulus will ensure that skills are coded and stored as **motor programmes** in the LTM, and those motor programmes will sit in the LTM until they are needed.

- The use of a method called **chaining**, when items of information are recalled as a sequence, so that one movement links to the next, helps to store information and is particularly useful in recalling serial skills (see Book 1, Chapter 2.1) such as a dance routine.

Memory tools

The strategies used to store information in the long-term memory can be remembered using the acronym:

Males And Females Can Run Charity Races

- Males – **m**ental practice
- And – **a**ssociation
- Females – **f**ocus
- Can – **c**hunking
- Run – **r**ewards
- Charity – **c**haining
- Races – **r**epetition

ACTIVITY

Have a look at a sporting clip from a media site such as YouTube. Make sure the clip is one that you have never seen before. Watch it once and then see if you can write down some fine details of the action such as which players were involved, which teams and what happened. If you can't remember the details accurately enough first time, then have another look. Did you use any of the above strategies to help you?

CHECK YOUR UNDERSTANDING

1 Draw a diagram to show the structure of the working memory.
2 Name three features of the long-term memory.
3 What is the first role of the working memory?
4 What are the four components of the working memory?

Schema theory (Schmidt): motor control and learning 1982

Schema theory suggests that rather than use a structured set of movements to develop skills, the core principles can be taken from an existing motor programme and then adapted, using some information from the environment and by using feedback from the senses. For example, the skill of throwing a javelin probably uses a motor programme that is made up of sub-routines such as grip, arm action and follow-through.

Figure 14 The javelin throw

The coaching points for the javelin throw could be adapted for use in the goalkeeper throw in football.

Throwing a javelin would be similar in concept to a goalkeeper throwing the ball out to team mates from the penalty box in football. But to make these two different skills applicable and precise to their respective sports, the grip and arm action may need to be adjusted to suit the sport and situation in which they are being used. While the sub-routine of the grip is a common concept to both types of throw, the narrow grip on the javelin may need to be adjusted to suit the wider grip on the football.

Parameters of a schema

When a schema is used to adapt an existing motor programme, there are four essential processes that must be used to make sure that the schema is effective.

A schema has two sections containing two parts each. The four parameters of a schema are as follows:

1 **Initial conditions**

The first process is called the **initial conditions** and it refers to information from the sporting environment that must be recognised before the schema can be used. This information may concern the position on the court, the placing of the limbs just prior to the action and the location of the performer with regard to other players. This first part of the schema can be summed up as 'Where am I?'

2 **Response specifications**

The second part of the schema is called the **response specifications** and in this part, the information from the environment is used to assess the available options open to the performer. How far away is the nearest player and therefore how far do I need to pass the ball? What type of pass is the best one to use in this situation? These are examples of some of the options that may be available to the performer just before the action starts. The response specifications can be summed up as, 'What do I need to do?' When using the first two parts of the schema, information is used from the motor programme in the memory system and therefore the first two parts of the schema are called the **recall schema**. The recall schema is responsible for initiating the movement and happens before the action has taken place.

Once the action is underway, the third and fourth parts of the schema are used. These are used to control the movement, are used during the action

Figure 15 The goalkeeper's throw in football

and are called the recognition parts of the schema. The **recognition schema** consists of the sensory consequences and the response outcome.

3 **Sensory consequences**

The **sensory consequences** concern the use of the senses to help guide the movement. For example, the grip on the netball or basketball may be controlled by using the sense of touch, or the strength in the pass may be controlled by the feel of movement during the arm action. Information from the senses is used to control and apply the movement to the situation – when a longer pass is needed to move the ball up the court, the arm action would be stronger and the grip firmer.

4 **Response outcome**

The final part of the schema is called the **response outcome** and here the schema and indeed the motor programme can be updated by getting knowledge of the result of the action. Did the pass reach the intended target? If the pass was successful, then the schema has been successful. If not, adjustments may be made for next time and the motor programme is adapted.

ACTIVITY

Consider the skill of a rugby pass.
Some of the points coaches might highlight when using this skill are:
1 Judging the distance needed to make that pass reach the team mate so that they do not slow down when catching the ball.
2 The recipient of the pass reaching out to catch the ball.
3 Scanning the pitch to see players who are available for the pass.
4 Weighting the pass using strong or soft hands to make sure it reaches the intended target.

State which of these coaching points are appropriate for use in the parts of a schema.
Which of the coaching points could be relevant for use in:
- the initial conditions
- response specifications
- sensory consequences
- the response outcome?

Now consider the skill of a javelin throw and these four coaching points:
1 The assessment of the number of steps to be taken in the run-up from the start of the throw.
2 The distance thrown.
3 The grip on the javelin during the throw.
4 The foot placement before the run-up starts.

Which coaching points would be relevant for use in initial conditions and response specifications (the recall schema)? Which would be relevant in the sensory consequences and response outcome (the recognition schema)?

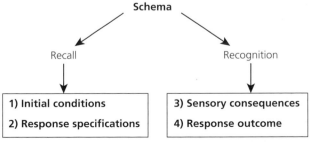

Figure 16 Schema theory: a summary

Implications for coaching when using schema

Since the use of schema is a good way to control skills, the coach may decide to employ a variety of strategies to make sure that the schema is used successfully. A good way to help a player become familiar with using a schema is to **vary the practice** conditions. When passing the ball in our examples of basketball or netball, the pass can be practised using a variety of drills and conditioned games such as 3 vs 2, attack vs defence or without opposition to encourage the player to continually adapt their approach. While such tasks are being undertaken, the coach should offer frequent feedback to the player to ensure that actions and motor programmes can be adjusted. The coach should point out and explain to the player when a schema can be used; for example, situations when the netball player may be able to adjust their netball pass for use on the basketball court should be highlighted. Parts of the skill that can be transferred should be pointed out. Should such adaptations be made successfully by the player, then the coach could offer reinforcement in the form of praise to the player to encourage further use of the schema in other situations. Such praise may offer the player motivation to continue using a method of skill development that enhances performance.

STUDY HINT

A variety of both practice and feedback help to build a schema.

CHECK YOUR UNDERSTANDING

1 What is a schema?
2 What is the function of recall schema?
3 What is the function of recognition schema?

Response time

In the previous sections we have looked at how information is processed; now we will look at what to do with the information once it has been sorted out. The first thing to do is to respond to that information and the faster that response is made, the more time sports players have to execute their skills – a huge advantage to the player. In team games, when a number of skills are open and unpredictable, it is very important to make decisions quickly so that the player can adapt to the changing situations faster than the opposition. Response time is often confused with reaction time, so to clear up any doubts here are some definitions.

Definitions of response time, movement time and reaction time

Reaction time involves no movement. It is the time taken from the onset of the stimulus to the onset of the response. It is the fraction of a second it takes us to process the available selected stimuli. At the start of a race, your reaction time would be the period from hearing the gun until you were just about to push against the blocks.

STUDY HINT

There is no movement in reaction time, just information processing.

ACTIVITY

Think back to the concepts used during information processing. Which of these concepts could be used by a sports performer during reaction time?

Movement time is the time it takes to complete the task after information processing has taken place. It is the time from the start to the completion of the action for the required task. In a 100 m sprint, the movement time would be the time between pushing against the blocks and hitting the tape.

Response time is the total time it takes from the onset of the stimulus to the completion of the task. In a 100 m race, the response time would be the time between hearing the gun and hitting the tape.

The relationship between reaction time and response time can be summarised as follows:

Response time = Reaction time + Movement time

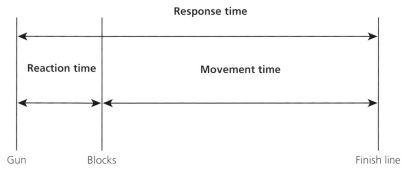

Figure 17 The relationship between reaction time, movement time and response time in a 100 m sprint

ACTIVITY

Figure 17 relates to a 100 m sprint. Consider the definitions of reaction time, movement time and response time and see if you can relate them to the skill of catching a ball hit by the batter in a game of cricket.

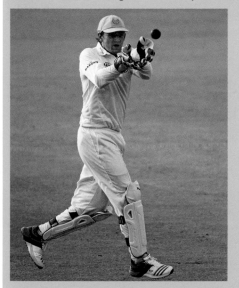

Figure 18 Catching a ball in a game of cricket involves reaction time, movement time and response time, but can you break this skill down into those components?

Simple reaction time and choice reaction time

A simple reaction time is when there is one specific response to one stimulus. An example would be the swimmer or the athlete at the start of a race responding to the starter's gun. This one choice should produce a fast reaction and response since the athlete has only one thing to think about before they react. Choosing from numerous stimuli is a choice reaction time and the response time now is much slower. A choice reaction time can also be made if the player has to choose a number of responses once the correct stimulus has been chosen. So in team games, for example, a key player with decisions to make such as a midfield player in hockey has to choose the correct stimulus from various indicators on the pitch and may also have to choose the correct response from various options. This process is much slower and indeed the number of choices is one of the factors that can affect response time.

Figure 19 A hockey player in midfield may have a number of choices to make and needs to learn to respond quickly

Factors that influence response time

The number of choices: Hick's law

The relationship between the number of choices and response time is summed up by **Hick's law**. This law states that as the number of choices increases, so does the reaction time. In sport, this law can be used to the player's advantage since you can try to keep your opponent guessing. When serving in tennis, for example, you can mix up your serves with direction or slice so that the opponent is never sure which one they are going to face. The variety will increase response preparation time and hopefully delay the actions of the opponent.

However, Hick's law is not always a straightforward linear relationship – it does not always work that reaction time increases at the same rate as choices increase. Players can become familiar with their environment and in our tennis example, as the game gets into its later stages, the opponent may have got used to the types of serves being played and the response becomes slightly quicker.

Figure 20 showing the relationship between the number of choices and reaction time according to Hick's law is shown on the next page. It clearly shows that as choices increase, the response time is slower; but it may also show a curved shape because the rate at which responses are slowed by increasing choice reduces as the environment becomes familiar. Hence the number of choices is reduced.

KEY TERM

Hick's law: Reaction time increases as the number of choices increases.

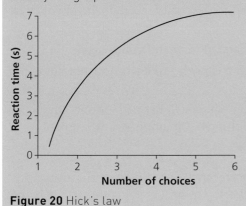
The following three concepts explain how timing and choice affect response time.

The single-channel hypothesis

This hypothesis states that stimuli can only be processed one at a time. Therefore, a second stimulus must wait until the first has been processed (like a car queuing at a set of traffic lights to merge from two roads into one) before it can be processed. Any following stimuli must also wait to be processed. The delay in processing a second stimulus increases response time and goes some way to explaining Hick's law: the more choices, the slower the response. The single channel hypothesis is shown in Figure 21.

How the timing of stimuli affects our reaction is explained by the psychological refractory period.

The psychological refractory period

This explains the delay that occurs because we can only process one stimulus at a time. The single-channel hypothesis has already told us that one stimulus must be processed through a single channel. So what would happen if a stimulus arrived before we had completed the processing of a previous stimulus? There would be a delay. The confusion caused by the arrival of a second stimulus before we had processed the first is called the **psychological refractory period (PRP)**. The performer might 'freeze' completely for the split second it takes to sort out the conflicting information. Imagine that you are playing tennis and the ball has been hit by your opponent to your forehand. You are set for the volley but the ball hits the net and deflects to your backhand. You have to sort out the new and correct stimulus, but first you have to disregard the old and now useless stimulus and this causes a delay.

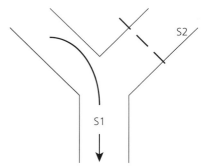

Figure 21 The single channel hypothesis: only one stimulus can be processed at a time

KEY TERM

Psychological refractory period: A delay when a second stimulus is presented before the first has been processed.

In sport you can use the PRP to your advantage – there are ways you can deceive your opponent to force a delay in their response. For example, performing a fake or dummy pass in a team game or by using fake body language to fool your opponent such as standing as if you are going to do a short serve in badminton and then hitting the shuttlecock long.

Figure 22 shows the concept of the psychological refractory period.

Figure 22 The psychological refractory period (PRP)

- S1 is the first stimulus, e.g. the ball to the right for a right-hand volley in tennis.
- R1 is the response to S1, a right-handed forehand volley.
- S2 is the ball hitting the net which means the volley is now not going to happen.
- R2 is the response to the deflection which will happen, or not, after a delay while S1 is dealt with, even though it might not now happen!

Anticipation

Anticipation is when a sports performer tries to pre-judge a stimulus. In other words, the performer tries to work out what is going to happen before it does, perhaps using information from the environment in the form of signals from the opponent or 'cues', which may include the body language and positioning of that opponent. The information could be learned prior to the game by researching the opposition or by learning from the actions of the opponent throughout the game.

In anticipation, there are two essential aspects of play that must be considered before the stimuli can be judged. **Temporal anticipation** is pre-judging when the stimuli is going to happen. **Spatial anticipation** refers to where and what the projected stimuli are going to be. In anticipation you need to know both, so that when judging the catch of a high ball in rugby, the player needs to know where on the pitch the ball is going to land and when it will get there.

Correct anticipation improves response time. As the information processing process is speeded up, the information has been processed before the action has happened, so the movement aspect of the response can happen immediately. However, sport performers should be aware of the effect of the PRP. If the anticipation is incorrectly judged and the stimulus that is presented is not the one expected, then there will be a delay while the actual and second stimulus are processed.

Improving response time

Players and coaches can improve response time in games by using strategies and tactics in training and during the game. These strategies are given below:

1 A player can use mental practice. By going over the task in the mind prior to the action, the response preparation process is improved and the

Figure 23 When catching a high ball from a kick in rugby, you need to know when (temporal) and where (spatial) the ball is going to land

KEY TERMS

Anticipation: Pre-judging a stimulus.

Temporal anticipation: When it is going to happen.

Spatial anticipation: Where and what is going to happen.

action can be predicted and so made quicker. Mental practice works well with closed skills and serial skills (see Book 1, Chapter 2.1) when the environment is predictable, such as the sequence about to be performed on the trampoline.

2 During practice the performer could train to the specific stimulus expected in the game. A goalkeeper might practise saving penalties to their left if the opposition penalty taker has a preference for aiming left when taking those kicks.

3 The performer could learn to focus and concentrate during the game so that the stimulus is picked up early. To help with concentration, the coach could make such stimuli intense. Pointing out the exact area in which to place the hands during a gymnastic vault and highlighting this area with coloured chalk might help.

4 Improving fitness improves reaction time; interval training and plyometrics might improve speed and power during the movement part of the response.

5 If appropriate, the player might also try to use anticipation to predict the stimulus, especially if the player has done their homework on the opponent.

Figure 24 A goalkeeper could practise saving penalties to improve reaction time

CHECK YOUR UNDERSTANDING

1 Define the terms reaction time, movement time and response time.
2 What is the relationship between reaction time, movement time and response time?
3 What is the difference between a simple reaction time and a choice reaction time?
4 What does Hick's law tell us?
5 What does the single channel hypothesis suggest?
6 What is anticipation?
7 Name two types of anticipation.

SUMMARY

This chapter has studied the ways in which information is collected, interpreted and used within the sporting arena. A logical and sequential approach was used to account for the features of information processing and the memory system. The three basic stages of information processing are – the input stage when the senses collect information, the decision-making stage when the memory system helps to make decisions, and the output stage when responses can be affected by the concepts of Hick's law. The psychological refractory period and the single channel hypothesis were outlined using various models. These models, such as Whiting's information-processing model and the memory model of Baddeley and Hitch supported the logical approach to information processing.

During the final stage of information processing, the actual response, movements could be adapted using schema theory and the four parameters of a schema have been outlined.

PRACTICE QUESTIONS

1 An impulse carried from the brain to the muscles that initiates movement best describes
which of the following processes? (1 mark)

   a) DCR

   b) Selective attention

   c) Effector mechanism

   d) Translatory mechanism

2 Games players use information processing to make decisions. Explain the types of sensory
information used in team games. (4 marks)

3 Effective sports performers use a process called selective attention.

   Using an example from sport, explain the term selective attention and evaluate
   the effectiveness of this process in helping a sports performer to make decisions. (8 marks)

4 During a tennis match, the ball hits the top of the net during a rally and the receiver
has to adjust their response. This causes a delay before the final response can be made.
Explain why this delay occurs. (3 marks)

5 Consider the sporting situations of an athlete at the start of a 100 m race waiting for
the starter's signal and a games player in midfield about to make a pass.

   a) Which performer do you think would have the faster reaction time? Explain your choice. (4 marks)

   b) What strategies could the athlete use to achieve a faster response time? (3 marks)

6 During sporting performance it may be necessary to process information using the memory system.

   What are the features and functions of the working memory? (8 marks)

7 A schema consists of 'recall' and 'recognition' components.

   Which of the following statements are features of recall schema? (1 mark)

   a) Occurs before the action and initiates movement.

   b) Occurs during the action and initiates motor programmes.

   c) Occurs before the action and controls movement.

   d) Occurs during the action and controls movement.

8 Schmidt's schema theory is based on four sources of information, called parameters,
which are used to modify motor programmes. Explain these four sources of information. (4 marks)

9 How can a coach organise practices to enable a schema to develop? (4 marks)

10 Explain the relationship between reaction time, movement time and response time, and explain
the strategies a coach or player could use to improve response time, showing how effective such
strategies may be. (15 marks)

Chapter 3.1 Injury prevention and the rehabilitation of injury

Chapter objectives

By the end of this chapter you should be able to:

- Identify acute and chronic injuries.
- Understand how screening, protective equipment, warm-up, flexibility training, taping and bracing are used in injury prevention.
- Describe how proprioceptive training, strength training and hydrotherapy can help rehabilitation.
- Give the physiological reasons why hyperbaric chambers and cryotherapy are used in injury rehabilitation.
- Explain how compression garments, massage/foam rollers, cold therapy, ice baths and cryotherapy can aid recovery.
- Explain the importance of sleep and nutrition for improved recovery.

Playing sport brings with it the risk of injury and lots of different injuries can occur to muscles, bones, joints, tendons and ligaments. The ankles and knees are two of the most commonly affected areas and injuries throughout the body can range from a muscle sprain to a serious fracture. Whatever the injury, the frustration at not being able to participate for anyone involved in sport is plain to see. For an elite performer, injury can affect their income and for a novice, it can affect progression. Injuries are often caused by inadequate preparation, poor equipment, poor technique, overloading too soon or simply from a collision or fall in competition. Sports science has improved our understanding of injury prevention and helps prepare performers better for exercise than ever before but the risk of injury is still prevalent.

Types of injury

There are two kinds of sports injuries: **acute** and **chronic**. An acute injury occurs suddenly during exercise or competition; for example, a sprained ankle or torn ligament, and pain is felt straight away and is often severe. A chronic injury occurs after playing sport or exercise for a long time. They are often called over-use injuries. They develop slowly, can last a long time and are often ignored by performers, which makes the injury worse, causing more problems.

Acute injuries

Any performer who experiences an acute injury can display the following signs:

- Sudden, severe pain
- Swelling around the injured site
- Not being able to bear weight

- Restricted movement
- Extreme leg or arm weakness
- A protruding bone or a joint that is visibly out of place.

Fractures

A break or a crack in a bone is a fracture and a bone can fracture in different ways. A simple or closed fracture is a clean break to a bone that doesn't penetrate through the skin or damage any surrounding tissue. A compound or open fracture is when the soft tissue or skin has been damaged. This is more serious as there is a higher risk of infection. As a bone can crack or break in more than one place or in different positions, there are many different types of fractures.

ACTIVITY

The table below highlights some of the different types of fracture. Find out either in your class or from your sport which of these is the most common type of fracture and look at how they occur.

TYPE OF FRACTURE	EXPLANATION
Comminuted	Here the bone breaks or splinters into three or more pieces
Spiral	A winding break
Longitudinal	A break that occurs along the length of the bone
Buckle	Occurs in children where the bone deforms but does not break
Hairline	A partial fracture of the bone that is difficult to detect
Greenstick	These fractures occur in children where the bone partly fractures on one side but does not break completely. This is because in young children the bone is softer and more elastic so it can bend.

Dislocations

Dislocations occur at joints and are very painful. It happens when the ends of bones are forced out of position. In sport, dislocations often occur with a fall or contact with another player, for example, in football tackles. They are often very easy to see as the bone looks visibly out of place.

Figure 1 A shoulder dislocation

Strains

Often called a 'pulled' or 'torn' muscle, a strain occurs when muscle fibres are stretched too far and tear. Strains occur regularly in team games from contact with other players and where the performer continually accelerates and decelerates suddenly. Elite athletes are also prone to strains where the intensity of their training is high and the overuse of specific muscle groups occurs regularly.

Sprains

Sprains occur to ligaments, which are strong bands of tissue around joints that join bone to bone. When playing sport where there is lots of twisting and turning, and excessive force is applied to a joint, a sprain can occur where the ligament is stretched too far or tears. In sport a sprained ankle is a very common injury.

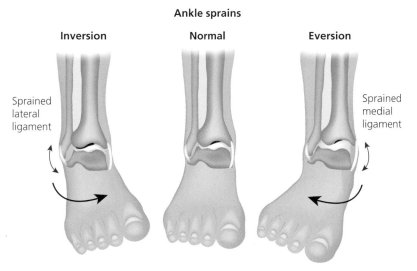

Figure 2 Ankle sprains

Figure 2 Ankle sprains

Chronic injuries

Most chronic or over-use injuries display the following signs:

- pain when you compete or exercise
- a dull ache when you rest
- swelling.

Achilles tendonitis

Tendons connect muscles to bones and are strong bands of soft tissue. When muscles contract they help to move the bones and joints. Tendonitis is an over-use injury that causes pain and inflammation of the tendon. The Achilles tendon is located at the back of the ankle and is the largest tendon in the body. It connects the gastrocnemius to the heel bone and is used for walking, running and jumping, so when we do a lot of regular activity it can be prone to tendonitis.

Stress fracture

A stress fracture is also an over-use injury where the area becomes tender and swollen. Stress fractures are most common in the weight-bearing bones of the legs, often when there is an increase in the amount of exercise or the intensity of an activity is increased too quickly. It happens when muscles become fatigued so they are no longer able to absorb the added shock of

> **STUDY HINT**
>
> Don't get strain and sprain confused. A strain happens to muscles and a sprain to ligaments.

> **ACTIVITY**
>
> Choose four different sports and compare the common acute injuries that can occur. Can you explain why these injuries happen?

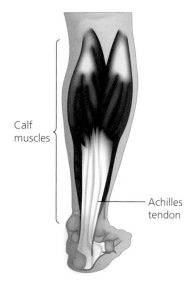

Figure 3 Achilles tendon

Calf muscles

Achilles tendon

exercise. The fatigued muscle eventually transfers the stress overload to bone and the result is a tiny crack called a stress fracture.

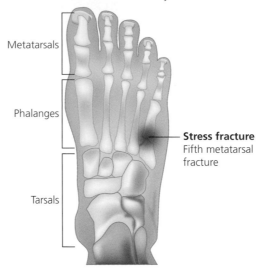

Figure 4 A stress fracture of the foot

'Tennis elbow'

Tennis elbow is an over-use injury and occurs in the muscles attached to the elbow that are used to straighten the wrist. The muscles and tendons become inflamed and tiny tears occur on the outside of the elbow. The area becomes very sore and tender. The medical term for tennis elbow is **lateral epicondylitis**. This is because pain is felt on the bony part of the outer elbow which is called the lateral epicondyle. Any activity that places repeated stress on the elbow can cause tennis elbow and, as the name suggests, this injury often occurs in tennis. (Pain that can be felt on the inside of the elbow is often known as 'golfer's elbow'!)

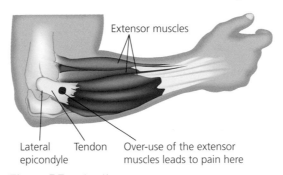

Figure 5 Tennis elbow

Injury prevention methods

Proper preparation before taking part in exercise can reduce the chance of injury. Improvements in sports science mean there are many injury prevention methods which everyone can put into practice, such as an adequate warm-up or using a foam roller. Other methods such as screening are available to elite performers whose training is much more intense.

Screening

In sport, screening can be used to help identify those at risk of complications from exercise, prepare performers for their sport, enhance performance and reduce injury. It can be used to detect a problem early before any symptoms occur. Screening can also save lives. For example, many young elite performers have CRY heart screening. CRY stands for 'cardiac risk in the young' and an **ECG** is used to assess and monitor a performer's heart. This test is encouraged by most sport governing bodies due to the demands of elite sport and the stress it can place on the heart.

Screening can also identify the musculoskeletal condition of an athlete which can highlight any past or current injuries. This will enable the performer to select a relevant conditioning training programme that will prevent further injury.

In professional sport, screening can be used to prevent injury. This involves assessing muscle imbalances, core strength, range of joint movement, postural alignment and mobility. If any problems are detected, a conditioner can select a specific training programme for improvement thus reducing the chance of a potential injury while at the same time enhancing performance.

However, screening can have disadvantages. Some screening tests are not 100 per cent accurate and may miss a problem (false negative) or can identify a problem that doesn't exist (false positive). It can also increase anxiety when an athlete finds out they have a health problem or are more susceptible to injury.

Protective equipment

Wearing the correct equipment can help reduce injuries in sport. The following table gives examples of protective equipment worn in a variety of sports.

Sport	Protective equipment
Football	Ankle and shin pads
Rugby	Scrum cap, gum shield, body armour
Cricket	Batting pads, thigh pads, box, helmet, gloves
Hockey	Leg guard, shin guard, pads, kickers, face mask for short corners, gloves, helmet
Squash	Eye guards

Whatever the equipment worn, it needs to fit correctly and meet National Governing Body regulations.

Warm-up

As already mentioned in Book 1, Chapter 4.2, Preparation and training methods, the warm-up helps prepare the body for exercise and should always be carried out before the start of any training session. Performing a warm-up will reduce the possibility of injury by increasing the elasticity of the muscle tissue. This happens because a warm-up will increase the body's muscle temperature. Heart rate and respiratory rate also increase, which increases blood flow and therefore the delivery of oxygen and nutrients to the working muscle. This prepares the muscles, tendons and joints for strenuous activity.

The first stage of any warm-up is to perform some kind of cardiovascular exercise such as jogging, which gently increases your heart rate. This will increase cardiac output and breathing rate and more blood is directed through the vascular shunt to the working muscles. Together, these three factors will increase the amount of oxygen being delivered to the muscles.

The second stage is the performance of stretching/flexibility exercises, especially with those joints and muscles that will be most active during the training session.

The third stage should involve the movement patterns that are to be carried out, for example, practising shooting in basketball or netball, or dribbling in hockey or football.

KEY TERM

ECG: Stands for an **electrocardiogram** machine where electrodes are placed onto the player's chest and the wires connect to an ECG machine and a printout is produced of the heart's electrical activity.

ACTIVITY

Can you think of another sport and identify what protective clothing is necessary?

ACTIVITY

Using your own sport or activity, design an appropriate warm-up.

KEY TERM

Active stretch: When a stretched position is held by the contraction of an agonist muscle.

Figure 6 Active stretching

KEY TERM

Passive stretch: Uses an external force to help the stretched position.

Figure 7 Here a partner is used as the external force to increase the intensity of the stretch

KEY TERMS

Static stretching: When the muscle is held in a stationary position for 10 seconds or more.

Ballistic stretching: Uses swinging and bouncing movements.

Figure 8 Static stretching

Flexibility training (active, passive, static and ballistic)

Flexibility training should involve the joints and muscles that will be most active during the activity.

Active stretching involves the performer working on one joint, pushing it beyond its point of resistance, lengthening the muscles and connective tissue surrounding it. An example is lifting your leg up and holding it in position. This involves strength in the agonist muscles, in this case, hip flexors. The tension in the hip flexors caused by holding the leg up in the air (see Figure 6) helps to relax the antagonist muscles being stretched (gluteals).

> ### ACTIVITY
> Can you think of some other active stretches?

Passive stretching is when a stretch occurs with the help of an external force, such as another part of your body, a partner or a wall.

> ### ACTIVITY
> Can you think of some other passive stretches?

Static stretching is stretching while not moving. It involves holding a muscle in the furthest point you can for up to 30 seconds, for example, trying to touch your toes. Here the hamstrings are the muscles that are stretched as they perform an isometric contraction.

Ballistic stretching involves performing a stretch with swinging or bouncing movements to push a body part even further. It is important that this type of stretching should only be performed by an individual who is extremely flexible such as a gymnast or a dancer who will try to push their body beyond the limits of their range of movement in comparison to a football player.

Taping and bracing

Taping a weak joint can help with support and stability to reduce the risk of injury. Ankle sprains are a common injury in sport and often taping is used during the recovery period to give the ankle extra support to prevent further injury. Taping can also be used on muscles. The tape used for muscles is more elastic than that used on joints and is applied directly to the skin to provide controlled support as the muscle moves. It is called kinesiology tape and expands as the muscle contracts.

Bracing is much more substantial than taping, often involving hinged supports, and is used to give extra stability to muscles and joints that are weak or have been previously injured. Their aim is to prevent further injury. Braces for the ankle and the knee are the most common in sport.

Injury rehabilitation methods

All injured sports performers want to know how long it will be before they can return to regular exercise. A long recovery time can be very frustrating. For elite performers there are recovery methods available such as hyperbaric chambers that can decrease recovery time. For those of us who cannot access these, there are training methods we can use to strengthen an injured area and make it less susceptible to injury again.

Proprioceptive training

Proprioception is a subconscious process using a system of receptor nerves (remember proprioceptors from your previous studies) located in the muscle, joints and tendons. For smooth co-ordinated movements, the brain needs to have an accurate knowledge of arm and leg position and how fast these body parts are moving. Proprioceptors deliver vital information about this, together with our visual and auditory senses and our sense of touch. Following injury, however, proprioception is impaired.

Proprioceptive training uses hopping, jumping and balance exercises to restore lost proprioception and teach the body to control the position of an injured joint subconsciously. For example, sprained ankles are a common sporting injury and a proprioceptive exercise used to help rehabilitate this type of injury involves a balance board.

A balance board (sometimes called a wobble board) is unpredictable and wobbles, so standing on one with an injured ankle strengthens the joint and at the same time re-educates the body to quickly react to the wobbly movements without thinking about it.

Figure 9 Andy Murray wears an ankle brace

Figure 10 Using a balance board to improve proprioception

Strength training

Strength training uses a resistance of some kind. This resistance can be weight machines or free weights, body weight or the use of therabands. Whatever the type of strength training, it prepares the body for exercise, reducing the chance of injury. The following table gives examples of different types of strength training that can be used to aid recovery.

ACTIVITY

Can you think of some other exercises where you use your body weight as the resistance?

Type of strength training	What is it?	Example
Free weights	Free weights such as dumb bells and kettlebells have to be controlled as they are lifted. By not relying on a machine, the muscles have to stabilise the weight as well as lift it.	

51

Type of strength training	What is it?	Example
Machine weights	Here the machine has a lot of the control so in the early stages of an injury the focus can be on just improving strength, starting with low weights and gradually building this up.	
Body weight	Using the body as the resistance often involves core body exercises such as the plank. Improving core strength helps balance and posture and reduces any imbalances that could lead to injury.	
Therabands	Therabands are made of latex and can have different strengths. Light resistance bands are used for rehabilitation and as the injury improves, bands with greater resistance are used.	

Hyperbaric chambers

The aim of hyperbaric chambers is to reduce the recovery time for an injury. The chamber is pressurised rather like an aeroplane (in some chambers a mask is worn) and there is 100 per cent pure oxygen. The pressure increases the amount of oxygen that can be breathed in and this means more oxygen can be diffused to the injured area. The excess oxygen dissolves into the blood plasma where it can reduce swelling and both stimulate white blood cell activity and increase the blood supply at the injury site. Many top rugby union, cricket and football teams use hyperbaric chambers.

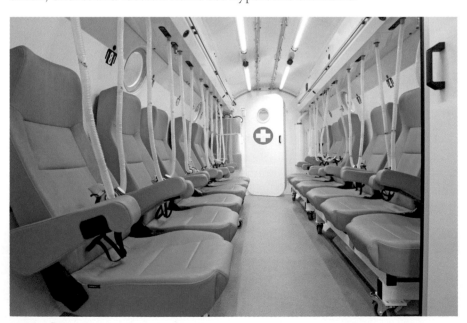

CHECK YOUR UNDERSTANDING
How can hyperbaric chambers aid injury rehabilitation?

Figure 11 Inside a hyperbaric chamber

Cryotherapy

Cryotherapy is the use of cooling to treat injuries. For common sporting injuries such as muscle strains, treatment for these is simply **RICE**. The RICE procedure involves the use of ice which has an analgesic effect and this can limit pain and swelling by decreasing blood flow to the injured area.

Ice baths are also a form of cryotherapy but are used for recovery after exercise (discussed in more detail later). Whole body cryotherapy (WBC) involves the use of cryogenic chambers to reduce pain and inflammation. The chamber is cooled by liquid nitrogen to a temperature below −100 degrees and the patient remains in the chamber protected with socks, gloves and a swimming costume for up to 3 minutes. The freezing gas surrounds the body so that the blood from the arms and legs flows towards the core in an attempt to keep the body warm and protect vital organs from the extreme cold. On leaving the chamber, the blood returns back to the arms and legs full of oxygen which helps heal injured cells.

Hydrotherapy

Hydrotherapy takes place in warm water and is used to improve blood circulation, relieve pain and relax muscles. Typically hydrotherapy pools are heated to approximately 35–37°C which increases blood circulation. Water can be used to make exercise easier and to alter exercise intensity. The main advantage of hydrotherapy is that the buoyancy of the water helps to support body weight, which reduces the load on joints and therefore allows for more exercise than is permitted on land. Exercising against the resistance of the water helps to strengthen the injured area.

Hydrotherapy exercises include squats, lunges, walking and running with or without a buoyancy aid in the water. Some hydrotherapy pools even have underwater treadmills. The faster these exercises are performed, the more resistance there is from the water.

Figure 12 Hydrotherapy pool with an underwater treadmill

KEY TERMS

Cryotherapy: The use of cold temperatures to treat an injury.

RICE: Stands for **R**est, **I**ce, **C**ompression, **E**levation.

CHECK YOUR UNDERSTANDING
How would you treat a muscle strain?

Recovery methods from exercise

Compression garments

Compression garments have been used in medicine for a long time to try to improve blood circulation and prevent medical problems such as **deep vein thrombosis (DVT)** occurring.

There is not a lot of research about the use of compression garments in sport but generally they are used by athletes to help blood lactate removal and reduce both inflammation and the symptoms associated with DOMS (delayed onset of muscle soreness). But a word of warning – be careful what you buy! You need medical grade compression garments (i.e. ones that deliver a special pressure to the body) and many sports stores do not sell these!

Figure 13 Examples of compression garments

Massage

Sports massage is a popular form of treatment which can prevent or relieve **soft tissue** injuries. Regular exercise can result in a build-up of tension in a muscle which will place stress on the muscle, as well as joints, tendons and ligaments. The benefits of sport massage include:

● Increases blood flow to soft tissue so more oxygen and nutrients can pass through to help repair any damage.
● Removes lactic acid.
● Causes stretching of soft tissue to relieve tension and pressure.
● Breaks down scar tissue which, if not removed, can lead to mobility problems in muscles, tendons and ligaments.

Foam rollers

Using foam rollers is a bit like self-massage. They can release tension and tightness in a muscle, as well as between the muscles and the **fascia.** They can be used to prevent injury and improve mobility. Foam rolling uses body weight and you literally roll your body on the foam roller to try to relax the muscle. If this hurts too much then it is important to support your body weight using your arms and add more weight as the muscle relaxes.

Figure 14 Foam rolling of the quadriceps muscles

Cold therapy

As a method of recovery, cold therapy is useful after intense exercise where it can target any minor aches and pains. Cooling the surface of the skin using ice gives pain relief and causes vasoconstriction of the blood vessels, which decreases blood flow and reduces any bleeding or swelling. A decrease in swelling (**oedema**) enables the muscle to have more movement. Ice can also reduce muscle spasms by decreasing motor activity. The conduction velocity of sensory and motor nerves (speed of the nerve impulse) slows down in cold conditions. Metabolic rate also decreases.

Ice baths

Ice baths are a very popular recovery method. After a gruelling training session or match, sports performers get into an ice bath for 5–10 minutes. The cold water causes the blood vessels to tighten and drains the blood out of the legs. On leaving the bath, the legs fill up with new blood that invigorates the muscles with oxygen to help the cells function better. The blood that leaves the legs takes away with it the lactic acid that has built up during the activity. Ice baths are now used among most professional sportspeople who train and play regularly. Most rugby super league teams do 'hot and cold' sessions where players spend 2 minutes in the steam room followed by 1 minute in the cold plunge pool. The purpose is to flush lactic acid from the muscles, reducing soreness for the week ahead. Despite its unpleasantness, the benefits can be felt immediately, especially in the legs. Some players include 'hot and colds' in their pre-match routine on game day.

Cryotherapy

From our discussion earlier, we already know that cryotherapy not only helps with injury rehabilitation, it can also help with recovery from exercise. Many sportspeople now use whole body cryotherapy (WBC) to aid their recovery which targets the whole body and not just a particular muscle. This is still a relatively new practice but whole body cryotherapy is a much quicker alternative to ice baths and, according to participants, more pleasant! Time spent in a chamber is up to 3 minutes and the body quickly returns back to normal. Research on the benefits of whole body cryotherapy has been mixed but it does appear to allow elite performers to recover quicker. The Welsh Rugby Union side believe in whole body cryotherapy so much that they have their own portable chamber in Cardiff!

Importance of sleep and nutrition for improved recovery

The amount of sleep you have and eating the correct foods can improve recovery times from exercise. How much sleep do I need is not an easy question to answer. It all depends on individual differences. One thing for certain is that a heavy exercise programme means you will need a long and good quality sleep. Some of the rebuilding of the damage done to muscle cells caused by strenuous exercise is done during sleep. Deep sleep is important for muscle recovery. The deepest part of sleep is the third stage of **non-REM sleep**. Here, brain waves are at their slowest and blood flow is directed away from the brain towards the muscles to restore energy. If sleep is too short then the time for repair is cut short! Most elite athletes have a minimum of 8–9 hours' sleep each night but your body will tell you if you need more.

KEY TERM

Oedema: A build-up of fluid which causes swelling.

Figure 15 Taking an ice bath

CHECK YOUR UNDERSTANDING
How does an ice bath help a performer to recover?

KEY TERM

Non-REM sleep (NREM): Means there is no rapid eye movement. It consists of three stages of sleep which get progressively deeper.

ACTIVITY
Think about how much sleep you have after heavy exercise. Is it enough? How do you feel the next day?

Nutrition is also crucial for recovery after exercise. During exercise, muscle glycogen stores decrease so they need to be replenished when exercise is finished. Research shows that replenishing glycogen stores during the first 20-minute window after exercise can then enhance performance the next day. In the 20 minutes immediately after exercise the body is most able to restore lost glycogen. Many elite performers drink chocolate milk within 20 minutes post-exercise to optimise recovery. This means they consume a 3:1 to 4:1 ratio of carbs-to-protein. This combination of carbohydrates to protein helps the body re-synthesise muscle glycogen more efficiently than carbohydrates alone. In addition, a liquid can be absorbed much faster than a solid and the performer can also rehydrate at the same time.

SUMMARY

You should now know that fractures, dislocations, strains and sprains are acute injuries and tennis elbow, stress fractures and Achilles tendonitis are over-use or chronic injuries. You need to be able to explain how screening, protective equipment, warm-up, flexibility training, taping and bracing can be used in injury prevention. Proprioceptive training, strength training and hydrotherapy can help the rehabilitation process, allowing an athlete to return to their sport quickly. In addition, hyperbaric chambers and cryotherapy are also used in injury rehabilitation but they are methods that are only available to elite performers. A hyperbaric chamber reduces recovery time from injury and cryotherapy has an analgesic effect, limiting pain and swelling by decreasing blood flow to the injured area. Compression garments, massage/foam rollers, cold therapy, ice baths and cryotherapy can all aid recovery. Sleep helps rebuild any damage done to muscle cells caused by strenuous exercise and it is important to replenish glycogen stores immediately after exercise.

ACTIVITY

With other members of your class, compare what you have to eat or drink after exercise and **when** you consume it.

PRACTICE QUESTIONS

1   The use of ice baths and cryotherapy can aid recovery. Analyse which of these methods you think is the most effective and give reasons why.   (4 marks)

2   What is the difference between an acute injury and a chronic injury? Use examples when you explain your answer.   (4 marks)

3   How can hydrotherapy help sports rehabilitation?   (3 marks)

4   Why is sleep important for improved recovery?   (3 marks)

Chapter 4.1
Linear motion

Chapter objectives

By the end of this chapter you should be able to:

- Define the scalars mass, speed and distance, giving equations and units of measurements.
- Define the vectors weight, velocity, displacement, acceleration and momentum, giving equations and units of measurements.
- Demonstrate the ability to plot, label and interpret biomechanical graphs and diagrams.
- Understand the forces acting on a performer during linear motion.
- Explain the relationship between impulse and increasing and decreasing momentum in sprinting through the interpretation of force/time graphs.

You have already studied some biomechanical principles of linear motion through Newton's laws of motion in Book 1 but this chapter develops your knowledge and understanding of motion and forces and their relevance in physical activity and sport.

Definitions, equations and units of vectors and scalars

There are several measurements used in linear motion and you should be able to define and explain how to calculate mass, weight, distance, speed, acceleration, displacement, velocity and momentum. All these measurements can be split into two groups:

- **Scalar quantity:** When measurements are only described in terms of size or magnitude – mass, distance and speed.
- **Vector quantity:** When measurements are described in terms of magnitude (size) **and** direction – weight, acceleration, displacement, velocity and momentum.

To help explain this further, speed is a scalar quantity because it just measures size. For example, when Usain Bolt set the 100 m world record he ran the race at an average speed of 10.49 m/s. Velocity is a vector quantity because it measures size and direction. For example, velocity measures speed with direction so in a penalty in football, we would talk about the velocity of a penalty kick as the striker kicks the ball towards the top left-hand corner at a velocity of 31 m/s.

Vectors are usually represented by arrows. The length of the arrow shows magnitude (if drawn to scale) and the longer the arrow, the bigger the size. Direction is shown by a line of application, a point of application and an arrow head (see Figure 1).

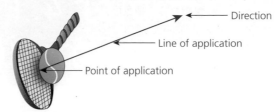

Length of the arrow = magnitude

Direction

Line of application

Point of application

Figure 1 Vectors

Mass versus weight

Mass is a physical quantity expressing the amount of matter or substance in a body. Our mass is made up of bone, muscle, fat, tissue and fluid and is measured in kilogrammes (kg). A sumo wrestler, for example, has a much greater mass than a gymnast. Mass is a scalar quantity because it does not have direction, just size.

Weight is the force on a given mass due to gravity. It is not measured in kg but in newtons as it is a unit of force. To calculate weight you use the following equation:

Mass (kg) × Gravity (9.8) = Weight (newtons)

So if a football player has a mass of 60 kg, their weight is 60 × 9.8 = 588 newtons. As the strength of gravity is the same everywhere on the surface of the Earth the gravitational force exerted on an object (its weight) is directly proportional to its mass. So, if the sumo wrestler has a mass, for example, three times greater than a gymnast, then the sumo wrestler's weight is three times that of the gymnast. This means that an object's mass can be measured indirectly by its weight. However the strength of gravity is different on the moon, for example, where it is one-sixth of that of the Earth, so if a gymnast has a mass of 40 kg their mass remains at 40 kg but their weight would be one-sixth of their Earth weight. Weight is therefore a vector quantity because it has both size and direction as it acts downwards from the centre of mass.

Distance versus displacement

Distance and displacement are quantities that are used to describe the extent of a body's motion. These measurements tell us how far a body has travelled. **Distance** is the length of the path a body follows when moving from one position to another. For example, a 200 m runner who has just completed a race has run a distance of 200 m. This is a scalar quantity because it just measures size.

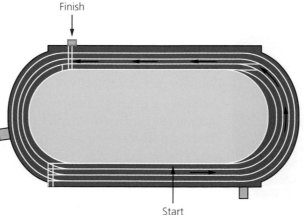

Figure 2 The distance from the start line to the finish line is 200 m

Displacement is the length of a straight line joining the start and finish points. For example, in a 200 m race on a track, the length of the path the athlete follows (distance) is 200 m but their displacement will be the straight line measurement from the start to the finish.

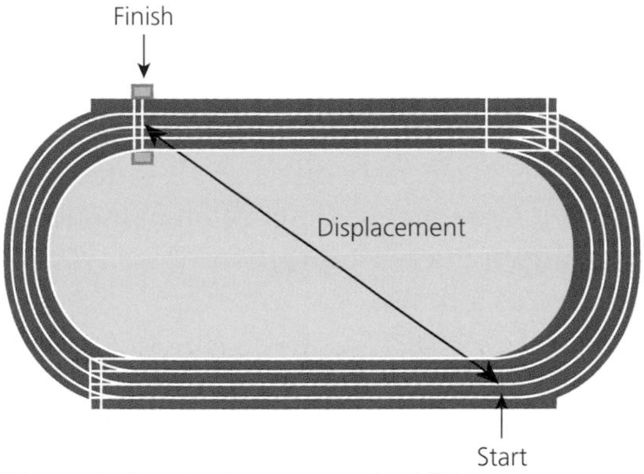

Figure 3 The displacement of a 200 m race

KEY TERM

Displacement: Measured in metres and is the shortest route in a straight line between the starting and finishing position.

Displacement is a vector quantity because it describes direction as well as size. Figures 4 and 5 show a javelin throw and a basketball free throw to further illustrate the difference between distance and displacement.

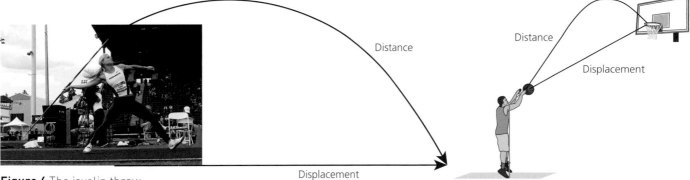

Figure 4 The javelin throw

Figure 5 A free throw in basketball

ACTIVITY

Work out the displacement from the following components of the triathlon:

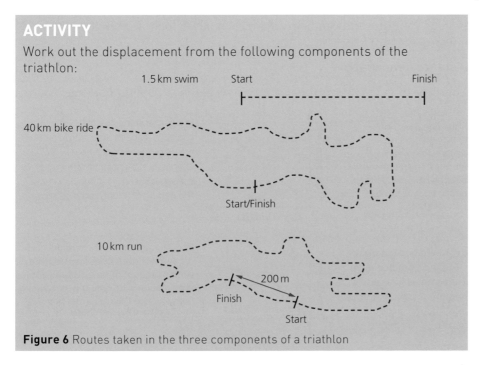

Figure 6 Routes taken in the three components of a triathlon

Speed versus velocity

Speed and velocity are measurements of how fast a body moves. Speed is the rate of change of distance. It is a scalar quantity since it does not consider direction and can be calculated as follows:

$$\text{Speed (m/s)} = \frac{\text{Distance covered (m)}}{\text{Time taken (s)}}$$

Velocity refers to how fast a body travels in a certain direction. It is the rate of change of displacement. Velocity is a more precise description of motion as it explains how fast a body is moving and in what direction. Velocity is a vector quantity and it can be calculated as follows:

$$\frac{\text{Displacement (m)}}{\text{Time taken (s)}}$$

ACTIVITY

Calculate the average speed and the average velocities for the components of a triathlon pictured in Figure 6 on page 59.

DISTANCE	TIME	DISPLACEMENT	AVERAGE SPEED m/s	AVERAGE VELOCITY m/s
1.5 km swim	30 mins 30 secs	1.5 km		
40 km cycle	90 mins	0.0 km		
10 km run	45 mins	0.2 km		

Graphs of motion

You should be able to demonstrate the ability to plot, label and interpret biomechanical graphs and diagrams. Graphs are one method of presenting information on motion from which changes and patterns in motion can be visually interpreted. Graphs of motion are often used in running activities such as sprinting and can help an athlete analyse their performance at different parts of a race.

Distance–time graph

This type of graph shows the distance travelled over a period of time:

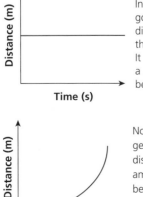

In this graph the line does not go up or down so there is no distance travelled. This means the performer must be stationary. It could be a netball player taking a shot or a goalkeeper in football before a penalty is taken.

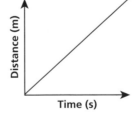

In this graph the line goes up in a constant diagonal direction. This indicates the distance run is changing at a constant rate and at the same speed. This could occur in the middle of a long distance race.

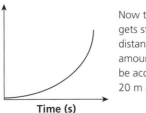

Now the line is curved and gradually gets steeper. This indicates that more distance is being covered in a certain amount of time so the performer must be accelerating, for example, the first 20 m at the start of a 100 m race.

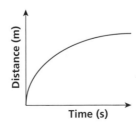

In this graph the curve starts to level off and less distance is travelled in a certain amount of time. This means deceleration is occurring which would happen once the performer has crossed the finishing line.

Figure 7 Distance–time graphs show the distance travelled over a period of time

The gradient of a graph

When looking at the gradient of a graph all this requires you to do is simply to look at the slope of the graph. This is determined by:

$$\frac{\text{Changes in the y axis}}{\text{Changes in the x axis}}$$

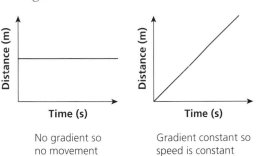
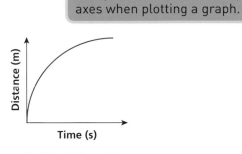

No gradient so
no movement

Gradient constant so
speed is constant

Gradient is increasing
so speed is increasing

Gradient is decreasing
so speed is decreasing

Figure 8 The gradient of a distance–time graph shows the speed of the movement measured

ACTIVITY

Now try to explain what is happening in this distance–time graph which is a combination of the above:

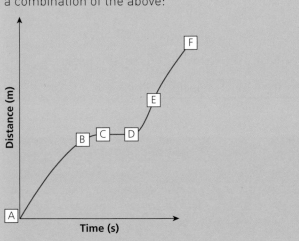

Figure 9 A distance–time graph showing changes in speed

Velocity–time graphs and speed–time graphs

These are essentially the same type of graph. The shape of the velocity graph will represent the same pattern of motion as the shape of a speed/time graph. These graphs indicate the velocity or speed of a performer or object per unit of time. The gradient of the graph will help you to decide whether the performer is travelling at a constant velocity, accelerating or decelerating.

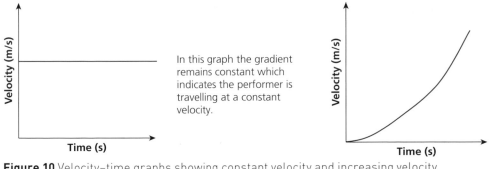

In this graph the gradient remains constant which indicates the performer is travelling at a constant velocity.

Now the gradient gets steeper (increases). This indicates that the performer is moving with increasing velocity or accelerating.

$$\text{Gradient of graph} = \frac{\text{Change in velocity}}{\text{Time}}$$

Figure 10 Velocity–time graphs showing constant velocity and increasing velocity

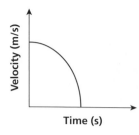

In this graph the gradient decreases. This shows the performer or object is moving with decreasing velocity or decelerating.

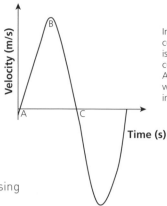

In this graph from A–B there is a positive curve above the x axis so the performer is accelerating. From B–C there is a negative curve so the performer is decelerating. At C the curve goes below the x axis which means there has been a change in direction.

Figure 10 (cont'd) Velocity–time graphs showing decreasing velocity and a more complex pattern of motion

Acceleration

Acceleration is the rate of change of velocity. When velocity increases, positive acceleration occurs and when velocity decreases, negative acceleration takes place. Acceleration is measured in metres per second squared m/s² and is a vector quantity.

Acceleration can be calculated as follows:

$$\frac{\text{Change in velocity (m/s)}}{\text{Time (s)}}$$

To calculate the change in velocity the following equation is used:

$$\frac{V_f - V_i}{T} \qquad \frac{\text{(Final velocity – Initial velocity)}}{\text{Time}}$$

The table below gives the 10 m split times and velocity for an elite 100 m sprinter.

10 m SPLITS	TIME (s)	TIME FOR EACH SPLIT (s)	VELOCITY (m/s)
10	1.87	1.72 (reaction time was 0.15)	5.8
20	2.89	1.02	9.8
30	3.81	0.92	10.9
40	4.68	0.87	11.5
50	5.52	0.84	11.9
60	6.36	0.84	11.9
70	7.20	0.84	11.9
80	8.05	0.85	11.8
90	8.91	0.86	11.6
100	9.77	0.86	11.6

From this table, calculate the sprinter's acceleration:
- from 10 m to 20 m
- from 20 m to 30 m.

Momentum

Momentum is the product of the mass and velocity of an object. It can be calculated as follows:

Momentum (kgm/s) = Mass (kg) × velocity (m/s)

Since momentum is calculated using velocity, it has magnitude and direction and is therefore a vector quantity. Momentum is dependent upon mass and velocity – if one of these increases then momentum increases.

KEY TERM

Momentum: Momentum (kgm/s) = Mass (kg) × velocity (m/s)

ACTIVITY

Complete the blanks in the table below:

PERFORMER	MASS (kg)	VELOCITY (m/s)	MOMENTUM (kgm/s)
100 m sprinter	80	11.9	
Prop	120		1080
Centre forward	70	10.5	
Middle distance runner	65	9.5	617.5

From this table it can be seen that a large mass, coupled with the ability to run at a high velocity, results in a greater momentum. If you had to stop any of the above performers, the prop would be the most difficult as his momentum is the greatest. Momentum can also be conserved. This occurs when a performer or object is in flight because neither mass nor velocity can be altered. When throwing a ball, for example, a fast arm action will allow the ball to travel at a greater velocity. But once in the air, this velocity cannot be changed unless an external force (such as gravity) acts upon it.

ACTIVITY

Copy the table below and complete the missing information and use it as a revision guide.

Measurements used in linear motion

MEASUREMENT	DEFINITION	UNIT OF MEASUREMENT	HOW TO CALCULATE? (IF RELEVANT)
Mass			
Distance			
Speed			
Weight			
Acceleration			
Displacement			
Velocity			
Momentum			

The forces acting upon a performer during linear motion

A force changes a body's state of motion; e.g. in a game of tennis when a serve is returned back across the net, a force has caused that change in direction. There are two types of force: **internal force** and **external force**.

- An internal force is applied when our skeletal muscles contract. For example, the force generated as the quadriceps contract concentrically to extend the knee in a jump.
- An external force comes from outside the body. For example, friction, air resistance and weight. Gravity is also an external force and is often described in terms of weight as weight is the gravitational force that the earth exerts on a body to pull the body downwards.

Both internal and external forces act upon a performer during linear motion. Internal muscular forces allow a runner to contract their skeletal muscles to generate the force required to produce movement. At the same time, external forces will act upon the runner. You should be able to identify and apply certain external forces which act upon a sports performer. These can be categorised as vertical forces, which are gravity and weight, and horizontal forces such as friction and air resistance (although air resistance can act vertically but this is negligible in most sports). An example of this would be dropping a piece of paper and a tennis ball vertically; the tennis ball will land first because of the air resistance acting vertically on the paper to slow down its descent.

Vertical forces

Weight

Weight is a gravitational force that the Earth exerts on a body, pulling it towards the centre of the Earth or effectively downwards. The greater the mass of the individual, the greater the weight force pulling the body downwards. Weight is equal to the mass of the body multiplied by the acceleration of a body due to gravity.

Reaction force

Reaction force is not mentioned in the specification but knowledge of a reaction force will help you to understand and apply your understanding of the forces acting on a performer during linear motion. Whatever the force acting on a performer during linear motion, a reaction force will be generated. Remember Newton's third law of motion:

For every action force there is an equal and opposite reaction force.

This means that there is always a **reaction force** whenever two bodies are in contact with one another. Consider a footballer kicking the ball. There is a reaction force at each point of contact so there is one between the foot and the ball and one between the foot and the ground. As the player kicks the ball, they generate a muscular force (action) which causes the ball to move and accelerate in the direction the force has been applied, but at the same time there is an equal and opposite reaction force applied by the ball to the footballer's foot. The other foot in contact with the ground applies an action force on the ground and the ground applies an equal and opposite

KEY WORDS

External force: Comes from outside the body.

Internal force: Is generated by the skeletal muscles.

KEY TERM

Weight: Weight = mass × acceleration due to gravity and is measured in newtons (N).

Figure 11 Reaction force

KEY TERM

Reaction force: This occurs when two bodies are in contact with one another.

reaction force which allows the player to transfer their weight forwards as they kick the ball.

Horizontal forces

Frictional force

There are two types of frictional force: static and sliding. Static friction force is the force exerted on one surface by another when there is no motion between the two surfaces. In other words, static friction occurs before an object starts to slide. Consider the friction generated between the surface of a netball court and the sole of the shoe. This is dry friction and when it acts between two surfaces that are not moving, it is referred to as static friction. As the netball player steps onto the court just before moving (sliding), there is a frictional force generated that holds the two surfaces static.

When dry friction acts between two surfaces that are moving relative to one another, sliding friction occurs. This is when there are two bodies in contact with one another that may have a tendency to slip/slide over each other. Friction acts in opposition to motion. This is often confusing but try to remember that friction resists the slipping and/or sliding motion of two surfaces and an arrow is therefore drawn in the opposite direction to this slipping, usually in the same direction as motion.

However, in skiing the friction arrow opposes motion as the slipping occurs in a forward direction.

Friction can be affected by the following factors:

● The surface characteristics of the two bodies in contact. Think of a 100 m sprinter who wears running spikes. These help to increase friction as the spikes make contact with the track and therefore maximise acceleration.

● The temperature of the two surfaces in contact. In curling, for example, the ice is swept in front of the curling stone. The sweeping action slightly raises the surface temperature of the ice which reduces the friction between the stone and ice, allowing the stone to travel further.

● The mass of the objects that are sliding. A larger mass results in greater friction.

Figure 15 The sweeping action in curling to reduce friction to allow the stone to travel further

Figure 12 Action force

Figure 13 Friction opposes the slippage between objects. For a runner the possible slippage of the feet is backwards so the friction arrow points forwards.

Figure 14 For a skier the slippage is forwards so the friction arrow points backwards

KEY WORD

Friction: Occurs when two or more bodies are in contact with one another.

Air resistance

Air resistance opposes the motion of a body travelling through the air and depends upon:

- The velocity of the moving body – the faster the performer moves, the greater the air resistance.
- The cross-sectional area of the moving body. The larger the cross-sectional area, the greater the air resistance. For example, think of the Tour de France and how the competitors crouch low over the handlebars, rather than sit upright.
- The shape and the surface characteristics of a moving body. A streamlined shape results in less resistance, as does a smooth surface; for example, most elite swimmers shave off all body hair or wear half/full body swimsuits so they create a smooth surface. Those who do not shave their head wear a swimming cap.

In water, air resistance is frequently referred to as 'drag'. Compare running in water to running on land. There is a much greater drag force in water due to its greater density.

How forces act upon the performer during linear motion

Forces are vectors and how they act upon a performer can be shown using an arrow on a free body diagram. The position, direction and length of the arrow are important and need to be drawn accurately.

The **weight** force is always drawn down from the centre of mass	The **reaction** force starts from where two bodies are in contact with one another. This contact can be the foot with the ground and is therefore drawn in an upward direction or can be the contact between sports equipment and a ball such as a tennis racket with a tennis ball.	The **friction** force starts from where the two bodies are in contact and is opposite to the direction of any potential slipping. It is drawn in the same direction as motion.	**Air resistance** is drawn from the centre of mass opposing the direction of motion of the body
a 	b 	c 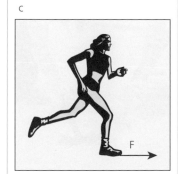	d 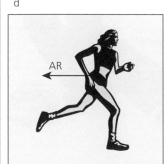

Figure 16 Free body diagrams

The length of the arrow drawn reflects the magnitude or size of the force: the longer the arrow, the bigger the size of the force.

Net force

This is the resultant force acting on a body when all other forces have been considered. Net force is often discussed in terms of balance versus unbalanced forces. A balanced force is when there are two or more forces acting on a body that are equal in size but opposite in direction. When standing, the weight force and reaction force are equal in size but opposite in direction. In this case, there is zero net force, and therefore no change in the state of motion.

An unbalanced force is when a force acting in one direction on a body is larger than a force acting in the opposite direction. When jumping in the air, the performer accelerates upwards as the reaction force is bigger than the weight force.

Similarly, if the friction force is equal in length to air resistance, then the net result is zero. If the friction arrow is longer than the air resistance arrow, the body will accelerate and if it is shorter, it will decelerate.

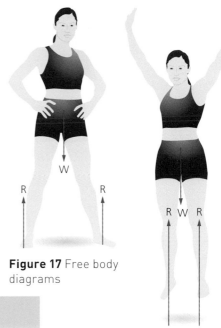

Figure 17 Free body diagrams

Figure 18 From left to right: F = AR so the net force is zero, F > AR shows acceleration, F < AR shows deceleration

The effects of internal and external forces can be represented as a vector diagram. In the high jump, the performer uses a large internal muscular force from the leg muscles to create a big action/reaction force in order to achieve as much vertical displacement (height) as possible. The relationship between the amount of vertical force and horizontal force provided by the muscles will lean towards the vertical component (V) as shown in Figure 20.

Figure 19 The forces exerted by the performer's leg muscles on the ground, when performing a high jump

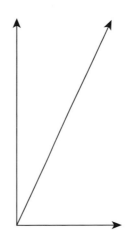

Figure 20 The forces exerted by the ground on the performer of a high jump

67

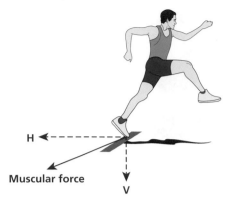

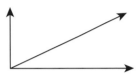

Muscular force

Figure 21 The forces exerted by the performer's leg muscles on the ground, when performing a long jump

Figure 22 The forces exerted by the ground on the performer of a long jump

As a result of the application of these forces, the resultant forces for the high jumper can be drawn as a vector diagram. The small horizontal force and the large vertical force provided by the muscles have a resultant force with a high trajectory (close to the vertical).

A long jumper, however, is trying to achieve as much horizontal distance as possible. This means there will be a greater contribution to the overall force from the horizontal component (H) as outlined in Figure 21.

As a result of the application of these forces, the resultant forces for the long jumper can be drawn as a vector diagram (see Figure 22).

CHECK YOUR UNDERSTANDING

Using arrows, draw the forces acting on the following bodies. Think carefully about the point of application, the size and direction of the force.

The relationship between impulse and increasing and decreasing momentum in sprinting

Impulse

Remember from Newton's first law of motion that a force is required to change a state of motion of a body. It will take a certain amount of time to apply this force. **Impulse** is the time it takes a force to be applied to an object or body and can be calculated as follows:

Impulse (newton seconds) = Force × Time

Knowledge of Newton's second law takes into account impulse and momentum. An increase in impulse will result in an increase in the rate of change of momentum, which causes a large change in velocity. For example, in tennis a player follows through with the racket to increase the amount of

KEY TERM

Impulse: Impulse = force × time.

time the racket is in contact with the tennis ball. This increases the outgoing momentum of the ball which causes the ball to travel faster. Consequently, impulse is equivalent to a change in the momentum of a body as a result of a force acting upon it:

Momentum = Mass × Velocity

Therefore, in a sporting environment impulse can be used to both add speed to a body or object, or slow them down on impact. Using impulse to increase momentum can be achieved through increasing the amount of muscular force that is applied. In basketball, for example, a large force is generated when jumping for a rebound in order to get as much height as quickly as possible to catch the ball. Using impulse to increase the momentum of a body or object can also be achieved through increasing the amount of time in which a force is applied. In the hammer throw, for example, three to four turns are used as opposed to just a single swing.

Using impulse to decrease the momentum of an object or body occurs by increasing the time forces act upon them. In any activity that involves a landing action such as a gymnast dismounting from the parallel bars, flexion of the hip, knee and ankle occurs, which extends the time of the force on the ground (how long the feet are in contact with the mat) and therefore allows the gymnast to control the landing and also reduces the chance of injury. Similarly at the end of an indoor 60 m sprint, the athletes have to stop quickly because the confines of the stadium mean there is not much track left. To do this, they push their feet hard into the ground to increase the contact time of the foot with the ground so they can decelerate quickly.

The interpretation of force–time graphs

Impulse is represented by an area under a force–time graph. The graphs in Figure 23 show various stages of a 100 m sprint. In the 100 m sprint, impulse is only concerned with horizontal forces. As the sprinter's foot lands on the ground, their muscles contract and a force is applied to the ground (action force) and the ground reaction force then acts on the foot which allows the athlete to accelerate forwards. The action of the foot in contact with the ground is referred to as a single footfall. It is important to note that in running/sprinting, negative impulse occurs first when the foot lands to provide a braking action; then positive impulse occurs next as the foot takes off for acceleration.

KEY TERM

Net impulse: A combination of positive and negative impulses.

Figure 23 Force–time graphs to show various stages of a 100 m sprint

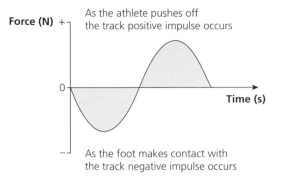

As the athlete pushes off the track positive impulse occurs

As the foot makes contact with the track negative impulse occurs

Middle of the race

Here both positive and negative impulses are equal (net impulse of zero). This means there is no acceleration or deceleration so the sprinter is running at a constant velocity.

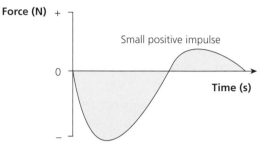

Small positive impulse

Large negative impulse

End of the race

Here the net impulse is negative which shows the sprinter decelerating.

Figure 23 (cont'd) Force–time graphs to show various stages of a 100 m sprint

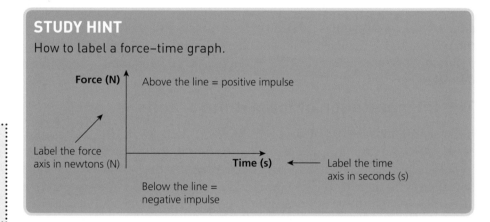
CHECK YOUR UNDERSTANDING

Can you explain how an athlete uses positive impulse during their sprint?

SUMMARY

You should now understand motion and forces and how they relate to sporting performance. To do this you need to explain and label the forces gravity, friction, air resistance, weight and muscular forces which generate equal and opposite reaction forces on a performer. Measurements of linear motion are divided into scalars and vectors and you need to be able to define and calculate these measurements and demonstrate the ability to plot, label and interpret biomechanical graphs and diagrams about them. Finally you should now be able to explain in sprinting how impulse can increase momentum by increasing the amount of muscular force that is applied and how impulse decreases momentum when the foot lands to provide a braking action. You need to be able to illustrate this in a force–time graph.

PRACTICE QUESTIONS

1 Sketch two vector diagrams representing the differing resultant forces for a long jumper and for a high jumper during take-off. (2 marks)

2 Ice hockey is often regarded as a very physical game, with many collisions occurring during normal play. A stationary ice-hockey puck was struck with an ice hockey stick and travelled across the ice until it struck and rebounded from a wall.

The diagram below shows the changes in horizontal linear velocity experienced by the puck. Assume that air resistance and friction on the ice are negligible, and describe and explain the horizontal motion of the puck associated with each of the periods of time identified as P, Q, R, S and T. (7 marks)

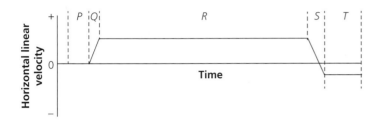

3 The graph below shows a velocity–time graph for an elite 100 m sprinter.

Use the graph to work out the velocity of the sprinter after 3 seconds and give a period of time when the sprinter's acceleration was the greatest. (2 marks)

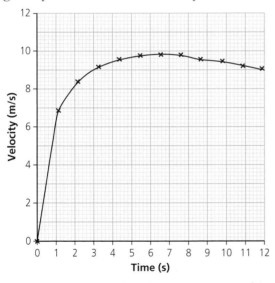

4 What is happening to the sprinter between 6 and 11 seconds? (1 mark)

5 The acceleration that a performer achieves when sprinting is related to impulse. What do you understand by the term impulse, and how can the athlete use impulse during their sprint? (4 marks)

Chapter 4.2
Angular motion

Chapter objectives

By the end of this chapter you should be able to:

● Understand and apply Newton's laws to angular motion.
● Define and give units for angular motion, angular acceleration, angular displacement and angular velocity.
● Explain how angular momentum can be conserved during flight using moment of inertia and its effect on angular velocity.

Angular motion

Angular motion occurs in sport all the time. It refers to rotation and involves movement around a fixed point or axis. It can involve the whole body in a somersault or a body part such as the arms when throwing the discus. Picture a runner – although they run in a straight line (linear motion), there is a significant amount of rotational movement in the running action in the arms and legs as they rotate around the joint (axis of rotation).

Figure 1 Three examples of angular motion: A somersault, throwing a discus or moving around the high bar in gymnastics.

Angular motion occurs when a force is applied outside the centre of mass. An off-centre force is referred to as an eccentric force.

ACTIVITY

To explain angular motion, lay a pencil on a flat surface. Its centre of mass is in the middle of the pencil. Tap it at one end so it turns. You have applied a force that is not through the centre of mass – an eccentric force. Eccentric forces cause rotations/angular motion. Tap it again at its centre of mass – the whole pencil moves in a straight line. You have applied a concentric force through the centre of mass and this causes linear motion.

ACTIVITY

Can you think of three sporting examples when a force is applied outside the centre of mass of an object or body to cause rotation to occur?

KEY TERM

Angular motion: Movement around a fixed point.

ACTIVITY

Can you think of examples from the shoulder joint for each axis of rotation?

When angular motion takes place, the body can rotate in one of three axes:

Transverse axis, which runs from side to side across the body	Sagittal axis, which runs from front to back	Longitudinal axis, which runs from top to bottom
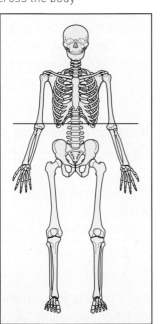	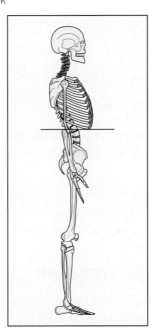	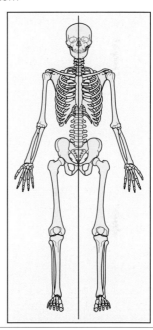
A somersault rotates a body in a transverse axis	A cartwheel rotates in a sagittal axis	A multiple spin in ice skating rotates in a longitudinal axis

Figure 2 Transverse, sagittal and longitudinal axes

KEY TERM

Torque: The rotational consequence of a force.

Angular motion occurs as a result of a **torque** (often called the moment). A torque is a turning force. It causes an object to turn about its axis of rotation. Increasing the size of the force increases torque. Applying the same force further away from the axis of rotation also increases torque. The easiest way to understand torque is to think of a door. A door rotates on its hinges and the rotation of the door depends on where you apply the force. If you exert a force close to the hinge, you have to apply a large force to make the door swing. If you apply a force at the edge of the door, you only need a small force to make the door swing. This means the perpendicular distance of the force from the pivotal point (moment arm) will increase the moment of the force. The moment of a force or torque (measured in newton metres) can be calculated as follows:

Moment of force or torque = Force × Perpendicular distance from the fulcrum
(newton metres)   (newtons)   (metres)

Angular analogues of Newton's laws of motion

It is possible to relate Newton's laws of motion to angular motion. In Chapter 5 of Book 1 we looked at Newton's Laws in relation to linear motion. Just by changing the terminology we can relate them to angular motion, except this time it is an eccentric reaction force that causes a change to angular motion.

Newton's first law

A rotating body will continue to turn about its axis of rotation with constant angular momentum unless an external rotational force (torque) is exerted upon it.

In practice, think of an ice skater spinning in the air. They will continue to spin until they land on the ice when an external force (torque) is exerted from the ice on their skates which changes their state of angular momentum.

Newton's second law

The rate of change of angular momentum of a body is proportional to the force (torque) causing it and the change that takes place in the direction in which the force (torque) acts.

In practice, the greater the torque exerted, the faster the rotation will be.

Newton's third law

When a force (torque) is applied by one body to another, the second body will exert an equal and opposite force (torque) on the other body.

In practice, as a goalkeeper tips the ball over the bar, they throw their arms up (eccentric action force on body), which causes the lower part of their legs to go back (reaction force).

Figure 3 Goalkeeper in action

Quantities used in angular motion

Knowledge of the following measurements can be used to describe the angular motion of a performer. You need to be able to define and give a unit of measurement for each of the following terms.

Angular displacement

This is the smallest change in angle between the starting and finishing point. **Angular displacement** is measured in degrees and **radians** (1 radian = 57.3 degrees).

Angular velocity

This refers to the rotational speed of an object and the axis about which the object is rotating. This term is a vector quantity as it makes reference to direction. This is because it refers to the angular displacement that is covered in a certain time. **Angular velocity** is calculated by dividing the angular displacement in radians (rad) by the time taken in seconds (s):

$$\text{Angular velocity (rad/s)} = \frac{\text{Angular displacement (rad)}}{\text{Time taken (s)}}$$

Angular acceleration

Angular acceleration is the rate of change of angular velocity. It is calculated by dividing the change in angular velocity in radians per second by the time taken in seconds:

$$\text{Angular acceleration} = (\text{rad/s}^2) = \frac{\text{Change in angular velocity (rad/s)}}{\text{Time taken (s)}}$$

To illustrate these measurements, look at the example of the gymnast spinning anti-clockwise on a bar in Figure 4.

CHECK YOUR UNDERSTANDING

Explain, using Newton's first law of angular motion, how a performer can alter their state of rotation.

KEY TERMS

Radian: The unit of measurement for angles.

Angular displacement: The smallest change in angle between the start and finish point of a rotation.

Angular velocity: The rate of change of angular displacement.

Angular acceleration: The rate of change of angular velocity.

STUDY HINT

Angular displacement and angular velocity are measured in radians: 1 radian = 57.3 degrees.

Figure 4 Gymnast spinning on a bar

The following calculations in the table below are from position X to position Y taken from Figure 4.

Angular displacement	Angular velocity	Angular acceleration
Angular displacement is the smallest change in angle from the starting point to the finishing point. In this case it measures: 110 degrees = 1.9 radians	$\dfrac{\text{Angular displacement (rad)}}{\text{Time taken (s)}}$ $\dfrac{1.9}{0.5} = 3.8$ rad/s	$\dfrac{\text{Change in angular velocity (rad/s)}}{\text{Time taken (s)}}$ Position X = 0 rad/s Position Y = 3.8 rad/s $= \dfrac{3.8}{0.5} = 7.6$ rads/s^2

ACTIVITY

Using Figure 5 below, now calculate the angular velocity and angular acceleration of the gymnast to get from position X to position Y if the time taken is 0.6 s.

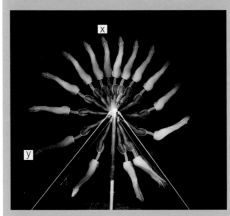

Figure 5 Gymnast spinning on a bar

STUDY HINT

How to calculate angular displacement, angular velocity or angular acceleration:

$$\text{Angular velocity (rad/s)} = \frac{\text{Angular displacement (rad)}}{\text{Time taken (s)}}$$

$$\text{Angular acceleration= (rad/s}^2) = \frac{\text{Change in angular velocity (rad/s)}}{\text{Time taken (s)}}$$

Moment of inertia

Inertia is a resistance to change in motion so moment of inertia is the resistance of a body to angular motion (rotation). This can be applied to the start of rotation when a body will resist angular motion; but once the rotation occurs, the body will want to continue to turn about its axis of rotation. Think about rotating doors in the entrance of a hotel. At first it is hard to start them rotating but once they get going, it is just as hard to stop them. Moment of inertia depends upon the mass of the body and the distribution of mass around the axis.

Mass of the body/object

The greater the mass, the greater the resistance to change and therefore the greater the moment of inertia. For example, a ten-pin bowling ball is more difficult to roll along the ground than a football, but once it starts rolling, it is more difficult to stop than the lighter ball.

Distribution of mass from the axis of rotation

The closer the mass is to the axis of rotation, the easier it is to turn, because the moment of inertia is low. Increasing the distance of the distribution of mass from the axis of rotation will increase the moment of inertia. In the example below, a somersault in an open position has a higher moment of inertia than the tucked somersault because in the straight position, the distribution of the diver's mass is further away from their axis of rotation. As a result, the open somersault is more difficult to perform than a tucked somersault.

Figure 6 Tucked and open somersaults

It is possible to look at the concept of moment of inertia to improve sprinting technique. All movements involve rotations at joints. Usain Bolt's upper leg action during sprinting rotates around his hip joint. His back leg is the drive leg, which is extending. As a result, the leg has a high moment of inertia as the mass is distributed away from the hip joint. As Usain recovers (front leg), he brings the mass of his leg closer to his hip joint which reduces his moment of inertia. This means he can bring his leg through quicker in order to start another drive phase. This is why a high knee lift is important in sprinting!

Figure 7 Usain Bolt's sprinting technique

KEY TERM

Angular momentum: Spin.

Angular momentum

Angular momentum (L) is the quantity of rotation a body possesses, or to put it more simply, spin. It involves an object or body in motion around an axis. It depends upon the moment of inertia (I) and angular velocity (ω).

Angular momentum = Moment of inertia × Angular velocity

These two are inversely proportional: if moment of inertia increases, angular velocity decreases, and vice versa.

Conservation of angular momentum

Angular momentum is a conserved quantity – it stays constant unless an external torque (force) acts upon it (Newton's first law). In sport it occurs during flight or on ice and snow where there is hardly any friction. In practice, when a diver performs a double front somersault from the 10 m board, the amount of angular momentum stays the same during flight and only changes when the diver hits the water on entry or changes their body position.

The conservation of angular momentum can also be highlighted when a figure skater performs a multiple spin, turning on a longitudinal (vertical) axis. Ice is a friction-free surface so there is no resistance to movement. Only the figure skater, therefore, can manipulate their moment of inertia to increase or decrease the speed of the spin. At the start of the spin, the arms and leg are stretched out. This increases their distance from the axis of rotation, resulting in a large moment of inertia and a large angular momentum in order to start the spin, so rotation is slow.

When the figure-skater brings their arms and legs back in line with the rest of the body, the distance of these body parts to the axis of rotation decreases significantly. This reduces the moment of inertia, which in turn increases their angular velocity and the skater spins very quickly.

Figure 8 The start of a spin

Figure 9 Increasing angular velocity during a spin

CHECK YOUR UNDERSTANDING

Why do you think a diver may want to increase their moment of inertia just before they enter the water?

SUMMARY

Angular motion refers to rotation where movement occurs around a fixed point or axis. Newton's laws of motion can be applied to angular momentum (angular analogues). In Newton's first law, rotation will remain constant unless an external rotational force is applied. Newton's second law applied means the greater the rotational force, the faster the rotation becomes. Newton's third law applied is when a rotational force by one body on another results in the second body exerting an equal and opposite rotational force on the first body.

Angular displacement and angular velocity are measured in radians. Angular momentum stays the same (conserved) but a performer can alter the speed of a rotation (angular velocity) by changing their body position to increase or decrease their moment of inertia. An increase in moment of inertia results in a decrease in angular velocity and a decrease in moment of inertia results in an increase in angular velocity.

PRACTICE QUESTIONS

1 Coaches use biomechanical analysis to help optimise performance. The diagram below is incomplete. When complete, it should show three curves representing the following parameters during a backward tucked somersault:

- angular momentum
- moment of inertia
- angular velocity.

Add the missing curve and label all three curves.   (3 marks)

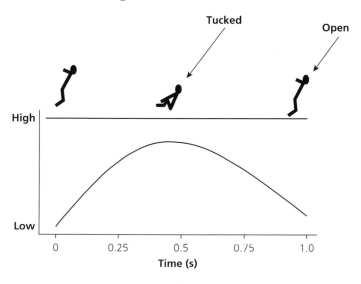

2 Explain Newton's first law of motion in relation to a dancer spinning.   (3 marks)

3 How does the gymnast alter her speed of rotation by changing her body shape?   (8 marks)

Chapter objectives

By the end of this chapter you should be able to:

- Identify angle of release, velocity of release and height of release as the factors that affect the horizontal displacement of projectiles.
- Identify the factors affecting flight paths of different projectiles.
- Understand the forces that affect the shot put and badminton shuttle.
- Identify the vector components of parabolic flight.

Projectile motion

Projectile motion refers to the movement of either an object or the human body as they travel through the air. In sport, as soon as a ball is released in a kick, hit or throw it becomes a projectile. The human body acts as a projectile in a variety of sporting situations such as the long jump and gymnastic vault.

Figure 1 The human body acting as a projectile

ACTIVITY

Can you think of other examples in sport when the human body becomes a projectile?

Factors affecting the horizontal displacement of a projectile

Three factors determine the **horizontal displacement** of a projectile:

- angle of release
- speed of release
- height of release.

Angle of release

To throw an object as far as possible, the angle of release from the performer's hand is important. This optimum angle of release is dependent upon release height and landing height. When both the release height and the landing height are equal, then the optimum angle of release is 45° (ignoring wind resistance and gravity). This would be the case for a long jumper as shown in Figure 2.

Figure 2 The long jumper takes off from the ground and lands on the ground

If the release height is below the landing height, then the optimum angle of release needs to be greater than 45°. Shooting in basketball highlights this (assuming the ring is the landing height).

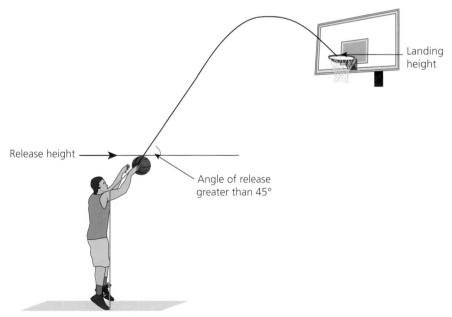

Figure 3 Shooting in basketball

If the release height is greater than the landing height, the optimum angle of release needs to be less than 45°. This can be seen in the flight path of the shot put where the hand is the point of release which is much higher than the landing point (ground) (see Figure 4).

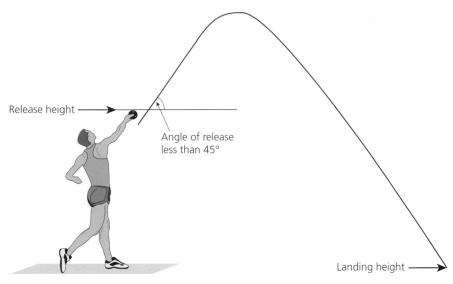

Figure 4 Throwing the shot put

Research has shown that the optimum angle of release for a world-class shot putter can be anywhere from 26° to 38°. Keeping the release angle smaller means more speed can be generated as the shot is released. The optimum angle of release for a shot putter will also depend on the size, strength and throwing technique of the athlete.

Speed of release

The greater the release velocity of a projectile, the greater the horizontal displacement travelled. In the shot put, the speed of the shift or rotation across the circle ensures that the shot leaves the hand at maximum velocity so a greater horizontal displacement can be achieved.

Height of release

A greater release height also results in an increase in horizontal displacement. The force of gravity is constantly acting on the mass of a shot put. This therefore means that technically the shot putter should try to release the shot at the highest point possible above the ground to gain maximum horizontal displacement. Similarly when fielding a ball in cricket, the taller the fielder, the further the horizontal displacement, providing the angle of release and velocity of release are the same. In order for a smaller fielder to achieve the same displacement, they will have to manipulate both their angle and velocity of release.

Factors affecting flight paths of different projectiles

Weight (gravity) and air resistance are two forces that affect projectiles while they are in the air. These two factors are crucial in deciding whether a projectile has a flight path that is a true **parabola** or a distorted parabola. A parabola is a uniform curve that is symmetrical at its highest point.

Projectiles with a large weight force have a small air resistance force and follow a true parabolic flight path. A good example is the shot put.

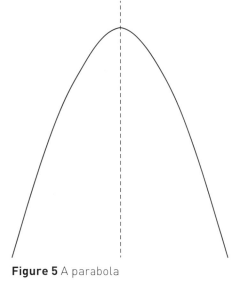

Figure 5 A parabola

KEY TERM

Parabola: A curve with matching left- and right-hand sides.

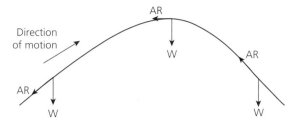

Figure 6 A parabolic flight path of a shot put

Figure 6 shows the forces acting on the flight path of a shot put at the start, middle and end of flight. As the shot put has a large mass there is a longer weight arrow.

The longer the flight path, the longer air resistance can affect a projectile and have a greater influence. In projectiles with a lighter mass, the effects of air resistance result in a flight path that deviates from a true parabola to a distorted parabola. The badminton shuttlecock is a good example of this.

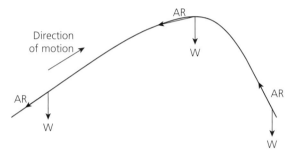

Figure 7 A non-parabolic flight path of a shuttlecock

Figure 7 shows the forces acting on the flight path of a shuttlecock. Compared to the shot put, the shuttlecock has a lighter mass and an unusual shape that increases its air resistance. In a serve the shuttle starts off with a high velocity, provided by the force of the racket. As the shuttle continues its flight path it slows down and the effect of air resistance reduces.

Vector components of parabolic flight

A shot put follows a parabolic flight path and as it is released at an angle to the horizontal, its initial velocity has a **horizontal component** and a **vertical component**. These two components can be represented by vectors. A vector is drawn as an arrow and it has magnitude (size) and direction. Drawing a bigger arrow means there is more magnitude and a smaller arrow less magnitude.

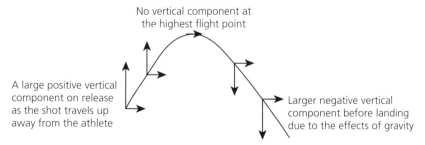

Figure 8 The forces acting on the flight path of a shot put

ACTIVITY

Can you identify the flight path of a golf ball, football and shot put and explain why they follow this flight path?

KEY TERMS

Horizontal component: The horizontal motion of an object.

Vertical component: The upward motion of an object.

This arrow represents the horizontal component	→
This arrow represents the vertical component	↑

Figure 9 shows both the both horizontal and vertical vectors on the flight path of a shot put as it follows a parabolic flight path.

Here the vertical component can only be affected by gravity which is why the vertical component decreases during flight. Air resistance is negligible so both the horizontal and vertical components are unaffected by air resistance. This means the horizontal component remains constant throughout the flight.

It is also possible to add the horizontal and vertical vectors together to get a resultant vector. This shows the true flight path of the shot put.

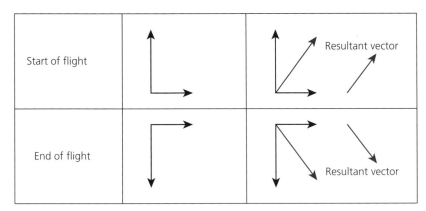

Figure 9 The true flight path of the shot put

SUMMARY

Make sure you can identify angle of release, velocity of release and height of release and explain how these affect the distance a projectile can travel. Understand how weight and air resistance act on the shot put and a badminton shuttle and recognise that a shot put follows a parabolic flight path as weight is the largest force; the shuttle follows a non-parabolic flight path as air resistance is the largest force. Make sure you can draw the horizontal and vertical components of a shot put's flight path and also give the resultant vector.

PRACTICE QUESTIONS

1 In a game of badminton the performer hits the shuttle into the air and it then becomes a projectile. Explain how the various forces act to affect the badminton shuttle *during* its flight. (3 marks)

2 Name three factors that affect the distance a shot put travels. (3 marks)

3 Draw a diagram to show the flight path of a shot put and on your diagram label and explain the changing vertical and horizontal vectors at the following points:
   ● the point of release
   ● the highest point of flight
   ● the point immediately before landing. (6 marks)

Chapter 4.4
Fluid mechanics

Chapter objectives

By the end of this chapter you should be able to:

● Understand what is meant by dynamic fluid force and relate this to drag and lift.

● Explain the factors that reduce and increase drag in sport.

● Explain the Bernoulli principle in relation to an upward lift force for the discus throw and a downward lift force for speed skiers, cyclists and racing cars.

Fluid mechanics

Fluid mechanics is the study of an object or the human body that travels through any liquid or gas. For example, swimmers travel through water and a tennis ball travels through the air. Both of these are slowed down by friction or drag. You need to be able to explain how a variety of sports can be affected by their fluid environment. You also have to look specifically at the effect of an upward lift force on the discus and a downward lift force on speed skiers, cyclists and racing cars.

Dynamic fluid force

Fluid dynamics is concerned with the movement of liquids and gases. It is a branch of fluid mechanics which is the study of fluids and how forces affect them. Drag and lift are dynamic fluid forces. These two forces have an effect on a variety of sports such as cycling, sprinting and swimming. Any projectile such as a ball, discus and javelin will also experience a drag and lift force.

Drag force

A **drag force** slows something down. Drag is the resistance force caused by the motion of a body travelling through a fluid. A drag force acts in opposition to the direction of motion and therefore has a negative effect on velocity. A drag force is produced from air resistance and friction. A cyclist, for example, will constantly try to minimise drag so they can increase velocity.

There are two different types of drag:

● *Surface drag* relates to friction between the surface of an object and the fluid environment. It is sometimes called 'skin drag'. Swimmers wear specialised smooth clothing and shave off body hair from their arms and torso to reduce surface drag.

● *Form drag* relates to the impact of the fluid environment on an object. It is sometimes referred to as 'shape drag'. The forces affecting the leading edge of an object increase form drag and the forces affecting the trailing edge reduce form drag. Form drag relates to streamlining and if we stick to swimming as an example, the swimmer has to create the thinnest and straightest form as they move through the water to decrease form drag. A large form drag also offers less turbulent air for anything that is following, e.g. in the slipstream. In cycling, for example, a cyclist will use another rider's slipstream (also known as 'drafting')

Figure 1 Slipstreaming in cycling

As the wind hits the front cyclist, it goes around the sides and the cyclist behind uses the air pocket that has been created. For it to work, the second cyclist has to ride very close to the bike in front (approximately 15–30 cm) and can save up to 30 per cent more energy as a result.

Factors that reduce and increase drag

Drag opposes the motion of a body travelling through the air. We have already looked at the factors that affect air resistance on page 66 but we can now look at them in more detail to explain how a sports performer can reduce and increase drag.

The velocity of the moving body

The greater the velocity of a body through a fluid, the greater the drag force. A racing car, sprinter or cyclist, for example, will experience greater air resistance in their competition, which increases drag. Consequently in a sport that is very quick, it is important to reduce the effects of drag and this is done by **streamlining** the body as much as possible.

The cross-sectional area of the moving body

The cross-sectional area of a moving body can reduce or increase drag. A large cross-sectional area increases drag. In some sports, reducing the effects of drag is crucial to ensure success. For example, in the Tour de France, the competitors reduce their cross-sectional area by crouching low over the handlebars, rather than sitting upright.

Figure 2 A cyclist crouching over their handlebars to reduce their cross-sectional area

Figure 3 A speed skier crouching low to reduce drag

Similarly, speed skiers reduce the effects of drag by crouching low. This will allow them to travel faster.

The shape and the surface characteristics of a moving body

A more streamlined, aerodynamic shape reduces drag. Sports scientists are regularly trialling drag-resistant clothing to achieve 'marginal gains' in speed to give competitors the edge over their opposition The speed skier has a helmet that extends to their shoulders to give them a more streamlined position and their special form-fitting suit and aerodynamic boots are also streamlined. In cycling, clothing with ridges and an aerodynamic helmet with air ducts have recently been designed to try to reduce the effects of drag even more. Elite swimmers shave off all body hair and wear half-body swimsuits (previously they wore 'fast suits' but these have now been banned) so they create a smooth surface. Those who do not shave their head wear a swimming cap.

The shape and surface characteristics of a badminton shuttle result in a much larger drag force from air resistance. The shuttle has an unusual shape with feathers and it is also very light. The larger drag force from air resistance means it loses speed quickly.

> **ACTIVITY**
>
> Can you think of some other examples in sport where the shape and surface characteristics of a moving body can increase or decrease drag?

> **CHECK YOUR UNDERSTANDING**
>
> Explain how increasing the cross-sectional area of a moving body can increase drag.

The Bernoulli principle

When the discus is thrown, it experiences an upward **lift force** during flight. A lift force enables the discus to stay in the air for longer, therefore increasing the horizontal distance it travels.

The more lift a projectile has during flight, the longer it will stay in the air and the further the horizontal distance it will travel. Lift is achieved when different air pressures act on an object. Air that travels faster has a lower pressure than air that travels slower. This is the **Bernoulli principle**. When a projectile such as the discus is released, the **angle of attack** is important.

KEY TERMS

Lift force: Causes a body to move perpendicular to the direction of travel.

Bernoulli principle: Where air molecules exert less pressure the faster they travel and more pressure when they travel slower.

Angle of attack: The tilt of a projectile relative to the air flow.

The angle of attack changes the flow of air around the discus so the air that travels over the top of the discus has to travel a longer distance than the air underneath. This results in the air above the discus travelling at a faster velocity, which therefore creates a lower pressure. This lower pressure above the discus creates an upward lift force and allows the discus to stay in the air for longer, resulting in a greater horizontal distance. If the angle of attack is too great, then lift is reduced and drag increases, causing the discus to stall. The optimum angle of attack that produces the best lift for the discus is anything between 25° and 40°.

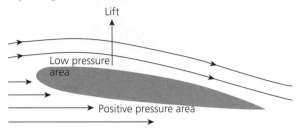

Figure 4 The flow of air over an object which creates a lift force

ACTIVITY

Try to explain what would happen if the angle of attack for the discus was 90°.

CHECK YOUR UNDERSTANDING

Describe how the javelin makes use of an upward lift force.

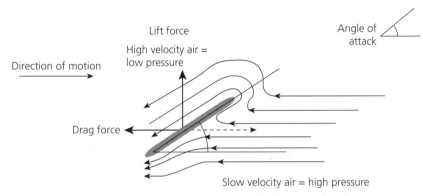

Figure 5 The Bernoulli principle producing a lift force on the discus

A lift force does not always have to work in an upwards direction. The Bernoulli principle can also be used to describe a downward lift force, such as that required by speed skiers, cyclists and racing cars. The car, bike and skis need to be pushed down into the ground so a greater frictional force is created. In a Formula 1 sports car, for example, the spoiler is angled so the lift force can act in a downward direction to push the car into the track. This happens because the air that travels over the top of the car travels a shorter distance than the air underneath, due to the angle of the spoiler. As a result, the air above the car travels at a slower velocity and at a higher pressure. This creates a greater frictional force so the tyres maintain a firm grip on the track as the car travels at high speed and around corners.

Here the shape and angle of the rear spoiler results in the lift force created by the Bernoulli principle acting in a downward direction.

Similarly with cyclists, the low streamlined body position over the handlebars means that the air that travels over the top of the cyclist has to travel a shorter distance than the air underneath. This results in the air above the cyclist travelling at a slower velocity which therefore creates a higher pressure. This higher pressure above the cyclist creates a downward lift force and allows the tyres of the bike to maintain a firm grip on the track.

Figure 6 A downward lift force is caused by the shape and angle of the rear spoiler

Figure 7 A downward lift force is caused by the cyclist leaning forward over the handlebars

Speed skiers need to stay in contact with the ice for faster speed because more downward acting lift means more force which melts the snow for a better friction-free surface.

SUMMARY

Drag and lift are dynamic fluid forces. Drag is a force that acts in opposition to motion and a lift force causes a body to move perpendicular to the direction of travel. The factors that reduce and increase drag are the velocity, cross-sectional area and the surface characteristics of a moving body. The Bernoulli principle is where air molecules exert less pressure the faster they travel and more pressure when they travel slower. Using this principle, an upward lift force is produced for the discus throw and a downward lift force for speed skiers, cyclists and racing cars.

PRACTICE QUESTIONS

1 Identify what is meant by a drag force and, giving an example from sport, explain how the effects of a drag force can be reduced. (3 marks)

2 Identify and explain two factors that can increase or decrease drag. (2 marks)

3 Explain the Bernoulli principle in relation to a downward lift force for a racing car. (4 marks)

Chapter 5.1
Psychological factors that can influence an individual in physical activities

Chapter objectives

This chapter concentrates on psychological theories and concepts which explain the impact that psychology has on the sports performer and the associated action. Some new terms, logical ideas and research-based theories are discussed and their impact on sports performance is explained.

After reading this chapter you should be able to:

- Explain the concepts of achievement motivation and the factors which influence a desire to be competitive.
- Look at the reasons sports coaches and players give for success and failure by examining the Weiner model of attribution and understand how this model can be used to encourage players to keep trying.
- Understand the factors which promote confidence in sport by looking at the theories of Bandura and Vealey.
- Examine the role of a sports leader and the factors that influence leadership style using the leadership models of Fiedler and Chelladurai.
- Discuss the methods coaches can use to reduce stress in the performer, including somatic and cognitive techniques.

Achievement motivation

Achievement motivation looks at how much desire a player has to keep on trying to succeed. It looks at two personality dimensions identified by the sports scientist Atkinson (1964). The first personality type is demonstrated by those sports people who keep on trying, even when things become particularly tough. These are the type of people who approach competition with enthusiasm; for example, the football player who volunteers to take a penalty in a penalty shoot-out at the end of the game even though there is a risk of missing the penalty and letting the team down.

Such personalities are said to display **approach** behaviour, known as the **need to achieve** or **NACH**, they are said to welcome competition and they also display, according to Atkinson and McClelland, some or all of the following characteristics:

1 *They welcome competition.* For example, in a squash league ladder competition they would want to play against someone of equal ability or slightly better than them so that even though there is a risk of losing, there is pride and satisfaction from winning: a strong incentive to win!

2 *They take risks.* People who have the need to achieve will attempt a more difficult route on a rock climb so that there is more satisfaction from reaching the top.

3 *They are very confident.* The need to achieve means that players have belief in their ability.

4 *They are task persistent.* One of the most important aspects of having the need to achieve is that a player will keep trying, even if they fail the first time. They will work in training to put right the things that went wrong so that they can do better next time.

5 *They attribute success internally.* People with the need to achieve will tell themselves that the reason for a win was a factor that was down to them, maybe the amount of effort they put into the game. (Attribution theory is discussed later in the chapter.)

6 *They welcome feedback and evaluation.* The need to achieve means that one of the first priorities after the game is to look at the statistics or to seek appraisal from the coach.

7 *They base their actions on trying to seek pride and satisfaction from their performance.*

The second personality type is one that shows a need to avoid competition and to seek safe and secure options rather than risky ones. Some coaches would argue that this is not a bad approach since towards the end of a close game, it might be better to play safe. In 2015, the Manchester United manager Louis van Gaal was criticised for a safe rather than risky approach to games, yet his team were close to the top of the league. The characteristics of those who show the **need to avoid failure** or **NAF** are:

1 *They will give up easily.* Those with NAF personalities will not have a second go if they fail the first time. They do not like to damage their self-esteem by losing, so their logic is, 'If I can't do it I won't bother'. Those with this personality type may even then go on to develop negative attitudes towards the activity; for example, lacking the flexibility for gymnastics might lead someone to stop doing the sport rather than increasing the stretching.

2 *They do not like feedback or evaluation.* NAF personalities will tend to avoid looking at the stats sheet in case they find something unwelcome that could affect future self-esteem.

3 *They take easy options.* In the league ladder, people with NAF characteristics will play either someone they can easily beat, perhaps at the bottom of the ladder or, perhaps surprisingly, someone at the very top of the ladder. This is because they can maintain self-esteem by either an easy win or by losing to an opponent they were not expected to beat.

KEY TERMS

Achievement motivation: The tendency to approach or avoid competitive situations. Summed up as the Drive to Succeed *minus* the Fear of Failure.

NACH: The need to achieve; approach behaviour. The player welcomes competition.

NAF: The need to avoid failure; avoidance behaviour. The player avoids risk.

Attributing success internally: Giving a reason for success that is due to the responsibility of the player.

Figure 1 The football player scoring a penalty has taken the risk of missing to gain the satisfaction and pride of scoring

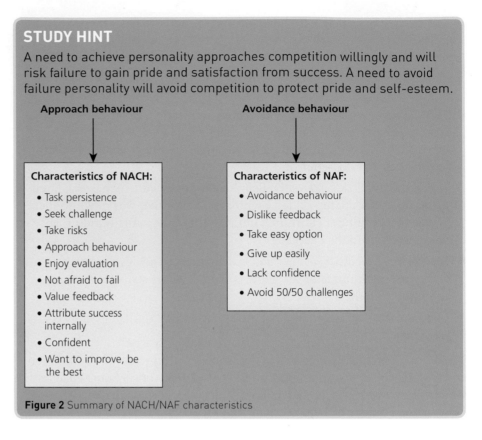

Approach behaviour   **Avoidance behaviour**

Characteristics of NACH:

- Task persistence
- Seek challenge
- Take risks
- Approach behaviour
- Enjoy evaluation
- Not afraid to fail
- Value feedback
- Attribute success internally
- Confident
- Want to improve, be the best

Characteristics of NAF:

- Avoidance behaviour
- Dislike feedback
- Take easy option
- Give up easily
- Lack confidence
- Avoid 50/50 challenges

Figure 2 Summary of NACH/NAF characteristics

The level of achievement motivation: what determines the NACH or NAF approach?

Achievement motivation can vary in sports performers. Sometimes and in some situations approach behaviour will be displayed and in other situations, avoidance will be shown. Achievement motivation can be defined as the drive to succeed *minus* the fear of failure. It is how sports performers approach or avoid competition and the definition used implies a balance between the personality of the performer and the situation. Therefore the level of achievement motivation shown depends on the **interaction** of personality and situation. The need to achieve or the need to avoid failure are situation-specific.

In terms of personality, some performers will have the need to achieve; others will have the need to avoid failure. This personality can be innate or developed (see personality, trait and social learning, Chapter 2.2, Book 1) and those with the trait of approaching competition will try hard in most situations.

In terms of the situation, the performer has to gauge the probability of success in the task and the incentive gained from that success. What this means is that a task that is easy will probably be completed successfully but will offer little incentive value or pride. The success is given, but no sense of pride is achieved. Such an approach may be adopted by a person with the need to avoid failure.

However, the undertaking of a task with a high degree of difficulty, such as a high board dive that requires some risky and difficult moves, may not be completed successfully, but if success is achieved then there is a large slice of pride and satisfaction to be gained, and a better score! A person with the need to achieve may adopt this approach to sport.

Figure 3 High board dive. The diver can play safe and include a well-rehearsed move but could also take a risk by including new and difficult moves which could gain a better score.

ACTIVITY

Look carefully at the graph shown in Figure 4. Make a copy of the graph and show in your copy two points on the line of the graph: one where you think a need to achieve performer will be and one where you think a need to avoid failure performer would be.

Figure 4

Interaction of

Personality   Situation

NACH   Probability of success

NAF   Incentive value

Figure 5 A summary of the influences on the level of achievement motivation

To develop the need to achieve

Most sports coaches would want their players to show approach behaviour when competing, even though a safe and risk-free approach is sometimes needed. The coach would often want players who will keep on trying and show confidence.

To develop approach behaviour in players, coaches might try the following strategies:

1 *Reinforcement.* The coach should offer praise and rewards to players who do well or who achieve their goals, so that the players keep the desire to do well in the future, thus promoting task persistence.

2 *Attribute success internally.* The coach should tell the player that any success achieved was down to something for which the player has responsibility. This could be the amount of effort the player put into winning the game or the good technique shown when executing skills. (See section on attribution theory on page 112.)

Figure 6 Basketball player doing a pass. This drill could be started without opposition to allow success

ACTIVITY

Use examples to show how a coach could allow success during practice.

KEY TERM

Confidence: A belief in the ability to master a task.

3 *Allowing success.* To encourage the belief in success and improve confidence, the coach could set tasks and training drills that can be accomplished with a little effort in the early development of the player and perhaps in the early part of training sessions.

4 *Improving confidence.* Later in this chapter we look at the concept of confidence, or self-efficacy in sport. Improving such confidence, using some of the strategies discussed here, will develop the need to achieve approach.

5 *Goal setting.* Coaches and players should set goals that are achievable with an amount of effort. This means that there is satisfaction to be gained from achieving the goal. Once a goal is reached, another challenge can be set so that the performer always has a realistic target to aim for. Goals set should just concern winning or the outcome. This is because, even in defeat, a narrow loss or a second place could involve an improved performance or technique when the performer reaches a process goal (a specific and agreed improvement in technique).

Achievement goal theory

Achievement goal theory suggests that motivation and task persistence depend on the type of goals set by the performer and how they measure success. Goals can be set to include an outcome which is based on beating others. It doesn't matter how the result was achieved as long as the goal is reached. If the performer succeeds then pride and satisfaction are maintained. The problem here is that if the performer fails to get the result, then confidence can be lowered. A task-related goal, however, is more concerned with the process of success, which is measured against the performer's own standards rather than against others, so that success can be achieved, regardless of the result and thus confidence is maintained. The performer will also consider their perceived level of ability when evaluating such goals.

> **CHECK YOUR UNDERSTANDING**
> 1 List three characteristics of a performer who displays approach behaviour.
> 2 List three characteristics of a performer who shows the need to avoid failure.
> 3 What is achievement motivation?
> 4 Name three things that influence the level of achievement motivation.
> 5 Suggest three things a coach could do to develop the need to achieve.

Confidence in sport

Confidence is such an important part of the make-up of a sports performer. Those with confidence tend to try harder and take more risks. They are more likely to show approach behaviour (see page 90) and, very importantly, those with confidence are more likely to win! The problem with confidence is that it can vary in intensity and with the situation. Confidence is another psychological concept that depends on interaction: the interaction of experience, personality and the situation. It makes sense to suggest that if you have experience of an activity you are more likely to perform better at it, especially if that experience has been positive, for example, a win. If a team has beaten their rivals quite heavily they are much more likely to think that they can beat them again the next time they play. If one of the players in that team has taken free kicks, set plays or penalties and scored from them, it might be that when a similar situation occurs again, the player with the experience in that specific situation is the one confident enough to step up and take the free kick.

In terms of personality, two types of confidence can be identified: trait confidence and state confidence.

Trait confidence is a consistent level of confidence shown in most situations when the player is happy to take part and anxiety is low. Trait sports confidence is concerned with how an athlete rates their ability to perform across a wide range of sports.

State confidence refers to a specific situation, such as taking a penalty or playing in front of a large crowd. This type of confidence may be temporary and can vary depending on the interaction of the influence of experience and personality. State sports confidence is concerned with how a performer rates their ability to perform at a particular moment.

The Vealey model of sports confidence

The interaction of factors that influence confidence was summarised by the psychologist Robin Vealey. She looked at the influence of trait confidence, state confidence, the situation and the competitive orientation of the performer. The **competitive orientation** refers to how much a performer is drawn to challenging situations.

Vealey suggested that confidence gained in one area of sport could be used to improve confidence in a different sporting activity. She used the idea of trait confidence, where the performer would rate their chances of doing well in a range of sports, and the idea of state confidence, where a performer would rate their chances of doing well in one specific situation. It was suggested that these two influences combine to produce a level of confidence in an **objective sporting situation**. The objective sporting situation is the combination of the type of skill being performed and the situation. If it is a skill that has been used successfully in the past, then both trait and state confidence would be high. The objective situation also looks at the conditions that the skill was performed in. It could have been in front of a large crowd or at a time when the score was close; in both cases the pressure was on.

The result or outcome of the performance of the skill in that situation is then evaluated by the player. The player makes a call as to how well they did, taking into account the objective situation. The result of that judgement may then lead to improved confidence in future activities and the player may go on to develop a competitive orientation. This means the player is prepared to compete and try hard in most sporting situations, which leads them to develop the characteristics of approach behaviour, as discussed in the previous section.

The judgement of the athlete is called the subjective outcome and if this judgement is good, then trait confidence and competitive orientation increase. If the subjective outcome is bad, then both trait confidence and competitive orientation decrease.

So if a player taking a penalty, when the scores are level and in the presence of a crowd, scores that penalty, then the outcome would be seen as good and the player would be confident of taking those penalties in the future. Not only that, but trait confidence would be improved and the player would rate their chances of doing well in other sports too.

Figure 7 Messi free kick: a player with experience of taking free kicks would be confident of taking them in a big game

KEY TERMS

Trait confidence: A belief in the ability to do well in a range of sports.

State confidence: A belief in the ability to master a specific sporting moment.

Competitive orientation: The degree to which a performer is drawn to challenging situations.

Objective sporting situation: The performance takes into account the situation in which the task is being undertaken.

STUDY HINT

According to Vealey, a player will evaluate their performance based on the outcome and the situation to produce a level of confidence for future events.

Figure 8 Hockey penalty in front of a crowd. A successful penalty is a good subjective outcome on which to base future confidence

ACTIVITY

Using a sporting example, explain how you would increase the confidence of a sports performer using Vealey's model.
A summary of the Vealey model is given below.

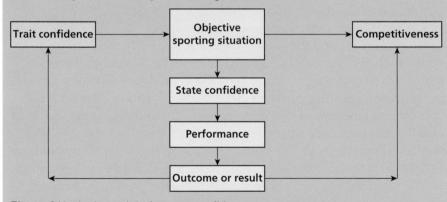

Figure 9 Vealey's model of sports confidence

Explanation of the Vealey model

The athlete approaches the sporting situation with a degree of trait confidence and a level of competitiveness related to the goal they wish to achieve. These two influences produce a level of state confidence related to the current sporting situation. Performance will be affected by the level of state confidence and then the performer, internally in terms of how the outcome was perceived and the causes of the result, can make an evaluation of the result. The evaluations made by the performer can then influence future competitiveness and the amount of future trait confidence.

Bandura self-efficacy theory

One of the types of confidence investigated by Vealey looked at confidence in specific situations. Bandura, 1977, looked at the concept of self-confidence in any one situation and suggested that confidence could vary with the situation and from moment to moment. Sports-specific self-confidence is called **self-efficacy** – accurately defined as the belief in your ability to master a specific sporting situation. Self-esteem often occurs as a

KEY TERM

Self-efficacy: A belief in the ability to master a specific sporting situation.

result of increased confidence, when the performer experiences a sense of satisfaction and inner pride from success. The willingness to compete and persist with the activity is increased.

Self-efficacy affects the confidence of both individual players and those players in teams. Tennis player Andy Murray had never won the Wimbledon men's singles tennis title, often losing at the semi-final stage. Under immense pressure from the 'home' crowd and the expectation to win, he seemed to lack the belief that he could ever lift the title, seeming to lose energy and belief at the end of the match. Then in 2012 he won the Olympic title and followed that up with winning the Wimbledon men's singles title in 2013. Murray has consistently been high in the world rankings in the years after his win. Confidence undoubtedly affects performance!

Factors affecting self-efficacy

Bandura suggested that such self-efficacy is influenced by four factors and he also suggested that a coach could use these four influences to improve player performance and confidence. If the four influences on performance are positive then the expectation to do well, or efficacy expectations, will be high.

The four influences are outlined below.

1 *Performance accomplishments*
This means that self-efficacy is influenced by what you have done in the past or your past experiences. For example, a high jumper at an athletics meet where the bar is at 1 m 20 would feel very confident of clearing that height if she had done 1 m 30 in training in the past week. A team that had beaten a rival 6–0 in the league would feel confident of beating the same team again in the cup. **Performance accomplishments** can be enhanced if the players not only achieved the win but enjoyed the experience too.

Figure 11 High jumper clearing the bar. If the high jumper has cleared a higher height in training than the one in the competition they may feel confident of success

2 *Vicarious experience*
Vicarious experience is concerned with watching others do the same task and being successful. The people being watched doing the task can be referred to as a 'model' and the effect of seeing others do the task well is even better if those models are perceived to have similar ability to the performer. In gymnastics, watching a fellow gymnast do a vault that has been practised in training may give the watching gymnast the confidence to go and do the vault themselves.

Figure 10 Andy Murray winning Wimbledon in 2013 gave him confidence in future events

KEY TERM

Performance accomplishments: What you have achieved already.

STUDY HINT

If the four influences on self-efficacy are positive then confidence is improved.

KEY TERM

Vicarious experience: Seeing others do the task.

Figure 12 Gym vault. If a gymnast sees a training partner clear a vault it may give them confidence to do it too!

3 *Verbal persuasion*

This refers to the power of reinforcement and encouragement. Praise from others such as the coach, fellow players or spectators gives a player a real incentive and confidence to repeat the successful attempt. Such encouragement from others is even more significant if it comes from those who are held in high esteem, such as family or the coach. They are known as significant others. For young players, the benefit of positive comments such as 'Well done, that was a great attempt' is essential in building confidence and future effort.

Figure 13 A coach giving a team talk. Giving encouragement improves confidence

4 *Emotional arousal*

Dealing with emotion in sport, such as keeping calm and maintaining your control and game strategy when you are very close to getting a big win, is essential to good performance. Such situations in sport cause an increase in anxiety and arousal and the key to **emotional arousal** is how the performer perceives the increased arousal before and during the activity. In our example, the player could think, 'What if we lose it now? We are so close!' The better judgement or perception of that situation would be, 'We've got this now, only a minute to go!' Teams and players that deal with the arousal better get the best results.

Figure 14 England Women's World Cup team, 2015. Players in tears after a loss to Japan in the semi-final. Dealing with the threat of increased emotional arousal is essential in securing top-class performance

Improving confidence

Coaches and players can use the four influences on self-efficacy, as identified by Bandura, to help improve and promote player confidence. Some of the things that the coach or player can do are as follows:

1 Control arousal with relaxation or stress management techniques such as visualisation. These stress management techniques will be discussed later in this chapter and there is a relationship between the level of anxiety or stress and the level of confidence: the lower the anxiety, the higher the confidence.

2 Give an accurate demonstration. This demonstration could be done by a role model who demonstrates accurately and is equal in ability to the performer.

3 Point out past successful performances. A coach of a team in a major tournament might point out that they have performed well in other similar tournaments and there is no reason why they should not do well again.

4 Give support and encouragement, for example, by saying, 'I know you can do it.'

5 Allow success during training by setting tasks within the capability of the performer. For example, lower the bar in high jumping to allow a beginner to clear the height.

6 Set attainable goals. Once these goals have been reached, a further more challenging goal can be set. The goals set should not always be about winning – performance and process goals that concern improvements in technique and getting a better personal result could also be set. It is important to note that the personal nature of these types of goals are important; they avoid social comparisons with other players.

7 Attribute any success achieved to the athlete, suggesting it is the athlete's ability or effort that produced a good result.

8 The coach or player may use the technique of mental practice to help the performer go over a routine or sequence in the mind. The coach can also offer a one-on-one coaching session, when the performer is given specific attention and help with weaknesses in their own individual performance.

STUDY HINT

Players and coaches can use Bandura's model of self-efficacy to develop strategies to improve confidence.

ACTIVITY

Study the four factors that affect the self-efficacy of the performer. Below are some strategies that would help coaches improve the self-efficacy of a performer. Write them in the correct boxes below.

- Realistic challenging goals
- Encouragement
- Attainable role models
- Coach one on one
- Attribute success internally
- Set goals on performance not outcome
- Avoid social comparison
- Use rewards
- Point out past successful performances
- Mental practice.

1 Performance accomplishments	**2 Vicarious experience**
Past success – have you done it before? *Improved by:*	Seeing someone else do the task. A demonstration, or watching a model of similar ability. *Improved by:*
3 Verbal persuasion	**4 Emotional arousal**
Encouragement – being convinced you can do it. *Improved by:*	Interpreting your arousal levels. Controlling anxiety. *Improved by:*

Self-efficacy increases positive attitudes, increases motivation, reduces fear of failure, reduces anxiety and helps to reach optimal arousal levels.

Figure 15 Strategies to improve self-efficacy

The home field advantage

The home field advantage is a balance between confidence and anxiety – the influence of the home crowd could increase confidence in the home team and cause anxiety in the away team. Often the team playing at home wins the game because the home audience support increases players' motivation and confidence. It seems logical to assume that not having to travel and the familiarity of the home environment can mean that more games are won at home than when playing away. Playing at home may mean the home team plays in a more fluent style since they feel more at ease and more confident. The home audience can cause 'functional assertive behaviour' in the home team, causing them to have more drive, more assertion and the correct choice of response. And since large crowds usually watch expert players, the effect of social facilitation could occur (see Chapter 6.2, Book 1). A good example of the positive effects of the home crowd came in the 2012 Olympics in London when the GB team won their highest number of medals for years!

Figure 16 GB athletes on the gold medal rostrum in 2012

In addition to helping the home team, the home crowd can have a negative effect on the away team, causing increased anxiety with hostile chanting. This can lead to a less effective performance: the away team sometimes commit more fouls due to anxiety and could suffer from the effects of social inhibition.

However, sometimes the home crowd can have a negative effect on the home team. The home crowd can cause the home team to 'choke' in big games, with the increased pressure of the game causing the catastrophe effect when the players suffer a dramatic reduction in performance. Indeed the more important the game, the less likely the home team is to win it. The effect of the home field advantage is increased in stadiums where the crowd are close to the pitch. In large stadiums the crowd may be far away and the help of the home support is ineffective.

The bigger and more supportive the crowd, the better the effect is for the home team; the more hostile the crowd is to the away team, the more negative the effect is for them.

STUDY HINT

The home crowd can have both positive and negative effects on performance, even though research shows the home team usually wins.

Figure 17 England football team playing at Wembley. More games are won playing at home.

Leadership

A **leader** is someone who influences you towards achieving your goals. In sport, there have been many examples of captains and coaches who have led by example and have those certain qualities that have helped their teams reach for success. Sir Alex Ferguson led Manchester United to 34 major honours during his 26-year tenure as the manager.

The leader plays a role in maintaining effort and motivation by inspiring the team and setting targets.

In this section we will examine the qualities and styles used by such leaders and look at the factors that influence the decision on the style of leadership to use. Getting this style right in sport can make a huge difference.

Types of leader

There are two types of leader. A **prescribed** leader is appointed from outside the group, perhaps from another group or a higher authority, often because the group might wish to take on new ideas and learn new methods. An **emergent** leader is appointed from within the existing group.

Figure 18 Sir Alex Ferguson had leadership qualities during 26 years at Manchester United

KEY TERMS

Leader: Someone who has influence in helping others to achieve their goals.

Prescribed leader: Appointed from outside the group.

Emergent leader: Appointed from within the group.

ACTIVITY

Can you suggest some examples from sport of prescribed and emergent leaders?

STUDY HINT

Prescribed leaders are new to the group; emergent leaders come from within the group.

Figure 19 David Moyes was appointed to Manchester United as a prescribed leader

Figure 20 Ryan Giggs emerged as a leader from within Manchester United

Leader qualities

In order to be effective, and certainly in the examples we have mentioned above, it is essential for the leader to possess certain qualities. These qualities include some or all of the following:

1 *Charisma*: This quality is hard to define but it is that certain demeanour and presence that the leader has which makes others listen and follow.

2 *Communication*: The leader has to get the message across.

3 *Interpersonal skills*: The leader needs to interact with other members of the team and sometimes those outside the group.

4 *Empathy*: The leader needs to be able to listen to others and take their views into account, showing an affinity with their views.

5 *Experience*: Leaders would have a wealth of knowledge in their chosen sport built up over many years.

6 *Inspirational*: Leaders need to encourage others and keep them trying even when the going gets tough!

7 *Confidence*: As we have seen in the previous section, confidence can be gained from others so a confident approach from the leader can spread to the players.

8 *Organisational skills*: A good leader would plan and prepare for training, linking it to the demands of the team.

> **STUDY HINT**
> A leader may use one or more of these leadership qualities at any one time.

> **ACTIVITY**
> Consider the qualities of a leader discussed above and give some examples from sport where you think those qualities were clearly shown.

Styles of leadership

The leadership style is the manner in which the leader chooses to lead the group. The choice of style is crucial to good leadership and if the correct style is used, then the group is more likely to be successful.

The three styles identified in a study by Lewin (1939) are as follows:

1 **The autocratic and task-orientated style**. In this approach, the leader makes all the decisions and dictates instructions to the group. An autocratic leader adopts a task-orientated style. In the task-orientated style, the concern of the leader is to get results and reach targets. An autocratic approach could be used by a coach who has made a specific plan to win a game, tells the players of the plan and makes them follow it in the expectation of a win. However, the coach will need to stay with the group and maintain contact throughout the session, since the group tends to switch off when this style is used if the coach is not there.

2 **The democratic and person-orientated style**. In this method, the coach adopts a more sympathetic approach to leadership and seeks the opinion of the group before making decisions, based on those suggestions. A democratic leader adopts a person-orientated style. The coach may use the quality of empathy to listen to the senior players after watching some video footage of the next opposition and then make a plan involving those players in the expectation of a win. In this style, the group usually continues to work when the coach is not present.

3 **The 'laissez-faire' style**. In this style, the leader does very little and leaves the group to it. It may be that the manager simply tells the players what the manager wants from them in a training session and then goes away to conduct some other business, safe in the knowledge that the senior players will conduct the session to help prepare the team for the expected win in the next match. There is a danger, however, that less motivated players will stop working if they are left alone.

KEY TERMS

Autocratic approach: Leader makes the decisions.

Democratic: Decisions are made by group consultation.

Person-orientated leadership: Concerned with interpersonal relationships.

Task leadership: Concerned with getting results.

> **STUDY HINT**
> The laissez-faire style can be used effectively when the group has plenty of experience.

All the above styles have their place in helping a group to achieve their goals. It is up to the leader to choose the right style at the right time. There are factors that the leader must take into account in order to choose the right style, including considerations of the situation, the group and the leader themselves. There is then an interactive approach to leadership when the leader must try to balance the requirements of the situation, the needs of the group and their own characteristics to try to choose the most effective leadership style. In order to make that choice easier, the leader might consider some of the following psychological concepts.

Fiedler's contingency model of leadership

Fiedler took into account one of the factors that influence leadership style: the situation. He suggested that the autocratic or task-orientated style of leadership is best used in two opposite situations: when everything is good **and** when everything is bad. Fiedler called a situation when everything is good, a most favourable situation; and when everything is bad, a least favourable situation.

In the middle ground, when the situation is between good and bad, he called it a moderately favourable situation and suggested that a person-orientated style is best used.

The task-orientated style of leadership concerns setting targets and reaching them quickly. It is results based and is best achieved with an autocratic style. The person-orientated style is best achieved with a democratic approach since it is concerned with developing the interpersonal relationships of the group.

How favourable the situation is, good or bad, depends on the task, the leader–group relationship and the leader's position of authority.

A most favourable situation is when:

- The leader has respect.
- There is good support within the group.
- The group is of high ability.
- There are high levels of motivation.
- The task is clear to the team.
- There is harmony between leader and group.

A least favourable situation is when:

- There may be hostility between the group members.
- There is little respect for the leader.
- The group has low ability.
- The group members do not support each other.
- Motivation is low.
- The task is unclear.
- The leader is weak.

A moderately favourable situation is when:

- There is a need or preference for consultation within the group.
- Motivation is moderate.
- There is limited support.
- The group has reasonable ability.

STUDY HINT

The task style of leadership is best in **both** a most favourable and a least favourable situation.

STUDY HINT

A person-orientated style is best used in a moderately favourable situation.

Task	Person	Task
Most favourable	Moderately favourable	Least favourable
Strong leader	Some harmony	Weak leader
Group harmony	Some motivation	Group hostility
Clear task	Some clarity	Unclear task
Respect for leader	Need for consultation	Little respect for leader
High ability		Low ability
High motivation		Low motivation
Support		Some support

Figure 21 The Fiedler contingency model

Chelladurai's multi-dimensional model of leadership

Chelladurai (1980) looked at other factors that influence the choice of leadership style, not just the situation. He assessed the idea that the leader must use an interactive approach to balance aspects of the situation and the leader and the group. His suggestion was that the more that the leader actually used a style that matched the requirements of the situation and the needs of the group, then the more satisfaction would be gained from the performance.

The importance of the situation would include the type of task being performed. An individual sport such as athletics could result in a different approach to leadership than a team game. A difficult or complex task may require more time to offer an explanation. The situation could be influenced by the amount of time available. An efficient approach might be needed during a time when there is a short turnaround for the coach between games, while during the off season there may be time to discuss issues concerning the team. The size of the group influences the situation. A large group might require an authoritarian approach to maintain control during training, while with a smaller group there may be opportunities for discussion. In a dangerous situation, an autocratic approach might be used to make sure instructions are given to eliminate the danger.

The features of the group affect the choice of leadership style. With a group of women, the use of empathy and consultation may be the best choice while men might prefer a more authoritarian approach to their training. With an able group, the coach could allow some flexibility and allow the group to use their experience to decide what they want to work on. Beginners might need to be told what to do. The age of the group is important; an older group may have some experience and knowledge to add to a discussion, while a younger group may welcome being told new information.

Figure 22 Snowboarding. An autocratic approach might be needed to eliminate danger in a sport such as snowboarding

ACTIVITY

How could the influence of the leader and the group affect the choice of leadership style?

Figure 23 The coach for female players may use a democratic approach

STUDY HINT

A leader must adopt an interactive approach to balance the requirements of the situation, the needs of the group and the leader's own preferences.

KEY TERMS

Required behaviour: What the situation demands.

Actual behaviour: What the leader decides to do in relation to leadership style.

Preferred behaviour: What the group wants.

Once the three influences on leader behaviour have been assessed, the leader can then choose how to behave with the group.

The **required behaviour** of the leader is a result of an assessment of the situation and may involve being autocratic during a quick break during play when giving out instructions.

The **actual behaviour** of the leader may be chosen to match both the situation and the group demands.

The **preferred behaviour** is the result of what the group want or prefer. A group of novice players may want instruction on new tactics and strategies, for example.

A summary of the Chelladurai model is given below.

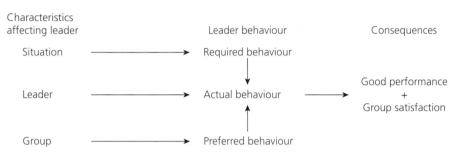

Figure 24 The Chelladurai model of leadership

As an example of the Chelladurai model, imagine an activity leader about take a group of Year 6 students climbing. The situation demands an instructive and autocratic approach because of potential danger. The group would want to be instructed since they have little knowledge of the activity. If the leader then uses the style that matches the requirements of the situation and the needs of the group, then the quality and satisfaction from the performance will be high.

CHECK YOUR UNDERSTANDING

1 What is the difference between a prescribed leader and an emergent leader?

2 Name three qualities of a leader.

3 What is the difference between a person approach and a task approach to leadership?

4 What is the laissez-faire style of leadership?

5 In a situation where the group is experienced, has respect for the leader and is clear in its goals, what style of leadership would you use?

6 Name some features of the group that could affect the style of leadership used.

ACTIVITY

Study the list of factors that influence the choice of leadership style. For each of the factors, give a justification of the correct choice of style to suit that specific influence. Use the table below to give your answer. An example has been done for you.

INFLUENCE	EXAMPLE/EXPLANATION
Situation: Time available Danger Type of task/sport	If lots of time is available, use the democratic style. If no time is available use the autocratic style. In dangerous situations, use the autocratic style. The democratic style can be used in a safe environment.
Leader: Characteristics Experience	
Group: Group size Gender Age Experience	

Stress management

Stress is the response of the individual to a threat. Stress is one of the most common emotions in sport. Players can feel stress during games or just before competitions. Managing and controlling stress is key to top-class performance. The surprising feature of stress is that it is not always a negative. At the end of an important game when the score is in your favour and, with only a few seconds to go, you realise that you are going to win, then a feeling of euphoria will be experienced that boosts your confidence and gives an internal feeling of satisfaction. This positive aspect of stress is called '**eustress**', and in some extreme sports, performers will often seek out this feeling by pushing themselves to more difficult challenges – sky diving from ever increasing heights, for example! The experience of 'eustress' can happen when a response to the threat of a difficult challenge is overcome and the feeling of success gives future confidence and motivation. Unfortunately more familiar to most sports people is the concept of stress which is a negative response to a stressful situation. Feelings of apprehension and anxiety are experienced, the performer may feel that they do not have the ability to cope with the situation and can experience both cognitive and somatic effects.

Stress and stressors

Stress can be positive and create the feeling of eustress discussed above or it can be negative and create the negative response of anxiety and **cognitive** and **somatic effects**. The cause of stress in sport is called a **stressor** and some of the stressors that may be relevant in sport would include:

- injury
- playing in an important match
- playing against really good opponents
- playing to get an important reward such as prize money
- fear of failure caused by pressure from being watched by significant others, pressure from the coach or pressure from your own expectations.

The stress experienced is the result of such stressors and it can be positive or negative, depending on how the performer perceives or views their ability to overcome the threat. Before an important athletics meeting, a runner at the start of the 3000 m race may experience the stressor of lining up against other top-class athletes in a major race. A positive response would be that the runner believes they are training well and that they will relish the challenge of testing themselves against this type of runner – *eustress*. A negative response would be that the athlete begins to think that they do not have the ability to compete against these athletes and is afraid of letting the coach down – *stress*.

The negative response gives rise to anxiety, and the negative effects of stress can be cognitive or somatic.

Cognitive stress

The cognitive experience of stress is psychological. It brings negative thoughts and feelings, including the irrational thinking of the inability to cope with the demands of the situation, such as the squash player taking their eye off the ball when returning a serve and losing the flight.

KEY TERMS

Stress: A negative response of the body to a threat causing anxiety.

Eustress: A positive response of the body to a threat.

Figure 25 Extreme sports such as sky diving can give the feeling of eustress

KEY TERMS

Cognitive effects of stress: These are psychological.

Somatic effects of stress: These are physiological.

STUDY HINT

Stress is a negative response linked to anxiety.
Eustress is a positive response to a threat.

ACTIVITY

Consider the different stressors outlined above. For each stressor, try to think of an example from a game or performance when that stressor happened to you. How did it make you feel and how did you overcome it?

Figure 26 A squash player may lose the flight of the ball when returning serve

The loss of concentration may be linked to the process called **attentional narrowing** when, as arousal and anxiety levels increase, the ability to take in information or cues from the environment is reduced; therefore some important information may be missed at higher levels of stress. The player may begin to experience some of the things associated with fear of failure and begin to worry about letting down the coach with a poor performance.

Somatic stress

Somatic stress is physiological and involves the physical response of the body to stress. This might include an increase in heart rate and an increase in sweating. In extreme cases, the player may suffer from nausea or feelings of sickness. One of the most damaging somatic responses is muscular tension, sometimes seen in sports performers when they are involved in high pressure, isolated situations such as serving for the match in tennis or taking a set shot in basketball. The muscular tension might cause an inaccurate or weak attempt.

Stress management techniques

The methods used to combat stress can be used to reduce either cognitive or somatic effects. Some methods can be used to reduce both.

Cognitive stress management techniques

The methods of cognitive stress management are:

Figure 27 A cricketer at the crease could use a learned cue to stop negative emotions

1 *Thought stopping*
   When negative and irrational thoughts occur, the performer uses a learned action or trigger to remove them. This learned physical action or cue can be a simple movement or rehearsed action that is linked to the negative thought to redirect attention to the task in hand. For example, the batter in cricket might prod the ground with the bat prior to the delivery of the bowler, to redirect attention to the pitch of the ball that they have previously found hard to pick up. The prior learning of the cueing action is vital to the success of this technique.

2 *Positive self-talk*
   Self-talk is when the performer replaces negative thoughts with positive ones. For example, a squash player who is struggling to retrieve an opponent's shot may think, 'I can get to the ball if I just move a little sooner and get on my toes.' Self-talk can also be used in other ways. It can

help the player to focus on a tactic or instruction from the coach and it can be used to overcome a weakness. The badminton player who has missed a couple of overhead shots might think about getting their feet in the right position, for example. Self-talk can overcome a bad habit. The golfer who keeps hitting the ball to the left of the fairway may begin to think about changing the grip on the club to correct the action.

3 *Imagery*

Imagery can recreate a successful image of the action from a past performance when the skill was performed successfully and the player can recall the feel of the actual movements in the mind. Imagery can go even further and use not only the actual feel of the movement, but the emotions associated with that successful action. The netball shooter who has scored a goal to win a close match would imagine the satisfaction and elation associated with that winning shot and use those emotions to build confidence for the current situation. Some players use imagery to avoid stressful situations by imagining a calm place, perhaps a favourite holiday destination, to use as a mental escape from the stress.

4 *Visualisation*

Visualisation also uses a mental image of the skill, an image perfected while performing the skill successfully in training. This image is then 'locked in' and re-lived when the skill is performed for real. In the real game situation, it is possible that the player might feel some pressure from the crowd or some aggression from other players. The player can visualise such feelings when practising and overcome them, so that when the skill is performed in real circumstances, such experiences have already been dealt with and the player has the confidence to deal with them again.

Visualisation and imagery can be internal or external. An external image is when the player has an image that concentrates on the environment, almost as if the player is watching themselves on television. Details of the pitch and the opponents may be used here. Internal imagery looks at the emotions and feelings involved in the skill, such as the sense of kinesthesis used to develop a feel of the movement or the satisfaction gained from completing the successful action.

5 *Mental rehearsal*

This is the process of going over the movements of a task in the mind before the action takes place. Mental rehearsal is especially useful for athletes about to perform a sequence of skills such as a routine on the trampoline. The idea is that if the required movements are rehearsed in order and in a spatial sequence, then the performer is less likely to forget the order of the moves or the required actions and therefore stress is reduced. Mental rehearsal is best done in a calm situation prior to the event (see Chapter 2.1, Book 1).

6 *Attentional control and cue utilisation*

One of the consequences of stress is that the performer may lose concentration and focus on incorrect stimuli from the environment. As stress and arousal increase, then the ability to take in information reduces – a problem called **attentional narrowing** (Easterbrook, 1959). The effect of emotion on cue utilisation suggested that the ability to take in information is directly linked to levels of arousal, an influence Easterbrook called **cue utilisation**. Therefore at low levels of stress and arousal, the performer is able to process plenty of cues from the environment. Sometimes though, when a high amount of information is

Figure 28 A player who has missed a few smash shots in badminton could use self-talk to remind themselves of good habits.

STUDY HINT

When imagery and visualisation are used to control stress, the mental image must be of a successful performance.

ACTIVITY

Think back to a game or performance in which you did really well. Try to recall some of the good things you did in the game and how you felt after the event. Did your recollections bring positive thoughts?

KEY TERM

Cue utilisation: The ability to process information is directly linked to the level of arousal.

STUDY HINT

At high levels of arousal, the ability to take in information is reduced.

taken note of, it may cause confusion and incorrect information could be mistaken for important cues. At high levels of arousal and stress, only limited information can be processed and this may cause important information to be missed – a problem known as **attentional wastage**. It means that important information has been ignored. Attentional wastage reduces the level of performance.

At moderate levels of arousal, the performer picks up the relevant information and performance can be successful.

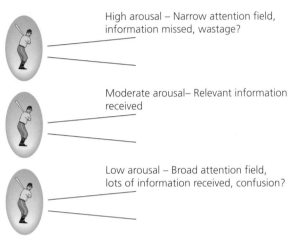

High arousal – Narrow attention field, information missed, wastage?

Moderate arousal– Relevant information received

Low arousal – Broad attention field, lots of information received, confusion?

Figure 29 Attentional narrowing and wastage!

To avoid the problem of attentional wastage and to ensure performance levels are maintained, Niddefer (1976, 'Test of attentional and interpersonal style', *Journal of Personality and Social Psychology*) suggested that the performer could choose an attention style that suits the situation. By using the features of selective attention (see Chapter 2.1), when important information is filtered from irrelevant information, the performer can control the style of attention required at any one moment and pick up relevant information.

There are four styles of attention that can be used in a sporting context. They are:

1 Broad, when a number of cues can be identified.

2 Narrow, when it is best to focus on one or two cues.

3 External, when information is drawn from the environment.

4 Internal when information is used from within the performer.

The four styles can then be combined as shown in the following table.

STUDY HINT

There are four styles of attentional control. The performer must choose the right style at the right time.

Broad, External Picking up wide range of cues from environment: e.g. position of players in a game.	**Broad, Internal** Mental analysis of numerous cues: e.g. analyse game and plan tactics
Narrow, External Focus is directed to one environmental cue: e.g. golfer concentrating on putting into hole.	**Narrow, Internal** Mental practice of one or two important cues: e.g. concentrate on weakness.

Figure 30 Attentional styles – Niddefer

So a broad external style is when a number of cues are drawn from the environment; for example, the midfield player scanning the field for information.

A narrow external style is when the player would focus on a specific cue in the environment such as the golfer concentrating on the hole when making a putt.

A broad internal style is when a coach or player would analyse information to come up with a tactic to use during the game.

A narrow internal style is when a specific weakness or coaching point can be mentally rehearsed such as the tennis player focusing on the weak backhand of the opponent.

The idea behind the use of attentional control is that if the correct style is chosen at the right time, then stress is lowered and performance is enhanced. During a game an experienced player may learn to switch styles as appropriate and therefore make correct choices. For example, the footballer in midfield could use a broad external style to select the player in the best position to receive a pass and then use a narrow external style to focus on making an accurate pass to that particular player's feet.

7 *Psychological skills training*
   The performer can train and practise using any of the methods explained as cognitive stress management techniques. Many professional sports clubs employ a sports psychologist to do just that. Players can be guided through aspects of visualisation and imagery.

Somatic stress management techniques

These techniques can be used to reduce the effects of muscular tension and increased heart rate. They include:

1 *Biofeedback*
   This technique uses a measuring device to help the athlete recognise the physical changes that will happen when under stress. Such measures would include the simple measure of heart rate; the galvanic skin response that measures increases in electrical activity when sweating; or electromyography that measures muscular tension with electrodes taped to the skin. The idea is that the athlete learns to recognise when such physical symptoms are happening and can eventually do so without the use of the measuring device. As soon as the signs are recognised, the performer can then use techniques to calm down and reduce stress.

2 *Progressive muscle relaxation*
   This is a physical technique, often conducted with the use of recorded instructions, when the performer alternates between a state of tension in a group of muscles to state of relaxation in those same muscles. The groups of muscles that are tensed, held and then relaxed are worked progressively from the periphery of the body to the core. The muscles of the arms, shoulders and legs may be worked on at first until the abdominal muscles are utilised.

3 *Centring*
   Centring is a form of breathing control when, at opportune times, the sports performer can learn to relax the shoulders and chest while concentrating on the slow movement of the abdominal muscles when taking deep controlled breaths. The use of the slow controlled breathing diverts the attention away from the stressful situation and once the technique has been mastered, the athlete can use it quickly when the need arises. You may have noticed games players using this technique before they attempt isolated skills such as the first serve in tennis or the kick at goal in rugby.

Figure 31 Rugby goal kickers often use breathing control just before they take a kick at goal.

CHECK YOUR UNDERSTANDING

1 What is a stressor?
2 Give three examples of a stressor.
3 Name two different responses to a stressor.
4 Name three methods of cognitive stress management.
5 Name three methods of somatic stress control.
6 What are the four styles of attentional control?
7 What is the difference between attentional narrowing and attentional wastage?

Attribution theory

An attribute is a reason given to explain something that has happened. It is a perceived outcome of events. In sport, reasons are often given for winning and losing, or for playing well or playing badly. Those reasons are given by the sporting leaders such as managers or coaches and, more importantly, by the players themselves. The reasons are vital to maintain motivation and effort and therefore attribution in sport is one of the most important factors in task persistence. The evaluation of performance by coach and player can give more confidence, bring satisfaction and make the expectations of the player higher. 'The coach says I played well last week so I'm looking forward to next week's match' may be a response to the coach praising the player's performance. The reasons given for winning and losing were classified by Weiner 1974 and he deduced that these reasons can fall into two sections, and he placed those sections on a matrix. Each section can be sub-divided into two parts, so that the locus of causality, which is simply the point where a reason might be placed, looks at the amount of control the player had over the result and can be external or internal. The stability dimension, which looks at how much the reasons for winning and losing can be changed, can be sub-divided into stable and unstable reasons.

Classification of sporting attributes

The locus of causality

The reasons for winning and losing can either be within the control of the performer or **internal**, or out of the performer's control – **external**. These two dimensions are known as the causality of the attributes and concern the amount of control the player has over the outcome of events. If you think the result was down to you, then you have some control over that result, perhaps by playing well. If you think the result was due to a decision by the referee, then you had no control over the outcome.

Weiner did some further study on his model in 1986 and came up with a reinforcement of the control aspect of attribution. He suggested that personal internal control includes the things that can be taken control of by the individual, such as effort, and that external control includes things over which the player has little influence, such as luck or the decision of the referee.

Figure 32 A referee decision is an external and unstable reason given for the result

The stability dimension

Reasons for winning and losing can also be changeable in a short time, so **unstable**, or relatively permanent, so **stable**. A **stable attribute** could change over a period of time but is not likely to change in the short term. The stability dimension is therefore concerned with how changeable the reasons for winning and losing are. If you think that you did not try hard enough in the game, then that can be put right and changed for next week, making this reason unstable. If you think that you are good at defending, then it is likely you will maintain that confident approach for the future. If the opposition are a good team, it is likely that they will still be a good team if you play them again later in the season, so this is stable.

KEY TERMS

Stable attribute: Unlikely to change in the short-term.

Unstable attribute: Can change in a short amount of time.

Figure 33 Barcelona football team. Playing a good team is an external and stable reason given for losing

Sporting attributes can be classified using the grid shown in Figure 32.

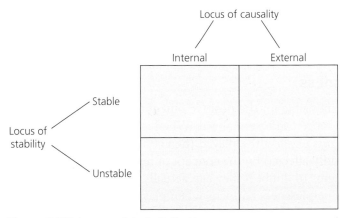

Figure 34 Weiner model of attribution

ACTIVITY

Here is a list of attributes that might be used by players and coaches to explain the reasons for winning or losing.

Look at the model in Figure 32, make a copy of it and then see if you can place the attributes listed in the correct area of the diagram.

The attributes are:

- Luck: 'We had two shots deflected!'
- The amount of practice done in the week: 'I worked hard this week in training.'
- The referee's decisions: 'That was a penalty – why didn't she give it?'
- My ability: 'The coach said I played well today, never let anyone past me.'
- Playing a good team: 'The opposition were two leagues above us.'
- The effort we put in: 'I did my best. I was shattered at the final whistle.'

Attribution and effort

Coaches and players can use attribution theory to make sure their players keep on trying, even after a defeat. In other words, attribution can be used to promote task persistence.

The concept of self-serving bias can be used to help in the process of promoting task persistence.

Self-serving bias

When players win games they like to think that it was down to them, so internal and stable reasons are often given for sporting success, while losing

KEY TERM

Self-serving bias: Using external and/or unstable reasons for losing.

is attributed to unstable and external reasons. **Self-serving bias** helps to promote self-esteem. So to keep your players happy and motivated, blame losing on a referee decision or a slice of bad luck. In other words, put the blame for defeat on external and unstable reasons. A coach should also make sure that the players feel a loss can be changed, so changeable and internal reasons can be used to explain a defeat – the coach could suggest that with a little more effort the game could be won next time. Other external reasons for a loss might be suggesting that a team played fairly well against a really good team – a reason that is external and stable.

To sum up, coaches and players should attribute losing to things that are either external and/or can be changed. Never give reasons for losing that are stable and internal, such as player ability, since this might cause the player to lose motivation. The problem of learned helplessness could occur.

STUDY HINT

To maintain motivation, blame losing on external stable reasons (e.g. good team), external unstable reasons (e.g. luck) or internal unstable reasons (e.g. more effort).

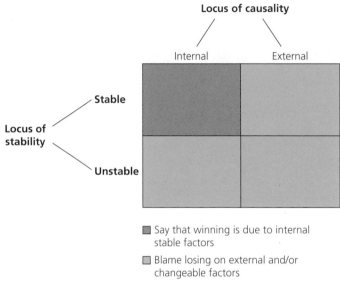

Figure 35 The Weiner model of attribution showing self-serving bias. In red are the reasons that should be given for winning and in blue are the reasons that should be given for losing

KEY TERM

Learned helplessness: Using internal stable reasons for losing.

Learned helplessness

When players feel responsible for the positive outcome of a game, then motivation and confidence can be enhanced. When self-doubt or a lack of belief in ability begins to affect the player, then confidence is lowered. Confidence can be badly affected by the concept of **learned helplessness**, when a performer begins to doubt if they can actually complete the task successfully. Learned helplessness happens when players blame losing on internal and stable reasons such as ability. The performer is so lacking in confidence that they think failure is inevitable and success is unlikely; there is no belief in their ability. The player may even give up even if success is possible and they could have actually won the game.

Learned helplessness can be so bad it becomes general, when the player begins to feel they are no good at sport overall or at a type of sport. An example of this would be a sports performer who feels that they are not very good at racket sports such as badminton and tennis since they have experienced little success when playing these sports. Learned helplessness can be specific to one sport or event, such as the player who thinks they are not very good at squash, as they are unable to read the bounce of the ball from the walls of the court and constantly make mistakes.

Learned helplessness can be developed not only by attributing success to internal and stable factors such as ability but by negative feedback and criticism from the coach or others. A lack of success or negative experiences can also develop learned helplessness, so that the player who loses consistently at a regular weekly squash match against his boss may begin to feel that he does not have the ability to succeed and only keeps on playing because he has to.

Attribution retraining

Learned helplessness can be overcome by **attribution retraining**, a set of strategies aimed at changing the reasons for failure. The key to attribution retraining is to change the perception and belief of the sportsperson by changing the reasons given for failure. To overcome learned helplessness, the coach should refer to the Weiner model – use the box! The coach could change internal stable reasons for failure into external unstable ones. Move away from blaming player ability so that the player begins to use external and changeable reasons for failure such as luck, or external reasons or task difficulty. The coach could provide motivation via reinforcement, allow early success so that confidence in ability is achieved, set achievable goals, and stress any personal improvement made during the game, even if the game was lost.

The strategies outlined above will help to promote self-esteem in players. In the example of the squash player regularly losing against their boss, the player could be encouraged to get some coaching, to learn new tactics, to play against others of similar ability or to change the racket, so the task is easier. It should be pointed out that the boss is an experienced player with high levels of success (task difficulty). The use of reinforcement may encourage more effort in practice sessions until the player improves in self-confidence and ability.

Learned helplessness is linked to confidence, so using some of the strategies that affect confidence will help to overcome learned helplessness, such as setting achievable goals and pointing out past success or giving demonstrations that are within the player's capability. Using cognitive and somatic stress management techniques, such as imagery or centring, will also help to avoid learned helplessness, and the use of encouragement and praise will give more confidence. The opposite of learned helplessness, a state of mind when the performer is high is confidence, has belief in their ability and thinks that success can be repeated whilst failure is both temporary and changeable is called mastery orientation. Sports performers with mastery orientation will show approach behaviour in competition and will continue to try even if at first they do not succeed.

Figure 36 Confidence can be affected by the attribution process

STUDY HINT
Learned helplessness can be general or specific.

KEY TERM
Attribution retraining: Changing the reasons given for success and failure.

STUDY HINT
Attribution retraining is changing the reasons given for winning and losing.

CHECK YOUR UNDERSTANDING
1 Why is using correct attributions so important in sport?
2 Name two external and unstable attributes.
3 Name two internal and unstable attributes.
4 What could happen if internal stable reasons are given for failure?
5 What is attribution retraining?
6 What is mastery orientation?

SUMMARY

This chapter represented a series of named psychological theories that attempted to explain various psychological factors that affect sports performance.

Atkinson and McClelland explained why some players take risks while others play it safe in the theory of achievement motivation. Sports scientists Bandura and Vealey examined the influences on sports confidence. Leadership was assessed by both Fiedler and Chelladurai and the reasons given for winning and losing were classified by Weiner in the section on attribution.

Each theory was discussed in terms of the impact on the performer. Strategies to overcome any negative influences or to promote positive aspects of the concepts discussed in each were outlined. Such strategies included the methods of controlling stress by both cognitive and somatic methods.

PRACTICE QUESTIONS

1 In terms of attribution theory, a coach should use Weiner's model of attribution to blame losing a game on factors that are:

   a) stable and internal   **c)** unstable and external

   b) stable and external   **d)** unstable and internal.   (1 mark)

2 Setting goals to improve confidence might help mostly to promote which of these four influences that are said, according to the psychologist Bandura, to affect self-efficacy?

   a) vicarious experience   **c)** performance accomplishments

   b) emotional arousal   **d)** verbal persuasion.   (1 mark)

3 Games players should be motivated when they approach competitive situations.

   i) Explain the influences that might determine a player's level of achievement motivation.   (4 marks)

   ii) How could a coach improve the approach behaviour of players in their charge?   (4 marks)

4 A good leader can influence the outcomes of sports performance.

   i) Outline the characteristics of a good leader and explain the difference between a prescribed and an emergent leader.   (4 marks)

   ii) What do you understand by the autocratic style of leadership and when, according to Fiedler, should this style be best used?   (4 marks)

5 Sports performers may benefit from high levels of confidence or self-efficacy. Using Bandura's model, explain how the influence of vicarious experience and emotional arousal affect the level of self-efficacy of a sports performer and show how these two influences could be improved.   (8 marks)

6 In the build-up to and during a tennis match, a player may experience increased levels of stress. Discuss and evaluate the techniques a coach or player could use to reduce the effects of cognitive stress.   (15 marks)

Chapter 6.1
Concepts of physical activity and sport

Chapter objectives

By the end of this chapter you should be able to:

- Identify and explain the characteristics of key concepts and how they create the base of the sporting development continuum (i.e. physical recreation, sport, physical education and school sport).
- Understand the similarities and differences between these key concepts.

Concepts of physical activity and sport

When participating in different types of physical activity, individuals often have different reasons for doing so (i.e. different types of activity have different functions). For example, a key reason for many participating in physical recreation is to improve their health and fitness.

When observing or watching people taking part in physical activity, you might notice a number of different features (i.e. **characteristics**). For example, at one end of the '**continuum**', there might be a relaxed atmosphere evident as opposed to a more serious attitude when watching sports performers.

Different forms of physical activity can be viewed on a **sporting development continuum**, with the 'foundation level' being the first introduction to physical activity/sport (e.g. at grass roots level in primary school PE programmes). This is followed by the 'participation level', with its emphasis on fun, socialising and developing friendships; participating in a recreational, relaxed manner. More dedicated, focused individuals can reach the 'performance level' where there is a commitment to regular involvement in sport where the emphasis is on winning, as we will discover later in this chapter.

Physical recreation

Physical recreation can be defined as 'the active aspect of **leisure**'. Leisure time is free time which can be spent actively or passively. If spent actively, it can be classified as physical recreation as it is entered into voluntarily during a person's free time and individuals have a choice in terms of the activities they take part in. The emphasis is on participation and taking part in physical recreation, without focusing on winning.

ACTIVITY

Leisure: Yes or no?

Identify whether or not you would consider the following as leisure time activities.

a) Working part-time at Burger King.
b) Going to the gym to keep fit after work.
c) Sending your friends a message on Facebook about going out.
d) Attendance at your A-level PE lessons.

KEY TERMS

Characteristics: Key features used to identify a particular concept (e.g. enjoyment in physical recreation or serious about sport).

Continuum: A scale representing gradual change.

Sporting development continuum: Participation in various forms of physical activity at various stages of development. For example, grass roots 'foundation stage' in primary school PE or 'participation stage' involvement as an adult in physical recreation.

Leisure: Free time during which individuals can choose what to do.

Participation level: An emphasis on taking part recreationally with enjoyment as a key motivator to participate.

ACTIVITY

State three characteristics of running as physical recreation.

The key characteristics of physical recreation

The following is a list summarising a number of characteristics commonly associated with physical recreation:

- It is fun, enjoyable, non-serious and informal in nature, so winning is not important; taking part is the main motive for participation.
- It is physically energetic, i.e. it involves effort being applied into physical activity.
- Participating is a matter of 'choice'; it is voluntary and up to you whether you take part or not in the free time you have available.
- It tends to involve adults at the '**participation level**' of the sporting development continuum.
- It is flexible in nature, so how long you take part for and the rules being followed can be adjusted by participants as they wish.
- It is self-officiated/self-regulated (i.e. any decisions during activities are made by the participants themselves).

The functions of physical recreation can be looked at in terms of positive outcomes for individuals, as well as how a society can benefit if more people increase their physical activity levels and recreation.

The functions of physical recreation for an individual

Regular participation in physical recreation increases an individual's health and fitness and helps in the development of physical skills (e.g. improvement of a golf swing).

It provides individuals with a challenge which, if they overcome it, will lead to a sense of achievement and increased levels of self-esteem and self-confidence. Recreation can provide a chance to refresh oneself and it can act as a stress relief from work, and help individuals to relax. Involvement in physical recreation can help people to socialise and meet up with friends (e.g. as members of a regular circuit training class at a leisure centre). As recreation takes place in a relaxed atmosphere, it provides people with a sense of fun and enjoyment. For many, it helps ensure participation in physical activity for as many years as possible, well into later life, as the emphasis is on taking part at your own level and pace, rather than trying to beat others.

Memory tools

Some of the benefits of physical recreation to individuals can be remembered via the 'S' factors!

- S = Develop self-confidence/self-esteem via a sense of achievement
- S = Stress reduction occurs
- S = Skills develop/fitness increases as a result of taking part in physical recreation activities
- S = Social skills improve
- S = Sense of fun/enjoyment is gained

The functions of physical recreation for a society

In addition to physical recreation having a number of benefits to individuals, there are also a number of positive outcomes of physical recreation for society in general.

Increased health and fitness helps reduce the strain on the NHS and lowers obesity rates. If more individuals from different social communities join clubs and socially interact, it can help increase social integration and improve community cohesion. This can lead to an increase in employment and economic benefits when more people use facilities and buy equipment to participate. A more positive use of free time by individuals increases social control and decreases crime statistics in a more socially inclusive society. If increased skill levels occur at the participation stage, this can lead to more individuals potentially progressing through to performance/elite levels.

The key characteristics and functions of sport

Sport can be viewed as a serious and/or competitive experience and can be identified by a number of key features (characteristics) including the following:

- It is highly structured and has set rules/strict rules (e.g. set time limits; set boundaries).
- It involves use of specialist equipment/set kit.
- Officials are present who are trained or appointed by national governing bodies to enforce the rules.
- Strategies and tactics are involved to try to outwit opponents and win.
- Rewards are received as a result of success, which can be extrinsic rewards such as medals/trophies, or intrinsic rewards such as gaining personal satisfaction from your performance.
- High skill levels/high prowess are visible in sporting performance.
- High levels of commitment and/or strict training are involved to maintain and improve fitness and skill levels.
- It is serious and competitive (i.e. winning is important).

Key characteristics of sport
Serious/competitive — 'win at all costs' attitude or sportsmanship (*how?*)
Prowess — high skill levels, particularly by 'professionals' (*who?*)
Organised — sport has rules/regulations (*how?*)
Rewards — available for winning (extrinsic) and intrinsic satisfaction (*why?*)
Time and space restrictions apply (*when?/where?*)

Figure 1 Key characteristics of sport

Taking part in sport has a number of important functions for individuals, as well as society in general. These are similar in a number of respects to the functions of physical recreation.

For individuals, it can help improve their health and fitness and physical skill levels.

Self-confidence often increases as a result of skill improvement and success, which can lead to a feel-good factor for participants where this is the case. Sport often provides increased social opportunities: for example, the chance to communicate, socialise and work as part of a team and make friends at sports clubs. Participation in sport can help develop positive sporting morals and attitudes such as fair play and sportsmanship which can influence a person's general behaviour and keep them out of trouble via positive use of their free time.

For society, sporting involvement has a number of functions as described below.

Regular participation in energetic sporting activities helps to decrease the strain on the NHS and to reduce levels of obesity as health and fitness improve. Levels of crime can be reduced too, as individuals make more positive use of the free time they have available to them. This increases social control within society. Increased social integration and equality of opportunity may result via increased participation in sport together by different socio-economic and ethnic groups. Increased participation in sport has economic benefits as people pay to participate and spend money on new equipment and the latest fashionable kit on the market. Employment opportunities can be created as a result of sports participation (e.g. via employment as sports coaches, lifeguards, fitness trainers, etc.).

Memory tools

The benefits of sports participation for society can be remembered via three 'S' factors and three 'E' factors!

- **S** – Strain on the NHS is reduced
- **S** – Social control is increased
- **S** – Social integration is increased, along with community cohesion/morale
- **E** – Employment opportunities increase
- **E** – Economic benefits result
- **E** – Equality of opportunity via 'sports participation' for all

The key characteristics and aims of physical education (PE)

The National Curriculum for Physical Education was introduced following the 1988 Education Reform Act. It has been reviewed and modified slightly since, but essentially its key characteristics and aims have remained broadly similar.

The key characteristics of PE can be summarised as follows:

- It is compulsory.
- It involves formally taught lessons.
- It has four Key Stages as part of the National Curriculum from ages 5–16.
- It begins at primary school 'foundation level'.
- Teachers are in charge and deliver lessons.
- Lessons are pre-planned; it is highly structured.
- It is in school time.

Physical education has a variety of different aims and functions, including the development of health and fitness, as well as positive attitudes which hopefully lead to healthy lifestyles being continued when PE is no longer compulsory. PE provides opportunities for increased participation in a

CHECK YOUR UNDERSTANDING
Lots of people take part in sport to increase their health and fitness.
Identify two functions of taking part in sport for an individual.

variety of activities, developing and improving a range of physical skills and competencies. The development of personal and social skills is an important aim of PE (e.g. teamwork; communication; leadership; co-operation). PE also aims to develop positive sporting ethics such as morality, fair play and sportsmanship. Cognitively, it can help improve problem solving, decision making and creativity (e.g. developing a new sequence in dance or gymnastics). PE also aims to develop pupils' skills of self-analysis, as well as learning to recognise strengths and weaknesses in performance and where improvements have occurred. Ultimately PE is about encouraging life-long participation and trying to create a sporting habit for life after pupils finish compulsory PE at the age of 16.

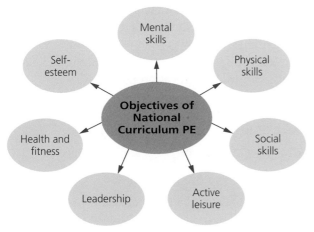

Figure 2 Objectives of National Curriculum PE

Memory tools

A number of the aims of PE can be remembered as '**P**' factors (i.e. they begin with the letter '**P**'!). For example, improving **p**hysical skills, **p**ersonal and social skills, **p**roblem-solving/decision-making skills.

Outdoor education as part of National Curriculum PE

Figure 3 Functions of outdoor and adventurous activities (OAA)

KEY TERM

Outdoor education: Activities which take place in the natural environment and utilise nature/geographical resources such as mountains, rivers, lakes, etc.

There are a number of functions of outdoor education for young people, as described below.

It helps children learn to appreciate and engage with the natural environment as well as increase its conservation. While in the natural environment, they are learning to develop new physical and survival skills (e.g. abseiling, climbing) which can result in increased self-esteem. Outdoor education activities such as climbing are physically challenging so result in increased levels of health and fitness.

Working with others is a key feature of outdoor education activities so increased co-operation, improvement in social skills and leadership skills often result. Mentally, there are a number of different functions to outdoor education including learning how to deal with a challenging situation, allowing the pupil to learn how to perceive risk, as well as learning to get excited as a result of participation in activities such as abseiling and climbing. Increased cognitive skills and improved decision making can also be gained by children as a result of outdoor education participation.

KEY TERM

Perceived risk: A challenge that stimulates a sense of danger and adventure for beginners or inexperienced performers in a safe environment, with danger minimised via stringent safety measures (e.g. wearing a safety harness when climbing).

ACTIVITY

Give examples of how outdoor education can be used to develop:
- physical skills
- social skills
- cognitive skills
- increase health and fitness.

Memory tools

The functions/benefits of outdoor education can be remembered via LEADS:

- **L** – Leadership skills
- **E** – Excitement/adrenaline rush
- **A** – Appreciation of the natural environment
- **D** – Decision making
- **S** – Social skills/self-esteem

PE Departments within schools face a number of problems offering outdoor education as a curriculum entitlement to pupils, including:

- a lack of time (e.g. time in the curriculum)
- a lack of money (e.g. high costs of specialist equipment)
- lack of qualified or motivated staff.

The location of a school can cause issues when trying to offer outdoor education activities as part of the curriculum, especially if it involves travelling a long distance to specialist facilities. In addition, health and safety concerns of parents, pupils and staff may act as a barrier when trying to offer such activities.

ACTIVITY

Using examples, identify three ways in which perceived risk can be experienced as part of a school's PE programme

CHECK YOUR UNDERSTANDING

OAA form a part of a school's overall PE programme. Identify the benefits of participating in OAA such as climbing.

A triangular model of PE

A pupil's experiences of PE should involve a number of different elements, including:

- Education (National Curriculum PE, as described above).
- School sport (e.g. extra-curricular competitive opportunities – inter-house competitions involving as many pupils as possible; inter-school competitions if you are chosen to represent the school in sport).
- Recreation (e.g. extra-curricular, non-competitive participation opportunities).

The key characteristics and aims of school sport

School sport is therefore different to PE as it mostly occurs in extra-curricular time as a choice for young children attending school. School sport is competitive and has been promoted as important by governments with initiatives introduced such as **School Sport Partnerships** and **School Games**. Schools sometimes use sports coaches to help increase the range of extra-curricular sporting opportunities available to pupils, as well as using their specialisms to develop pupils' talents to the full.

There are a number of benefits to participating in school sport. Physically, increased activity levels increase health and fitness and skill levels, which can increase a child's self-esteem. Socially, new groups can be formed and new friendships developed via extra-curricular involvement in school sport. Improved cognitive skills can result in improved decision-making capabilities, as well as an improvement in academic achievement if pupils become more motivated to attend and achieve at school.

Having considered the concepts of physical activity and sport mainly in isolation, it is also important to consider how they compare and contrast in a variety of different ways.

Similarities and differences between these key concepts

Similarities and differences between physical recreation and sport

Sport and recreation are *similar* in that they both involve physical activity, which helps increase health and fitness. They can be performed in a person's free time as voluntary activities, with individuals gaining intrinsic benefits as a result of participating; for example, achieving a sense of personal satisfaction as a result of achieving goals/aims.

Sport and recreation have a number of *differences* including those identified below.

Table 1 Physical recreation compared to sport

Physical recreation	Sport
Available to all/voluntary/choice	More selective/obligation/for some an occupation
Emphasis on taking part/participation focus	Emphasis on winning/serious/competitive
Limited/varied effort/commitment required	Involves a high level of effort/commitment, e.g. to train for a specific event/competition
Rules can be modified ,e.g. timings, numbers involved	Set rules apply
Self-officiated/self-regulated	External officials enforce rules
Mainly intrinsic rewards	Extrinsic rewards available for success, e.g. winning trophies/medals
Varied skill/fitness levels	Higher skill/fitness levels
Basic equipment and clothing used or worn	High tech equipment and clothing used or worn

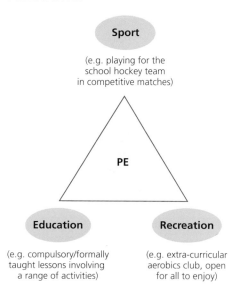

Figure 4 A triangular model of PE

123

Similarities and differences between physical recreation and physical education

Physical recreation and physical education are *similar* in that they both develop physical skills and are energetic, so have health and fitness benefits. They can both be enjoyable and fun to participate in so have intrinsic benefits.

The *differences* between physical recreation and physical education can be summarised via the table below, directly comparing key features of these two concepts of physical activity.

Table 2 A comparison of physical recreation with physical education

Physical recreation	Physical education
Voluntary/choice	Compulsory
In a person's free time	In school time
Informal/relaxed	Formal teaching and learning
Participants control activity themselves; self-regulated	Teacher in charge
Participation level	Foundation level at primary school level
Simple/limited organisational structure	Highly structured

CHECK YOUR UNDERSTANDING

Identify three similarities and three differences between PE and physical recreation.

STUDY HINT

You should aim to be able to identify the differences between compulsory National Curriculum PE and voluntary participation in school sport.

CHECK YOUR UNDERSTANDING

Identify four differences between school sport and National Curriculum PE.

A comparison between PE and school sport

As mentioned above, the overall concept of PE can be experienced in a number of different ways.

A direct comparison can be made between PE as a compulsory National Curriculum subject and school sport as a choice for young people, as illustrated in the table below.

Table 3 National curriculum PE compared to school sport

National Curriculum PE	School sport
In lesson time; curriculum time	In free time; extra-curricular
Compulsory	Element of choice; voluntary involvement
For all	For the chosen few; elitist
Emphasis on taking part	Emphasis on winning; competitive
Teacher led	Coaches involved
Wide variety of activities experienced	Specialisms develop

SUMMARY

In this chapter you have gained a clear understanding of the key features and purposes of various forms of physical activity (concepts) such as physical recreation, sport, physical education and school sport. You should now be able to identify what shared features these concepts have in common, as well as describe any differences between them where these exist.

PRACTICE QUESTIONS

1   Which of the following statements best describes the characteristics of sport?   (1 mark)

   a) Voluntary; a choice with an emphasis on participation.

   b) The participation level of the development continuum with an emphasis on fun.

   c) Rules are flexible and self-regulated.

   d) The performance level of the development continuum with an emphasis on winning.

2   What are the functions of physical recreation for the individual?   (3 marks)

3   Identify the benefits of participating in sport to society.   (3 marks)

4   Outline the functions of National Curriculum PE in schools today.   (4 marks)

5   Identify the problems schools face in offering OAA within their school PE programmes.   (3 marks)

6   Using an example, explain what is meant by perceived risk.   (3 marks)

7   Cycling has enjoyed a recent increase in participation among all ability levels.

   Compare cycling when it is performed as a physical recreation activity with cycling when it
   is performed as a sporting activity.   (4 marks)

8   Explain the potential benefits to society of increased participation in sport and physical
   recreation.   (8 marks)

Chapter 6.2
Development of elite performers in sport

Chapter objectives

By the end of this chapter you should be able to:

- Identify the personal, social and cultural factors required to support progression from talent identification to elite performance.
- Understand the generic roles, purpose and relationship between organisations in providing support and progression from talent identification through to elite performance (e.g. national governing bodies; national institutes of sport such as the English Institute of Sport; UK Sport).
- Identify the key features of national governing bodies' Whole Sport plans.
- Describe the support services provided by national institutes of sports for talent development.
- Explain the key features of UK Sport's World Class Performance Programme, Gold Event Series and Talent Identification and Development.

Development of elite performers in sport

There are personal, social and cultural factors required to support progression from **talent identification** to elite performance and these are discussed below.

Personal factors

It is important that all young, talented athletes in the UK are able to fulfil their sporting potential and have in place all they need to support and develop their talents. When considering the factors necessary in order to progress through to the **elite** performance level, a useful point to start is to identify some key **personal qualities** viewed as important in talented athletes.

On a personal level, talented performers need to be goal orientated. This means that they have firmly established and measurable short-term and long-term goals which provide them with progressive stepping stones to success and provide a framework to advance up to the elite level.

These young athletes also need to be good communicators and be willing to offer opinions and listen to the advice from a team of people who work with them, supporting their sporting progression. For example, coaches and athlete **mentors** play a key role in providing advice and support to sports performers as they develop their talents, as long as the performer is prepared to listen and act on the advice, as appropriate.

At a personal level, athletes need to have a clear focus on what they want to achieve and how to achieve it. Young performers with a sporting talent can sometimes be too easily distracted and consequently fail to reach their true potential (e.g. by devoting too much time to meeting the demands of sponsors as opposed to training).

Patience is another important personal factor an individual needs in order to develop through to elite performance level. The ability to set out a clearly defined path of progression and stay on it over a number of years can be crucial in young elite performers developing their talents in a progressive manner. This can particularly be the case when 'failure' or a lack of expected progress occurs. The important thing here is to remain patient and learn from any training sessions and competition failures so they can ultimately progress towards their end goal of succeeding in elite sport.

Having dedication, determination to succeed, and motivation from within themselves to advance and excel in sport are all important personal factors as they help to ensure enjoyment and the commitment to putting in the necessary time and energy to fully develop their sporting talents.

One particularly important personal quality necessary to develop as an elite performer is that of self-confidence. This is often based on an individual's self-belief linked to their high technical skill levels and having the physical attributes necessary to succeed in top level sport. Confidence, resilience and perseverance are often required when faced with challenges on the pathway from talent identification to elite level performance.

A summary of key personal factors and qualities necessary to develop as an elite performer:

- Commitment and self-discipline
- Determination to succeed, as well as being single-minded and mentally tough
- Highly motivated with the desire to achieve
- Willing to self-sacrifice in order to succeed
- High pain tolerance
- High levels of self-confidence and self-efficacy
- Highly skilled physically and/or naturally talented
- High level of physical fitness.

Social and cultural factors

A wide range of social and cultural factors can influence the progression of a young talented individual through to elite performance level.

Of key importance is the support of friends and family when starting out in sport and trying to progress. Having friends and family present in the crowd at sports events to support and encourage is viewed as very important, both socially and emotionally. The financial resources of a family can be important in an individual's development as money is required to pay for specialist equipment, travelling expenses, specialist coaching and medical support. An important social and cultural influence on performer progression is therefore an individual's **socio-economic status**.

As indicated above, participation and progression in sport can cost a lot of money so an individual's socio-economic status is an important factor in them achieving their potential, particularly when financial support is not available to them at an early stage of their development (e.g. from sponsors or the National Lottery.)

KEY TERMS

Talent identification: The multi-disciplinary screening of athletes in order to identify those with the potential for world class success.

Elite: The best, highest level sports performers at 'excellence' level.

Personal qualities: The attributes and personality characteristics of an individual person.

Mentor: An individual who helps and guides another person's development (e.g. Olympic silver medal-winning diver Leon Taylor acted as a mentor to Tom Daley in the run-up to London 2012 and Rio 2016.)

Figure 1 Leon Taylor, pictured on the right, an athlete mentor in diving

ACTIVITY

Identify three physical and three psychological qualities you feel are necessary for an individual to develop as an elite performer.

KEY TERM

Socio-economic status: An individual's position in the social structure, which depends on their job, level of income and area they live in.

Figure 2 Jessica Ennis-Hill is a high-profile sports performer who acts as a role model to inspire others

Another factor influencing elite progression is the presence or absence of equal opportunities policies and anti-discriminatory practice within the sport an individual is competing in. Such policies and practices are important in working against any potential barriers which can negatively impact on an individual's progression through a sport. For example, if there are issues linked to **sexism**, where opportunities for women to develop in a sport are negatively affected by negative male perceptions of their capabilities, action must be taken to challenge such perceptions.

To help combat sex discrimination, **equity** targets have been set for all sport National Governing Bodies (NGBs) by Sport England which help increase the participation of women and girls in sport and help more of them progress through to elite level.

Educational providers such as schools, colleges and universities are another important social and cultural factor influencing a young person's sporting progression. If the experience of sport at school, for example, is a positive one, and there are strategies, policies and practices in place to encourage talented individuals to aspire to and progress towards, then they are more likely to progress. This can be through links to local clubs with high level coaches and specialist facilities to train in.

Indeed, educational providers such as those identified above should be part of a co-ordinated programme, linked to sports clubs, designed to identify talent and provide the opportunity to progress through structured levels of competition; for example, from school, to local area, to county, regional and then national levels.

Another important social factor is the level of media coverage a sport has which can influence its initial status with youngsters and their willingness or desire to participate and develop their talents in such an activity. The presence or absence of role models to aspire to can, therefore, be an important social factor, influencing involvement and progression in a sport. For example, in football, high levels of media coverage show many top-class performers to aspire to, whereas in a sport like hockey, with relatively low amounts of media coverage, there are few well-known elite performers to aspire to.

A summary of the social and cultural factors necessary to develop as an elite performer:

● High socio-economic status
● Evidence of equal opportunities and anti-discriminatory practice within a sport and setting of equity targets
● High quality, supportive educational provision
● Structured levels of competition to progress through
● High levels of media coverage and role models to aspire to.

Organisations providing support and progression

Three organisations are focused on within the syllabus as being particularly important when considering talent identification and elite performer progression. UK Sport, the English Institute of Sport (EIS) and the **national governing bodies** of sport (**NGBs**) will each be considered in turn, with any inter-relationships between them explained as and when appropriate.

UK Sport

UK Sport has a single focus on developing high performance sport in the UK. Their work is aimed at developing and implementing various strategies to increase sporting excellence in this country. Their primary role is to strategically invest and distribute National Lottery funding for elite performer development in order to maximise the performance of UK athletes in the Olympic and Paralympic Games.

They do this via two main channels. The first of these is to provide funding to NGBs which enables them to operate a World Class Programme (see the explanation of this programme later in this section) covering all funded summer and winter Olympic and Paralympic sports. The second channel provides funding directly to athletes via an Athlete Performance Award which contributes to their living and sporting costs once they have reached elite performance level. In terms of financial support at elite performer level, UK Sport also provides funding for the National Institutes of Sport such as the English Institute of Sport (EIS) and the British Olympic and Paralympic preparation plans for the Olympic and Paralympic Games; for example, Rio 2016 and the preparation camp at Belo Horizonte.

UK Sport is therefore the nation's high performance sports agency investing in Olympic and Paralympic sport. Working with partner organisations, they run a number of centralised strategic support services across the UK including the development of 'World Class Coaches' for example, via the Elite Programme. This is delivered in conjunction with Sports Coach UK and is aimed at developing programmes and innovations to support coaches involved in the World Class system.

UK Sport is a lead agency involved in running Talent ID programmes with the EIS providing host venues, as explained in more detail below. As part of such programmes, UK Sport is keen to develop lifestyles in young performers which enable elite performer progression to occur unimpeded by personal issues or work demands. Personal Lifestyle Advice has been developed by UK Sport and delivered at National Institutes of Sport to help with mentor support and advice on issues such as time management, budgeting and so on.

UK Sport promotes positive sporting conduct and ethics at elite level in the UK's high performance athletes. UK Sport also sees it as important to develop and manage the UK's international sporting relationships, e.g. via liaison with International Federations on the International Voice programme.

National institutes of sport

One example of a national institute of sport is the EIS.

The EIS is a subsidiary of UK Sport and wholly owned by them. The EIS receives a grant of £40 million over four years from UK Sport and generates its own income by providing services to NGBs such as performance analysis, sports medicine and so on. In the year of London 2012, for example, NGBs invested £6.1 million in EIS services to help and support elite performer development in their sports. It is UK Sport's science, medicine and technology arm which acts as the team behind many of Team GB's most successful Olympians and Paralympians. Their job is to increase the probability of a potential elite athlete being successful by providing a range of different services to improve their health, fitness, training and preparation.

Figure 3 The National Lottery funding elite sporting success

CHECK YOUR UNDERSTANDING
Describe the role of UK Sport in elite performer development.

Figure 4 An EIS centre at Sheffield

129

In terms of such sporting services, the EIS operates 'World Class Performance' environments via nine 'High Performance' centres, as well as numerous other training bases across England. Their 'partner sites' include the Team GB Intensive Rehabilitation Unit at Bisham Abbey, as well as Holme Pierrepont National Water Sports Centre in Nottingham, and St Mary's University College, Twickenham. Its staff work with high level coaches and NGB performance directors to help improve the performance of their best athletes, by delivering a range of services to enable them to optimise training programmes and maximise performance in competition. Examples of such services include top class staff providing expertise in the following areas necessary for the development and progress of sporting excellence:

- **Sport science:** Exercise physiology is one aspect of sport science provided at the National Institutes of Sport, including the EIS. Work in this area is highly important in elite performer development as it helps evaluate training as it happens, allowing coaches and athletes to objectively monitor the impact of training on the body. Other sport science support provided at National Institutes of Sport includes performance nutrition, performance psychology, performance analysis and so on.

ACTIVITY

Visit **www.eis2win.co.uk/pages/Physiology.aspx** and identify three ways in which exercise physiology services are improving elite performers at the EIS.

- **Medical:** Sports medicine is particularly important to athletes at the high performance level. It is made available as quickly as possible at National Institutes of Sport such as the EIS and includes services such as physiotherapy and strength and conditioning coaches.

- **Performance Lifestyle Support:** This is available to all athletes on the World Class Performance Programme. It provides a personalised support service specifically designed to help each athlete create the unique environment necessary for their success. This support aims to minimise potential concerns, conflicts and distractions which could be detrimental to performance. It also helps with time management, budgeting, dealing with the media, sponsorship and career development, etc. (See **www.eis2win.com/pages/Performance_Lifestyle.aspx**.)

The EIS has a dedicated Performance Solutions team of scientists who work in partnership with UK Sport alongside coaches and NGB Performance Directors. Together they feed the pipeline of talent into sports and facilitate the transition from talented junior to elite international performer via Performance Pathways, i.e. Talent ID, Recruitment and Progression. The **UK Talent Team** is a collaboration between the EIS and UK Sport, supporting the World Class Programmes to identify and develop talented athletes via projects like the national athlete recruitment projects. The UK Talent Team's work focuses on the hundreds of Podium and Podium Potential athletes with the capability to positively impact future Olympic and Paralympic Games. Successful graduates of Talent ID programmes included GB rower Helen Glover (Sporting Giants) at London 2012 and Skeleton Gold medallist Lizzy Yarnold (Girls4Gold) at Sochi in 2014.

Sports technology and engineering underpin the sport science and sport medicine services the EIS delivers by developing equipment and technology to support practitioners, as well as sports performers. Transferred from UK Sport in August 2013, the EIS has a Research and Innovation team

Figure 5 Talent ID graduate, Helen Glover

which aims to ensure that Britain's top athletes have the best equipment and technology available to them when competing on the global stage. The team looks at innovation in a number of different areas, including training science, performance medicine, sporting equipment and coaching technologies. Working directly with NGBs, the EIS Research and Innovation team provides funding and expertise to support projects which have a beneficial effect on elite level athletes now and in the future.

Memory tools

A number of the roles and purposes of the National Institutes of Sport can be linked to the word 'SPORT':

- **S** = Sport science and sport medicine support
- **P** = Performance Lifestyle Programmes are provided
- **O** = Organisations work in partnership (e.g. EIS and UK Sport)
- **R** = Research and innovation
- **T** = Top quality facilities and high level coaches are provided.

National governing bodies of sport

NGBs can help ensure the development of elite performers in a number of different ways. Initially, they can promote and increase participation in their sport, providing equality of opportunity for all.

Memory tools

'PAMPER' can be used to remember different ways that NGBs try to provide equality of opportunity:

- **P** = Positive role models used to promote sport to target groups.
- **A** = Accessible facilities provided and developed for groups with a particular need.
- **M** = Meet government policies on sport and recreation (e.g. in their Whole Sport Plans).
- **P** = Policies put in place to target certain under-represented groups (e.g. ethnic minorities).
- **E** = Employment of sport-specific Sport Development Officers (SDOs) to promote the sport to under-represented groups.
- **R** = Resources invested in inner city areas.

They can also use regional scouts and talent identification schemes to try to identify young sporting talent. Once young talent has been identified, it needs supporting in a number of different ways.

NGBs are the organisations which make decisions on who in their sport should receive funding, for example, from UK Sport's World Class Programme. They work with organisations such as the National Institutes of Sport and UK Sport to provide elite performers with various support services necessary to help them develop and progress. For example, high quality coaches and top-class training facilities are important in enabling performers to develop their talents to the full. NGBs are the organisations that provide sport-specific coaching awards from basic, low level qualifications through to the high levels necessary to support and develop elite performers in their sport.

For example, in tennis the Lawn Tennis Association (LTA) has developed a Coaching Pathway from Level 1 Coaching Assistant through to the Level 5 Master Performance which develops players to an elite standard.

As described above, performance lifestyle support, as well as research and innovation, sport science and sport medicine services available to NGBs at National Institutes of Sport, all play an important part in elite performer development. In addition, performers need to be part of developmental

Figure 6 The EIS - an example of a home country institute of sport

STUDY HINT

It is important to link the key services of the National Institutes of Sport to the level of service they provide. They don't just provide facilities and coaches; they provide high quality facilities and high level coaching to develop performers.

CHECK YOUR UNDERSTANDING

The home nations of England, Northern Ireland, Scotland and Wales all have National Institutes of Sport. Identify five ways in which these National Institutes are aiding the development of the UK's elite athletes.

KEY TERM

Whole Sport Plan: A business plan/document submitted to Sport England outlining National Governing Body strategies to increase participation and enhance talent in the sport(s) they are responsible for. For the four-year period the Whole Sport Plan is in operation, i.e. 2013–17, £83 million has been allocated to develop talented young athletes.

ACTIVITY

Research British Rowing's Rowability and Indoor Rowing schemes (e.g. via Sport England or British Rowing websites) and identify which groups in society they are particularly aimed at.

Figure 7 Sir Ben Ainslie, pictured on the left

training squads with progressive levels of competition to gradually develop their talents in a structured and organised manner.

British Cycling is the NGB for cycling in this country, home to the successful Team GB Cycling Team, and its aims, as always, are to win world and Olympic medals across all the cycling disciplines.

British Cycling has a number of stages of identification, confirmation and development of talent in their sport. For example, the Olympic Podium Programme supports highly skilled elite cyclists on a full-time programme largely based near the GB cycling team's headquarters in Manchester. The Olympic Academy Programme provides a finishing school for 18–23-year-olds to fine-tune their skills, enabling them to make the jump to the senior Olympic Podium Programme.

Key features of national governing bodies' Whole Sport Plans

A **Whole Sport Plan** is a lottery-funded, Sport England 'approved' outline of how an NGB intends to increase participation in the sport it is responsible for, as well as identify and develop talent in it. In 2012, NGBs submitted their Whole Sport Plans to Sport England, giving information on how investment in their sports would nurture young talent.

British Rowing is one example of an NGB that developed a 2013–17 Whole Sport Plan and it received over £5 million for participation schemes such as Rowability and Indoor Rowing.

Funding was also allocated to British Yachting's Whole Sport Plan (2013–17) which included its plans for Talent Development. Similar to other NGBs, increasing the number of talented young athletes coming through the ranks is of continuous importance to British Yachting. Its England Talent Programme, designed to find the next Ben Ainslie, identified the need to provide more locations for talent support when trying to provide more intensive support to sailors and coaches with the greatest potential to progress to world-class level. It also highlighted the need to enhance the domestic competition programme to align it with world class selection. Junior Racing and training programmes were also viewed as important in identifying and developing talent, with those progressing being exposed to appropriate international regatta experience to further test them.

ACTIVITY

Research the Royal Yachting Association (RYA) Whole Sport Plan (2013–17) via **www.sportengland.org/our-work/national-governing-bodies/**. Identify and explain four different elements of the RYA England Talent Programme.

Talent development and support services

Working in partnership, UK Sport, the National Institutes of Sport (e.g. EIS) and national governing bodies (NGBs) of sport are committed to systematically unearthing sporting talent with the necessary potential and mind-set to win medals and world titles. This is done through talent identification programmes.

Various reasons for using talent identification programmes can be made by such organisations, including the following:

- It means all potential performers can be screened.
- Performers can be directed to the sports most suited to their talents.

- The development process can be accelerated as a result of the information gained.
- Efficient use can be made of available funding for Talent ID schemes.
- The chances of producing medallists are improved.
- They provide a co-ordinated approach between organisations such as NGBs, the EIS and UK Sport.

Possible disadvantages of Talent ID programmes include the following:

- They may miss late developers.
- They require high levels of funding.
- They require large numbers to be tested to be of use.
- There are no guarantees of success.
- Many sports are in competition for the same talent pool; high profile sports may attract more performers or the best performers.

What makes a talent identification programme effective? That is, what helps improve the chances of the success of talent programmes undertaken within the National Institutes of Sport such as Girls4Gold?

- There is a simplicity of administration and record keeping, evidenced through clear and appropriate division of roles. Performers can be analysed via a clear database of physiological information.
- Talent identification monitoring systems are used that are built on good practice and use appropriate tests.
- Well-structured competitive programmes and development squads are provided at various levels appropriate to participants' current level of performance and provide a structured route through to elite level.
- Specialist, high quality training facilities to support progression are provided; testing facilities are of a high standard.
- Funding is allocated to young up-and-coming performers at different stages of their development.
- Talent spotting is undertaken via high quality coaches and high quality talent scouts.
- There is high level provision of support services (e.g. sports scientists, physiotherapists) to support performers during their identification and progression.
- Organisations involved in Talent ID work together (e.g. EIS, UK Sport and NGBs).
- Equality of opportunity is ensured by allowing anyone who feels they meet the initial criteria for a programme to apply to be part of it.

Figure 8 Girls4Gold

Memory tools

You can remember key features of an effective Talent ID programme via TALENT:

- **T** = Testing facilities are of a high standard
- **A** = Analysis of performers via a clear database
- **L** = Links between organisations involved in Talent ID ensure a co-ordinated approach
- **E** = Equal opportunities for all to apply
- **N** = National development squads/programmes exist to develop through
- **T** = Talent spotting via high quality coaches.

STUDY HINT

When identifying the key characteristics of an effective Talent ID programme, consider how the things the programme provides links to talent identification, e.g. they provide high quality coaches to talent-spot.

The EIS is one of the National Institutes of Sport which provides various support services to help ensure talent development. Its Performance Pathways Team works with UK Sport to support the World Class Programme in identifying and developing talented athletes by providing them with the necessary support services to ensure their progress. The Team has identified four main areas of support as important for the identification and development of talent:

1 **Pathway Frontline Technical Solutions:** These are designed to meet the specific needs of each sport when identifying and developing talent (e.g. to design talent recruitment and confirmation programmes for different sports such as UK Athletics Futures programme).

2 **Pathway Education:** This provides educational opportunities for development coaches covering a variety of topics linked to elite performer development.

3 **Pathway Analytics:** This gives sports the ability to provide meaningful measurements of the effectiveness of their performance pathways by using a range of diagnostic tools; they can also take a 'Performance Pathway Health Check'.

4 **Performance Pathway Health Check (PHC):** The PHC is an important diagnostic tool, supporting summer and winter Olympic and Paralympic sports. It provides a review of current systems and practices for supporting the development of potential medal winners in any given sport. It includes a review of the sport's long-term vision and strategy for elite development, as well as a consideration of the coaching and training environments a sport has in place to develop elite performers.

5 **Pathway Strategy:** This is designed to assist sports to develop and put in place a clear progressive pathway from Podium Foundations level to Podium level in their sport.

The ultimate aim of support services provided by National Institutes of Sport, such as the EIS, is to identify new athletes with clear sporting potential, help them progress onto the World Class system and successfully represent Great Britain in major international sporting events.

One example of the work of the EIS Pathway Team is its partnership with UK Sport and the British Army, which was launched in October 2014 with the aim of representing Team GB at the 2020 Tokyo Games. It involves projects such as Talent Transfer (Girls4Gold: Army) and Shooting (Troops2Targets). These schemes give female soldiers the chance to take part in a number of assessment days in EIS centres to see if they have the potential to be successful in major international shooting competitions, with the 2020 Olympics as the ultimate aim.

Key features of UK Sport's World Class Performance Programme, Gold Event Series, Talent Identification and Development

World Class Performance Programme

It can take athletes many years to develop the necessary high level skills and competitive maturity required to be successful at the top level of international sport. UK Sport has therefore adopted a funding philosophy which reflects potentially long journeys to the top. This works on the basis of two clear, distinct levels which make up the World Class Pathway for

Performance Pathway Team: A combination of EIS and UK Sport expertise used to identify and develop world-class talent.

ACTIVITY

Identify three features of an EIS Performance Pathway Health Check (PHC).

individuals on the World Class Performance Programme (WCPP). The WCPP covers all funded summer and winter Olympic and Paralympic sports. The two levels are:

1 **Podium:** Designed to support athletes with realistic medal-winning capabilities at the next Olympics/Paralympics (i.e. a maximum of four years away from the podium).

UK Athletics, like other NGBs, receives funding from UK Sport and the National Lottery which enables them to offer financial support to a selected group of performers in their sport via the WCPP. In the lead-up to Rio, UK Athletics funded 21 podium group athletes in 2015–16 including Jessica Ennis-Hill, Mo Farah, Adam Gemili and Laura Muir.

2 **Podium Potential (previously known as Development):** Designed to support athletes whose performances suggest they have realistic medal-winning capabilities at subsequent Olympic/Paralympic Games (i.e. a maximum of eight years away from the podium).

Beneath Podium Potential is the 'Talent' level which provides funding and support to identify and confirm athletes who have the potential to progress to the world class pathway. The 'Futures Programme' in place for British Athletics underpins the WCPP and was designed to provide financial and medical support to young, talented athletes (typically aged 17–20) and their coaches.

Gold Event Series

UK Sport is the lead agency attempting to ensure the UK successfully bids to host and stage major sporting events. They have a flagship programme called the Gold Event Series which is working hard to bring 100 targeted major international sporting events to the UK during the ten years it is operating (i.e. from 2013–23). Successful bids were made as part of the programme to host the UCI Track Cycling World Championships in London in 2016, as well as the World Athletics Championships at the Olympic Stadium in 2017. The Gold Event Series focuses mainly on attracting World Championships, European Championships and premium world circuit events to the UK. Prior to developing event bids, UK Sport works with the sport and host location, helping it to draw up a detailed business plan and giving a budget to work to. When UK Sport agrees a financial award to support an event bid, it continues to work with the NGB involved to develop and support their planning and delivery of the actual event. Ultimately, UK Sport has a number of objectives it aims to achieve as a result of staging major international sporting events in the UK, including:

● Supporting high performance success

● Creating high profile opportunities for people to engage in sport

● Using and demonstrating the legacy of London 2012 and Glasgow 2014

● Driving positive economic and social impacts for the UK.

Talent Identification and Development (Talent ID)

UK Sport is a lead agency in running Talent ID programmes with National Institutes of Sport, such as those in the EIS, acting as host venues. The co-ordinated work of the EIS with UK Sport supporting talent identification and development is described in detail earlier in this section. Additional information contained here focuses more on UK Sport's specific roles when looking to discover sporting talent of the future.

Figure 9 Adam Gemili – Britain's hope for athletics success on the world stage

STUDY HINT

If asked to *explain* the World Class Performance Programme, you should use the correct terms to identify the different levels of the pathway before providing clear/correct explanations of the levels to distinguish between them.

CHECK YOUR UNDERSTANDING

Identify three key objectives UK Sport aims to achieve through its Gold Event Series.

UK Sport has a clearly defined mission to drive forward Olympic and Paralympic Performance Pathways which help to ensure continued success at future Games events. Its Performance Pathway Team supports World Class Programmes to identify and develop talented athletes and construct the necessary support systems needed to help ensure success. Frontline Technical Solutions are provided via the Pathways Team, looking to create a 'talent profile' which is capable of predicting future Olympic and Paralympic potential. It is also involved in possible positive transfer of sporting talent from one sport to another, following in the footsteps of dual Olympic medal winner Rebecca Romero who successfully switched from rowing to cycling.

The Pathway Team also provides specialist knowledge for Olympic and Paralympic talent and development managers and coaches on the issues they face in identifying and developing future generations of elite performers. UK Sport's educational work involves creating a unique learning programme for talent development managers and coaches nominated into the WCPP by their NGB. It draws on best practice in developing excellence from many areas of life other than sport, including astronauts, junior surgeons and musicians, to try to learn from 'gold standard' examples of how to create successful opportunities to progress for elite performers.

Pathway Analytics, as described earlier, enables sports to measure and benchmark the effectiveness of their performance pathway using a Talent Health Check which is delivered every four years by the Performance Pathway Team. It discusses topics such as junior to senior transition, as well as retention and attrition rates of athletes on the pathway. Overall, UK Sport looks to develop and implement a clearly defined pathway, vision and strategy, from foundation through to podium level.

UK Sport's talent recruitment and confirmation programmes involve a number of different phases. Campaigns start with a 'talent search' which can involve the general public and/or the sports community. Interested athletes are invited to submit an application form to UK Sport for them to consider, with successful applicants invited to Phase 1 testing, hosted at venues around the home nations. Phase 1 involves performing a range of different fitness and skill tests linked to the sport. Results from these influence progression onto Phases 2+3, which further assess an athlete's suitability for a sport via medical screening, performance lifestyle workshops and psychological/behavioural assessments.

Following these assessment phases, selected athletes then embark on a 6–12-month 'confirmation phase' where they are totally immersed into the sport's training environment, with exposure to a carefully constructed developmental experience. Rates of progression are tracked to see if individuals are suitable for the sport and potential funding on their WCPP.

UK Sport also operates a 'World Class Talent Transfer' initiative for athletes exiting an Olympic or Paralympic World Class Programme who are interested in exploring their possible potential to achieve elite level performance in another sport.

One example of a Talent Identification scheme supported by UK Sport is GB Canoeing's 'Girls4Gold Canoeing'. It is the first programme in a series of Girls4Gold campaigns aiming to increase the female talent pool in various sports, including canoeing, so they can challenge for more medals in Tokyo 2020 and beyond.

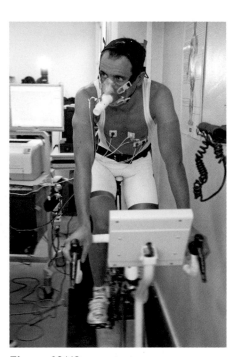

Figure 10 VO$_2$ max test

CHECK YOUR UNDERSTANDING

Describe the four key phases of UK Sport's Talent recruitment programmes.

SUMMARY

After reading this chapter you should have gained a clear understanding of a range of personal, social and cultural factors which are required when developing talented sports performers to reach their potential. Knowledge and awareness of the key roles and functions of various organisations involved in elite performer development such as national governing bodies of sport (e.g. their Whole Sport Plans) and institutes of sport (e.g. the EIS) will also have been developed. You will be able to identify and explain a number of different features of UK Sport programmes supporting elite performer development in the UK, including the World Class Performance Programme and its Gold Event Series.

PRACTICE QUESTIONS

1 Which of the following is a national governing body of sport? (1 mark)

   a) UK Sport

   b) English Institute of Sport

   c) British Cycling

   d) Gold Event Series

2 What are the personal qualities necessary for an individual to progress toward elite level sport performance? (3 marks)

3 UK Sport plays a key role in co-ordinating Talent ID programmes to help achieve its aim of developing elite performers.

   Identify the characteristics of an effective Talent ID programme. (4 marks)

4 Explain how the structure of the World Class Performance Pathway is supporting the development of elite athletes in the UK. (3 marks)

5 Discuss the advantages and disadvantages of introducing structured Talent ID programmes in the UK to support the development of elite performers. (8 marks)

6 The Gold Events Series is a 10-year programme running from 2013 to 2023 which aims to attract major sporting events to the UK.
   Discuss the suggestion that hosting major championships will benefit the individual performer and the sport. (8 marks)

Chapter 6.3
Ethics in sport

Chapter objectives

By the end of this chapter you should be able to:

- Describe the definitions and key features of amateurism, the Olympic oath, sportsmanship, gamesmanship and the win ethic.
- Explain the definitions and examples of positive and negative forms of deviance in relation to the sports performer.

Ethics in sport

Amateurism

Amateurism was a nineteenth-century code or ideal of sporting ethics which developed among upper then middle classes during the Victorian era.

In the nineteenth century, elite sport was dominated by the upper and middle classes who had high status in sport, as well as in society. Upper and middle class amateurs held a higher status than professionals at the time. The code of amateurism encouraged socially acceptable behaviour in sport and was based on playing sport to clearly set rules. These rules were put in place by middle and upper classes which then formed many national governing bodies (NGBs); for example, the Football Association (FA) in 1863. The development of written rules gave sports a clear structure and fairness, such as having equal numbers on a team.

Amateurism closely adhered to a code of ethics (dominant at the time) which involved playing sport to a high set of moral values which included fair play and sportsmanship, immediate acceptance of the rules and refereeing decisions, etc.

Being wealthy and part of the social elite, with plenty of free time for sport, meant the upper and middle classes could afford to play sport for the love of it, rather than for monetary gain ('It's not the winning but the taking part that counts').

Participation in sport was seen as more important than winning and taking part was viewed as a character-building exercise. The middle and upper classes played sport according to their God-given abilities and training was frowned upon, as this would constitute professionalism! Anyone who developed competency in a number of sports was viewed with high regard as an all-rounder and this was the elite performer model of the time. The amateurs were therefore the 'elite performers' of the nineteenth century and were very highly regarded in society for their sporting talents.

In modern-day British sport, 'amateurism' is still evident in a number of ways including through:

- Fair play/sportsmanship: This is still viewed positively, encouraged and promoted in a number of ways. For example, the Fair Play Awards in football; shaking of hands prior to and at the end of sporting contests; and through the Olympics with the 'Olympic ideal' based on principles of amateurism.

- Sports such as Rugby Union which maintained their amateurism until late into the twentieth century and still have codes of conduct based on such principles, such as calling the referee 'Sir'.

The Olympic oath

Written by Baron de Coubertin, the founder of the modern Olympics, the Olympic oath was first taken at the 1920 summer Olympics in Antwerp. It is a promise made by one athlete as a representative of each of the participating competitors, one judge as a representative of the Olympic officials who commit to impartiality at the opening ceremony of each Olympics and one coach.

The oath of the athlete reads as follows:

> *'In the name of all competitors I promise that we shall take part in these Olympic Games, respecting and abiding by the rules which govern them, committing ourselves to a sport without doping and without drugs in the true spirit of sportsmanship for the glory of sport and honour of our teams.'*

You could argue that it is still relevant in modern-day sport because the Olympics are still viewed by large numbers of people as a festival of sport with fair play and sportsmanship very much in evidence. However, there are unfortunately lots of examples of doping and positive drugs tests at Olympic Games, which some argue leaves the relevance of the Olympic oath in question (e.g. Ben Johnson at the Seoul Olympics in 1988). Ben Johnson is thought to have sparked a significant increase in drugs testing and a tightening up of procedures and practices, following his positive test for drugs the day after winning the 100 m gold medal, breaking the World Record in the process. In addition, with professional athletes now allowed to compete in the Games, more examples of 'win-at-all-costs' behaviour and stretching of the rules to their absolute limit are occurring in Olympic sport, which further questions respect and adherence to the oath. Team GB Olympic gold-winning cyclist Philip Hindes became involved in a potential 'cheating' scandal in London 2012 when he claimed that he 'fell' from his bike as part of a plan, seconds into the start of his race because he felt he was 'losing' as the race started. In the team sprint in cycling, if you crash like this, it is considered a 'false start' and the race is restarted. Hindes claimed he felt he made a poor start which led to his perceived need to crash on purpose to get a restart and improve his chances of winning gold. The actions of Hindes were technically within the rules, but perhaps not in the true spirit of the Olympics or reflecting its oath.

To find out more about the Olympic oath (1920–80), you can visit: http://olympic-museum.de/oath/theoath.htm

ACTIVITY

Research further the examples of sports performers breaking or stretching the Olympic oath to the limit, and identify why this might lead some to suggest that such an oath is irrelevant in the modern-day Olympics:

a) Ben Johnson at the 1988 Seoul Olympics
b) Philip Hindes at London 2012.

KEY TERMS

Amateurism: Participation in sport for the love of it, receiving no financial gain; it is based on the concept of athleticism (i.e. physical endeavour with moral integrity).

Athleticism: A fanatical devotion to sport involving high levels of physical endeavour and moral integrity.

STUDY HINT

Amateurism can refer to the nineteenth century, so it is important to consider the code of amateurism when it was at its height in the 1800s, when the upper and middle classes controlled sport (i.e. who played it, and how they played it).

Figure 1 Baron de Coubertin, founder of the modern Olympics

Figure 2 Ben Johnson at the Seoul Olympics in 1988

Sportsmanship

Sportsmanship involves playing by the written rules to a high code of ethics. Fairness, maintaining self-control and treating others fairly are all positive virtues associated with sportsmanship. It also involves maintaining high levels of etiquette to ensure fair play is clearly evident in a sporting contest. It therefore involves playing the game in a positive spirit, with respect shown for opponents and officials alike. Examples of sportsmanship at elite level include professional footballers returning the ball to the opposition when it has been kicked out of play to allow an injured player to have treatment, and cricketers 'walking' before being given out when they know they have made contact with bat on ball and it has been caught. Professional sports performers sometimes show 'good grace' when returning to play at former clubs and not celebrating the scoring of a goal or try as a mark of respect to their old club.

In modern-day sport, sportsmanship is under attack as winning becomes increasingly important. For example, when a team is winning they often stretch the rules and waste time in order to ensure a victory. Some performers (like professional footballers Wilfried Zaha at Crystal Palace and Ashley Young at Manchester United during the 2014–15 season) earned a negative reputation for **simulation**/diving in the penalty area to try to unfairly win a penalty. In addition, violent actions have seemingly replaced the civilised behaviour more evident in the amateur era of many sports. On occasions, performers constantly question the decisions of referees or refuse to adopt sporting etiquette with their opponents. For example, Luis Suárez and Patrice Evra refused to shake hands prior to the start of a Liverpool vs Manchester United Premier League game, even though this forms part of the FA's 'Respect' initiative for promoting fair play and sportsmanship!

However, sportsmanship can be encouraged in a number of ways, including the following:

- Use of NGB campaigns promoting sportsmanship/fair play (e.g. FA Respect).
- The giving of awards for fair play to encourage it in top level sport, therefore providing positive role models for youngsters to follow. UEFA Fair Play Awards include a place in a European competition awarded on the basis of fair play/sportsmanship.
- Use of technology to help match officials reach the correct decisions and allow performers to be **cited** after matches for behaviour which goes against the rules, e.g. a dangerous tackle missed by the referee in rugby.
- Introduction of NGB rules promoting fair play (e.g. banning high or late tackles, etc.)
- Punish foul play and unsporting behaviour on the field of play and within the sporting event, e.g. officials can 'sin bin' – book or send a player off.
- Punish foul play and unsporting behaviour after the event, e.g. fines or bans imposed by national governing bodies of sport.
- Use of positive role models to promote sportsmanship and fair play.
- Use of rigorous drug testing to try to ensure fairness in sporting contests and catch out drugs cheats.

> **CHECK YOUR UNDERSTANDING**
> Give three ways in which elite level sports performers fail to adopt the sportsmanship ethic; and identify three ways in which sportsmanship is encouraged and maintained in high level/elite sport.

Gamesmanship

Gamesmanship can be described as the art of winning games by cunning means, but without actually breaking the rules. Although on many occasions, it is a very fine line between gamesmanship and actually cheating! Gamesmanship therefore involves stretching the rules to the limit and failing to follow the etiquette of the game or sporting contest. There are many examples of gamesmanship in elite level modern-day sport, such as:

- Delaying play at a restart to get back in defence (e.g. by keeping possession of the ball).
- Time wasting when ahead in a game to try to ensure victory.
- Verbally 'sledging' an opponent to distract or upset them, e.g. in cricket, a bowler or fielder might say something to upset the concentration of a batsman in an effort to get them out.
- Psyching out an opponent at a pre-match press conference.
- Taking an injury time-out, toilet break or appealing a decision to the umpire even when it is not necessarily needed, to upset the concentration or rhythm of an opponent (e.g. in tennis or cricket).
- Deliberate deception of an official to try to gain an advantage, e.g. over-appealing for a wicket in cricket or a penalty in football and claiming for a decision which is not necessarily theirs! Another example is when a performer over-reacts to a challenge in a bid to put pressure on a referee to book or send off an opponent.

In the long history of cricket, one particular incident stands out as an example of gamesmanship. In 1981, Australia played New Zealand in a one-day international which went down to the last ball, with New Zealand needing six to win. The Australia captain Greg Chappell told his brother Trevor to bowl the last ball underarm, making it virtually impossible to score a six. Australia therefore won the game as the ball was legal and within the rules at the time as the umpire had been informed that the ball was going to be bowled underarm. This caused huge uproar as it was a clear stretching of the rules to their absolute limit in order to guarantee a victory.

Figure 3 Appealing a line call in tennis can be a way to deliberately upset an opponent's concentration

KEY TERM

Gamesmanship: Bending the rules and stretching them to their absolute limit without getting caught; using whatever dubious methods possible to achieve the desired result.

STUDY HINT

Gamesmanship does not refer to breaking the rules, cheating or taking performance-enhancing drugs. Remember, it is about bending the rules in order to win.

ACTIVITY

Identify three different examples of gamesmanship in:
a) Football
b) Cricket.

CHECK YOUR UNDERSTANDING

Identify two similarities and two differences between gamesmanship and deviance in sport.

Win ethic

The win ethic links to the sporting ethic of 'win at all costs', where coming second is not viewed as an option and the outcome is all that matters. The win ethic has sometimes been called the 'Lombardian ethic' after the Green Bay Packers American football coach, Vince Lombardi. Lombardi claimed that for him, '…winning was not a sometime thing, it was an all-time thing'. The highly successful Liverpool FC manager in the 1960s and 70s, Bill Shankly, had a similar win ethic to Lombardi when he was quoted as saying, 'Football is not a matter of life and death. It is far more important than that.'

In modern-day rugby, where the code of amateurism was protected until late in the twentieth century, top-level coaches have even resorted to using fake blood capsules to mimic a blood injury so that a specialist kicker can enter the field at a crucial game stage, when kicking a penalty is required to win. Performers also try to ensure victory when the stakes are so high by cheating in various ways. Diego Maradona was famous for his 'hand of God' which involved illegally punching a ball into the back of the net to help Argentina to victory over England in the 1986 Football World Cup. Seemingly, winning is all that matters when the rewards for winning are so high and livelihoods are at stake. The win ethic is evident in modern-day elite sport via the following examples:

- No drawn games, i.e. there is always a winner in basketball, American football, League Cup football in England.
- Managers and coaches are fired if unsuccessful.
- High amounts of deviance (see next section), e.g. violence; over-aggression; doping.
- Media praise for winners; positive newspaper headlines.
- Media negativity for losers.

Positive and negative forms of deviance in relation to the sports performer

Positive deviance

Deviance is behaviour which goes against the norms of society and is deemed to be unacceptable. In terms of sports performers, **positive deviance** involves over-adherence or over-conformity to the norms and expectations of society. For example, a performer might over-train or try to compete in a sporting event, despite being injured. Retired marathon runner Paula Radcliffe is one example of an elite performer doing her best to win for her country at the 2004 Athens Olympics, despite carrying an injury which ultimately led to her pulling out of the race part-way through. Another example of positive deviance is where a performer is striving to win within the rules or etiquette of a sport, who accidentally and without intent injures another player.

Negative deviance

Negative deviance in sports performers involves under-conformity to the norms and expectations of society. The motivation to win at all costs encourages performers who lack moral restraint to act against the norms of

---

CHECK YOUR UNDERSTANDING

The Lombardian ethic is a dominant sporting ethic in twenty-first century elite sport. How is such a 'win at all costs' ethic displayed in sporting contests?

KEY TERMS

Positive deviance: Behaviour which is outside the norms of society but with no intent to harm or break the rules. It involves over-adherence to the norms or expectations of society.

Negative deviance: Behaviour that goes against the norms and has a detrimental effect on individuals and society in general.

society and sport in various ways and cheat. Examples of negative deviance include the following:

- Taking illegal performance-enhancing drugs.
- Deliberately fouling or harming an opponent through aggression or violent actions.
- Accepting a bribe to lose; match-fixing.
- Diving to win a penalty or free kick.

SUMMARY

After reading this chapter, you will be able to define and give practical sporting examples of various ethical terms used in sport. In addition, you will develop an understanding of the impact of various ethics on sport with amateurism, the Olympic oath and sportsmanship compared to negative deviancy, gamesmanship and the win ethic. You will gain an awareness of lots of different sporting examples linked to sporting ethics to help you understand the terms and apply your knowledge on this topic area, as appropriate.

ACTIVITY

Identify two examples of positive deviance and two examples of negative deviance.

CHECK YOUR UNDERSTANDING

Using examples, explain the terms positive and negative deviance.

PRACTICE QUESTIONS

1 Which of the following statements best describes an example of gamesmanship? (1 mark)

   a) Shaking hands with an opponent at the end of a game.

   b) Arguing with the officials at the end of a game.

   c) Time wasting at the end of a game.

   d) Applauding the fans at the end of a game.

2 Using examples, explain the difference between sportsmanship and gamesmanship. (4 marks)

3 The development of professionalism has led to a 'win-at-all-costs attitude' being the dominant ethic in twenty-first century sport (e.g. Alonso and Ramos deliberately getting sent off in a Champions League match in late 2010 when playing for Real Madrid to avoid possible suspension at the knock-out stage).

   Discuss the view that sportsmanship has declined over the last century or so. (15 marks)

4 Give reasons why an elite performer may display behaviour which is deemed unacceptable by coaches, managers and officials. (3 marks)

5 Outline strategies sporting authorities such as national governing bodies could use to encourage higher standards of individual performer behaviour. (3 marks)

Chapter 6.4
Violence in sport

Chapter objectives

By the end of this chapter you should be able to:

- Identify the causes and implications of violence in sport in relation to the performer, spectator and sport.
- Explain strategies for preventing violence within sport in relation to the performer and spectator.

Violence in sport

Causes and implications of violence in sport in relation to the performer

A number of sporting ethics were introduced and explained in the previous chapter and, of these, the 'win ethic' in particular can help explain why performers become aggressive and ultimately violent during sporting contests. The emotional intensity or importance of a result (e.g. if it is a local derby or a Cup Final) can increase the pressure on performers to win at all costs. On occasions, pre-match media hype and intense build-up to a key contest can 'over-psych' a performer and lead them to become aggressive. This was the case when Wigan Rugby League prop Ben Flower was sent off for a vicious attack on St Helens player Lance Hohaia just two minutes into the Grand Final in 2014. Flower appeared to take exception to Hohaia's use of a forearm on him and very quickly engaged in a violent assault which ended in Flower being sent off and given a lengthy ban from the game.

Figure 1 Rugby is an example of a sport where players sometimes react violently to provocation!

Frustration with decisions made by match officials may create a sense of injustice and increase frustration for sports performers, which ultimately leads them to become violent on the field of play (for example, performing a late tackle or retaliation against an opponent). Performer violence might also occur as a result of abuse or provocation from opponents and/or the crowd. One famous example of performer violence as a reaction to abuse and provocation from an opponent was when Zinedine Zidane head-butted Marco Materazzi after Materazzi tugged his shirt and allegedly made negative personal comments against some of Zidane's family members. This occurred during extra time, with the scores level at 1–1 in the 2006 World Cup Final, which resulted in Zidane being sent off and France ultimately losing. Eric Cantona kicked a Crystal Palace fan, Matthew Simmons, who was sitting at the front of the stand. This is an example of a violent reaction by a top-level performer to racial insults and having a missile 'hurled' at him by a spectator. This action cost Cantona dearly as he was fined £20,000, banned from playing for his club Manchester United for nine months and stripped of the captaincy and his place in the French national team.

Some sports are viewed as naturally more violent than others as aggression and high levels of physical contact are part of the game. For example, in American football, ice hockey and rugby, there is lots of physical contact when body checking or tackling opponents.

While the examples of Cantona and Flower given above illustrate that severe punishments have been handed out for violent acts on the field of play, it has been argued that another cause of performer violence is a lack of deterrents and relatively low-level punishments for violent actions from national governing bodies (NGBs) and the players' respective clubs.

Memory tools

Causes of player violence can be remembered via 'WINNER':

- **W** = Win ethic and high rewards for success
- **I** = Importance of the event (e.g. local derby/Cup Final)
- **N** = Nature of the sport
- **N** = National governing bodies are too lenient with their punishments
- **E** = Excitement/over-arousal
- **R** = Refereeing decisions leading to frustration

Strategies for preventing violence within sport in relation to the performer

The frustration caused by poor officiating can be decreased by using more officials to help reach decisions as actions occur on the field of play. For example, extra officials have been trialled and adopted in the Europa League, where two extra officials are employed to help with decisions close to goal and one extra official is situated on each goal line. Off the field of play, contests can be stopped and video technology used to help reach the correct decision, e.g. via a fourth official. This can help decrease performer frustration with officials and any perceived injustice in them, as the decision is taken out of the referee's hands and given to an individual in the stands, using technology to help them reach the 'correct' decision. For example, in rugby the **television match official (TMO)** involves an official reviewing plays by looking at TV footage as and when asked to by the on-field referee.

KEY TERM

Violence in sport: Physical acts committed to harm others in sports such as American football, rugby, football and ice hockey.

CHECK YOUR UNDERSTANDING
Suggest three possible reasons why a performer becomes violent during a sporting contest.

KEY TERM

Television match official (TMO): Rugby League use a television match official who is a referee who can review plays by looking at TV footage as and when asked to by the on-field referee.

Figure 2 Awaiting the TMO decision

If a lack of punishment or effective deterrents are a cause of violence, then the sporting authorities/NGBs and even the law need to apply tougher sanctions. These sanctions could include longer bans, higher fines on players, or the deduction of points from clubs. In extreme cases, where there are particularly violent actions by performers on the field of play, court action might be taken and a possible prison sentence imposed. This happened to Rangers player Duncan Ferguson, who received a three-month prison sentence for his head butt on Raith Rovers player Jock McStay in 1994. In most sporting situations where particularly aggressive actions have occurred, it is normally the NGB of the sport which is responsible for discouraging performer violence and promoting higher standards of behaviour. Controlling violent behaviour in their sport is therefore an important responsibility of the NGBs, who are keen to present a positive image to fans and future performers, as well as potential sponsors. They can take a number of actions to try to prevent player violence, including:

- Supporting the decisions of match officials when dealing with violence by performers by using a TMO/video replays to check decisions being made, changing/clarifying rules on violent acts (e.g. 'high tackles'), and training officials to develop the skills necessary to diffuse or calm down match situations which could potentially develop into aggressive behaviour.

- Punishing violence by performers missed by officials after the match by using video evidence.

- Use of post-match video evidence where individuals have been cited by referees as performing violent actions worthy of further investigation; e.g. the Rugby League 'on-report' system allows a referee who sees what they believe to be an act of foul play to highlight the incident immediately to independent reviewers.

- Promoting performers with good disciplinary records as positive role models in their sport.

- Imposing harsh punishments for violent actions on the field of play (e.g. long bans or heavy fines).

- Introducing education campaigns and/or awards linked to Fair Play. For example, the FA and its Respect campaign: West Ham qualified for the Europa League after topping the Premier League Fair Play table in 2014–15.

ACTIVITY

Research and identify three ways in which the sport of rugby (i.e. League or Union) has tried to reduce the number of violent acts during matches.

Causes and implications of violence in sport in relation to the spectator and the sport

Spectator violence has been particularly evident over the years in the sport of football, so it will be the focus of this section, which reviews a number of different causes of **football hooliganism** before considering the negative implications of such violence.

Figure 3 Riot police separating hooligans from the rest of the crowd at a football match

A variety of different causes and reasons can be identified as causing football hooliganism, including the following:

- Emotional intensity and the ritual importance of the event, e.g. a local derby, team loyalty taken to extremes.
- Too much alcohol and the 'highs' caused by drug taking.
- Pre-match media hype stirring up tensions between rival fans.
- Poor policing, stewarding and crowd control. (This was one of the key reasons identified for the Hillsborough Stadium disaster in 1989.)
- Lack of effective deterrents and punishments to deter individuals from involving themselves in violence at football matches.
- Diminished responsibility by individuals in a large group (i.e. a football crowd); organised violence as part of a gang and peer pressure to get involved in violence.
- Reaction of working class who perceive the middle class to be taking over 'their game'.
- Poor officiating or frustration with match officials heightens tensions between rival fans.
- Violence by players on the pitch is reflected in the crowd.
- Religious discord, e.g. at a Celtic vs Rangers match, tensions are particularly high between rival fans.
- A negative violent reaction may result in chants and taunts by rival fans.
- Frustration at one's own team losing can lead some in the crowd to become violent.
- Violence is sometimes used by young males as a display of their masculinity caused by an adrenaline rush when attending a match.

Possible **solutions** to try to combat football hooliganism include:

- Ban on or control of alcohol sales; for example, ban pubs where known trouble-makers gather from opening prior to kick-off.
- Increased use of police intelligence and improved liaison between forces across the country to gather information on known or potential hooligans.
- Imposing tougher deterrents like bans from matches, higher fines and prosecution/imprisonment for violent offenders, banning individuals from travelling abroad. For example, following the Heysel Stadium tragedy in 1985 where 39 fans died as a result of violent fighting between Liverpool and Juventus fans within a football ground, UEFA excluded all English clubs from international competitions for five years and Liverpool for six years.
- Using CCTV around stadiums to identify and then eject or arrest individuals for crowd disorder.
- Removal of terraces, building of 'all-seater' stadiums, segregation of fans, and family zones to create a better, 'more civilised' atmosphere at football matches, promoting football as family entertainment.
- Encouraging responsible media reporting prior to matches, decreasing the hype and potential tensions between rival fans.
- Playing games at kick-off times imposed by the police (e.g. early kick-offs to try to avoid high levels of alcohol consumption).
- Passing specific laws preventing 'trespass' onto the pitch to try to stop pitch invasions and potential clashes between rival fans in the ground.

ACTIVITY

The Hillsborough Stadium Disaster Inquiry report is a document overseen by Lord Justice Taylor concerning the causes and consequences of the Hillsborough disaster in April 1989.

Research the **Taylor report** via its summary document and identify three of its recommendations for improving crowd control and decreasing football hooliganism.

Figure 4 An all-seater football stadium

When football hooliganism was at its height towards the end of the twentieth century (i.e. in the 1970s and 1980s), there were a number of **negative consequences** for the game of football.

Firstly, media images of fans openly involved in violence caused the image of football to decline, which put some people off encouraging it as a sport to participate in. A decline in the participation of football as a sport was accompanied by a decrease in the numbers actually going to matches and watching them. If parents believe a sport is likely to bring their children into contact with violence, they are unlikely to allow their children to take part in or go to watch that sport.

Some of the measures introduced negatively impacted law-abiding fans who were further discouraged from attending matches due to restrictions such as bans on all supporters of a club travelling to and attending a match, due to previous incidents at matches.

At club level, some teams were banned from entering competitions due to the negative behaviour of their fans. (As mentioned above, Liverpool were banned by UEFA from competing in Europe for six years following the violent clashes between their fans and those of Juventus prior to the European Cup final in 1985.)

Hooliganism also had negative implications for clubs as a result of the ever-increasing costs of security and policing before, during and after matches. This was particularly the case for clubs in the lower leagues where money was tighter.

The negative images of football hooliganism involving English 'fans' at home and abroad were often viewed globally and portrayed England as a nation of violent thugs who were out of control. This then had a negative influence on relations with other countries and on bids to host international sporting events.

> **CHECK YOUR UNDERSTANDING**
> Identify three negative effects of hooliganism for law-abiding football fans.

> **STUDY HINT**
> When considering negative consequences of spectator violence, remember the consequences themselves and not just the solutions or strategies you could use to solve such violence.

> **CHECK YOUR UNDERSTANDING**
> Explain the negative implications of hooliganism for the sport of football.

SUMMARY

After reading this chapter you should have gained an understanding of different causes of performer violence in sport, linked to a variety of examples of where such violence has occurred, along with increased knowledge of the strategies used to try to combat such aggression. You should also have gained a clearer understanding of examples of where football hooliganism has occurred and what caused such violent acts to occur before, during and after matches. You will now also have improved knowledge of various strategies that try to combat football hooliganism, along with an understanding of the negative implications and effects hooliganism has had on football that were very much evident when violent fan behaviour was at its height in this country in the 1970s and 1980s.

PRACTICE QUESTIONS

1 Which of the following is a technological aid or innovation that can be used in a sport to help try to decrease performer violence in that sport? (1 mark)

   a) Use of closed circuit television (CCTV)

   b) Use of Hawkeye to review close line calls in tennis

   c) Use of a television match official (TMO) in Rugby League

   d) Use of extra match officials in Europa League football

2 Outline strategies sporting authorities such as national governing bodies could use to encourage higher standards of individual performer behaviour. (4 marks)

3 Identify the possible solutions to violent behaviour among spectators in high level sports such as football. (4 marks)

4 While hooliganism has declined since the 1970s and 1980s, clashes between rival fans at Euro 2016 in France illustrate the fact that it has not been completely eliminated. Discuss how football clubs, the community and the players themselves can work together to keep spectator violence at football matches down to a minimum. (15 marks)

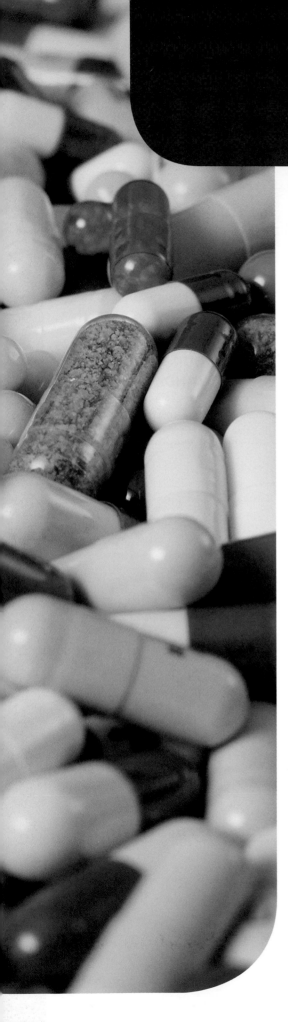

Chapter 6.5
Drugs in sport

Chapter objectives

By the end of this chapter you should be able to:

- Understand the social and psychological reasons behind elite performers using illegal drugs and doping methods to aid performance.
- Explain the physiological effects of drugs on the performer and their performance.
- Identify the positive and negative implications to the sport and the performer of drug taking.
- Outline strategies for elimination of performance-enhancing drugs in sport.
- Describe arguments for and against drug taking and testing.

Illegal drugs and doping methods to aid performance

The use of illegal drugs and **doping** methods to enhance performance at elite level continues to be a major issue in sport in the twenty-first century. This chapter starts with a focus on a consideration of the social and psychological reasons behind such usage.

The social reasons for drug taking and using doping methods to enhance performance illegally include the following:

- A win-at-all-costs attitude which dominates modern-day elite sport.
- The fame and fortune attached to success at elite level (i.e. the very high level of extrinsic rewards/money received for sporting success via prize money, sponsorship deals and so on).
- The high levels of pressure to win from a variety of different sources such as coaches, family and media expectations. (Coaches might persuade athletes to take drugs illegally because their main competitors are and they won't be able to compete with them on a level playing field if they don't.)
- The lack of effective deterrents and firm belief that they will get away with it and not get caught.
- Poor role models set a bad example that drug taking in certain sports is viewed in some way as being acceptable (e.g. athletics/cycling, etc.).

In addition to a variety of different social reasons, elite performers also use illegal performance-enhancing drugs and doping to aid their psychological performance in a variety of different ways. Some may use beta-blockers to steady their nerves where fine motor control is required (e.g. snooker players), while others may use anabolic steroids to increase their aggression in high contact sports (e.g. rugby players). When athletes are suffering from a lack of confidence, stimulants can be used to raise a performer's belief that they can achieve, even when the competition is of the highest standard like at the Olympic Games.

Physiological effects of drugs on the performer and their performance

All athletes want to improve their performance and there are both legal and illegal methods, in addition to training, of achieving this. In the table below there is a list of illegal drugs that some athletes feel the need to use.

Method of enhancement	What are they?	Reasons why this method is used (i.e. benefits)	Which athletes might use them?	Side-effects
Anabolic steroids	Artificially produced hormones, e.g. **THG**	They aid in the storage of protein and promote muscle growth and development of muscle tissue in the body, leading to increased strength and power. They also lead to less fat in the muscle; a lean body weight. They can improve the body's capacity to train for longer at a higher intensity and decrease fatigue associated with training.	They are particularly beneficial to power athletes such as sprinters.	Liver damage, heart and immune system problems. Acne and behaviour changes such as aggression, paranoia and mood swings.
Beta-blockers	Help to calm an individual down and decrease anxiety by counteracting the adrenaline that interferes with performance by preventing it from binding to nerve receptors.	They can be used to improve accuracy in precision sports through steadying the nerves. They calm performance anxiety and aid performance by keeping the heart rate low and decreasing the tremble in the hands. They work by widening the arteries, allowing increased blood flow and reducing involuntary muscle spasms.	Particularly relevant in high precision sports such as archery, snooker and golf.	Tiredness due to low blood pressure and slower heart rate which will affect aerobic capacity.
EPO	A natural hormone produced by the kidneys to increase red blood cells. Now it can be artificially manufactured to cause an increase in haemoglobin levels.	It stimulates red blood cell production which leads to an increase in the oxygen-carrying capacity of the body. This can result in an increase in the amount of work performed. It therefore increases endurance and delays the onset of fatigue. An athlete can keep going for longer and recover more quickly from training.	Tends to be used by endurance performers (e.g. long-distance runners and cyclists) who need effective oxygen transport in order to succeed in their sport.	Can result in blood clotting, stroke and, in rare cases, death.

Figure 1 Lance Armstrong was stripped of his Tour de France titles after an investigation by the US Anti-Doping Agency

Positive and negative implications to the sport and the performer of drug taking

In terms of 'the sport', drug taking and doping threatens the spirit and integrity of sport. It is cheating and negatively damages the reputation of a sport and decreases interest in it. Certain sports are strongly associated with drugs cheats such as Ben Johnson and athletics; Lance Armstrong and cycling. Such a strong association with drugs creates suspicion which clouds the successes of 'clean athletes' such as Chris Froome in the 2015 Tour de France and Mo Farah in the 2015 World Athletics Championships in Beijing.

The Tour de France has a long history of association with doping offences, including a particularly bad year in 2007 when it was referred to as the 'Tour de Farce', following daily positive tests which negatively impacted on the image of the Tour, as well as the sport of cycling in general. It provides negative role models to young children as well as developing young athletes in the sport who perceive that they cannot compete if they don't take drugs.

In terms of 'the performer', drug taking can positively impact performance and bring fame and fortune for those who manage to evade detection. But there are a number of negative implications of drug taking. It provides negative role models which set a bad example to young people. It can also be very damaging to a performer's health (steroids can lead to high blood pressure; EPO can increase the risk of heart disease and strokes). There are also a number of negative social consequences as athletes involved in doping may lose their good reputation following a positive test. Future career prospects may be negatively impacted, with a loss of income and sponsorship deals resulting from doping infringements being widely reported in the media. In certain cases it can result in legal action against an individual who can be fined, banned from competing, stripped of medals and earnings and even end up in jail, like Marion Jones as part of the **BALCO** scandal.

Doping can lead to social isolation from peers, as well as having a negative effect on an individual's emotional and psychological well-being.

Strategies for elimination of performance-enhancing drugs in sport

UK Anti-Doping (UKAD) is the organisation responsible for protecting UK sport from the threat of drug taking and doping. It administers the testing programmes for over 40 sports and has a number of anti-doping strategies designed to try to eliminate the use of illegal performance enhancers in sport.

Educationally, UKAD works with athletes and their support staff (e.g. coaches) to increase their knowledge and understanding of the dangers of drugs and the moral issues associated with doping. They promote ethically fair, drug-free sport via their '100% Me' programme. This programme is delivered to athletes at all stages of the performance pathway and includes

KEY TERM

BALCO: The 'Bay Area Laboratory Cooperative' which was behind one of the biggest scandals in drugs history as the source of THG, with several athletes implicated and subsequently banned from sport, including sprinters Dwain Chambers and Marion Jones.

Figure 2 Marion Jones was implicated in the BALCO scandal

rising stars at the 'School Games' as well as elite athletes preparing for the Olympics and Paralympics.

Investment in drug detection technology, science and medicine is also used by UKAD to try to ensure that they can prevent and detect doping. They work in a co-ordinated manner with other organisations involved in drug detection and prevention such as the **World Anti-Doping Agency (WADA)** and the national governing bodies of sport. Such a co-operative approach is important when trying to develop and enforce stricter testing procedures to try to catch out the drug-takers. These procedures include random testing, out of competition testing, and the '**whereabouts system**').

Once detected and caught, it is important that organisations punish the drugs cheats as harshly as possible to act as a deterrent to those considering following a similar route to success. Harsher punishments might include longer or lifetime bans and the return of career earnings and money gained from sponsorship. It is important to try to adopt a standardised, consistent approach between different countries and different sports when punishing drugs cheats so elite performers who are 'clean' gain confidence from a unified system which deals strongly with convicted drugs cheats.

Where positive role models exist, they should be used to promote ethically fair, drug-free sport (e.g. Sir Chris Hoy and the 100% Me campaign, which promotes the fact that winning clean is possible). In addition, drugs cheats should be 'named and shamed' to try to dissuade others from following their negative example.

While the fight continues to eradicate drugs in sport, a number of problems still exist including those described below.

- Sometimes it is difficult to gain immediate access to athletes who may be training abroad.
- There is ongoing development of new drugs/masking agents which keep the performers who take drugs one step ahead of the testers.
- The fact that sometimes drugs can be taken accidentally means some individuals claim their 'innocence' despite the fact that they are ultimately responsible for what they put into their body (e.g. taking medication when ill).
- Different countries and sports have different regulations and testing procedures so it is very difficult to get a unified approach to eliminating drug usage in sport. Such a unified approach would have a number of positives as it would help to ensure equality between sports for competitors and clarify for all a standard list of banned substances, testing procedures and punishments. It would also enable the high costs of testing to be shared between all sports and countries involved and enable random, out-of-competition testing to occur via improved access to performers who would not be able to pick and choose sports based on drug testing procedures and practices.

Memory tools

You can remember a number of strategies being used to decrease drug usage via 'DOPING':

- **D** = Drug-free culture created via education programmes (e.g. 100% Me)
- **O** = Organisations involved in drug detection/enforcement need to work together
- **P** = Punishments need to be harsher
- **I** = Investment is required into new testing programmes/technology
- **N** = Name and shame negative role models
- **G** = Guilty lose funding/sponsorship deals

KEY TERMS

Whereabouts system: A system designed to support out of competition testing which requires athletes to supply the details of their whereabouts so that they can be located at any time and anywhere for testing, without advance notice.

WADA (the World Anti-Doping Agency): A foundation created in 1999 through a collective initiative led by the IOC to promote, co-ordinate and monitor the fight against drugs in sport.

ACTIVITY

Visit **https://elb.wada-ama.org** and identify three key elements of the World Anti-Doping Code.

ACTIVITY

Visit **www.ukad.org.uk/athletes** and identify three ways in which the 100% Me programme is promoting ethically fair, drug-free sport.

CHECK YOUR UNDERSTANDING

Explain the advantages of all sports in all countries testing for performance-enhancing drugs.

Figure 3 Skier Alain Baxter with his Olympic medal at Salt Lake City before he lost it after testing positive for a banned stimulant taken 'accidentally' in a cold cure

Arguments for and against drug taking and testing

Various arguments can be used *for* the legalisation of drugs in sport, allowing them to be just another training aid. These are outlined below:

- The battle against drugs is expensive and time consuming.
- Drugs are quite easy to access and some would argue that they are very difficult to eliminate and the money spent on testing could be better spent on things like participation initiatives and/or investment in elite sport.
- Detection is not always effective; drug testers are always one step behind as new drugs become available and masking agents are developed.
- Sometimes it is difficult to define what is a 'drug', compared to a legal supplement; other technological aids are not regulated such as oxygen tents and nutritional supplements, etc.).
- Drugs are sometimes taken 'accidentally' (e.g. stimulants in cold cures, as with skier Alain Baxter).
- Sacrifices made by a performer are personal choice.
- If everyone takes drugs, it levels the playing field and increases performance standards physiologically and psychologically.
- If drug taking is properly monitored, health risks may be lessened.
- Athletes do not ask to be role models and individuals have a right to choose as it is their body; drugs can be particularly helpful to athletes to recover more quickly from gruelling training.

The majority of people, however, would argue *against* the points above and point out that drugs should continue to be banned in sport for a variety of different reasons. These are outlined below:

- There can be health risks and dangerous side-effects (addiction/heart disorders).
- Drug taking creates negative role models who set a poor example to the young who might then be tempted to use them.
- Drug use gives a negative image to certain sports (e.g. weight lifting, cycling, athletics).
- Pressure to take drugs increases from coaches and peers who take drugs.
- Success in sport should be about hard work and natural talent and drug use is outside this concept.
- Drugs give an unfair advantage and are immoral, unethical and against the fair play ethic.
- Taking drugs is cheating.
- Only richer countries can afford them.
- There are a variety of different negative consequences if caught doping, such as loss of sponsorship, loss of medals and loss of lottery funding.
- Drug taking is illegal.

SUMMARY

After reading this chapter, you should understand the different reasons why elite performers continue to take illegal performance-enhancing drugs in an attempt to prove themselves as world number one and achieve fame and fortune as a result. Your understanding of the physiological impact of drugs such as EPO, beta-blockers and steroids should have been increased, along with your ability to link such knowledge to sports where they are particularly valuable in aiding performance. You should have increased awareness of the ethics of drug taking which involves consideration of a number of issues, including the impact of doping on sport and sports performers, as well as the legalisation debate considered from both sides of the argument. When looking at possible solutions to drugs in sport, you should have more knowledge of a variety of different strategies being implemented in the continuing battle against their usage.

PRACTICE QUESTIONS

1 Which of the following is a key psychological reason why an elite performer takes drugs in order to improve their chances of success? (1 mark)

   a) Increased power

   b) Increased confidence

   c) Increased endurance

   d) Increased anxiety

2 Elite athletes continue to take performance-enhancing drugs despite obvious risks to their health and the negative implications of being caught. Give reasons why drug taking continues at elite sporting events such as the Olympics. (4 marks)

3 Describe the physiological reasons why an elite performer might use anabolic steroids just like any other training aid. (3 marks)

4 Outline the strategies being used by sports organisations to try to decrease the use of drugs by elite performers. (4 marks)

5 Explain the problems which are being faced by drug enforcement agencies in the world of sport (e.g. WADA/UK Anti-Doping) in their fight to eliminate performance-enhancing drugs at the elite performer level. (8 marks)

Chapter 6.6
Sport and the law

Chapter objectives

By the end of this chapter you should be able to:

● Understand the use of sports legislation in relation to performers (contracts, injury, loss of earnings), officials (negligence), coaches (duty of care) and spectators (safety and hooliganism).

Sport and the law

Sport and the law have traditionally been considered as separate areas of life as they have rarely overlapped. However, the number of deviant acts in sport appears to have increased. In addition, the increased level of professionalism and commercialisation involved in sport has led to a stricter adherence to legal standards. This has led the authorities to make all those involved in sport as accountable as other social and business institutions. The needs of various groups including performers, officials, coaches and spectators need to be considered in relation to sport and the law.

Uses of sports legislation in relation to the performer (injury, loss of earnings and contracts)

Lots of injuries occur to performers while playing sport and more often than not, they are seen as being an expected side-effect of participating in sport. However, sometimes injuries can occur that are not considered as part and parcel of the sporting contest and involve a deliberate act by a participant to injure another. In certain instances, these are illegal. For example, criminal cases have been brought for dangerous tackles and violent actions such as punches in football matches, which have resulted in serious career-ending injuries.

Figure 1 Matt Holmes, a professional footballer who successfully claimed damages for a career-ending tackle.

ACTIVITY

Research and identify two examples of professional footballers who have successfully claimed damages for career-ending tackles on the field of play.

In such cases, civil claims (e.g. for injuries suffered and/or loss of earnings) can be made against the person who has committed the illegal act. In order to be successful, claims made by sports performers for injury or loss of earnings need to prove that the act was outside the playing culture of the sport; the incident must be shown to be an unacceptable means of playing the sport. For example, in football, a foul might be considered an acceptable means of playing the sport, depending on the nature of the foul, but a stamp or a punch would not be.

Issues relating to player violence are mostly dealt with by the national governing bodies (NGBs) of sport, but on occasions players involved in on-pitch violence may be prosecuted.

The first example of violence leading to prosecution and a jail sentence was Duncan Ferguson in Scotland in 1995. More recently, Gateshead player James Cotterill, who was the first English player to be convicted, was jailed for an offence on the pitch in 2006 when he punched Bristol Rovers player Sean Rigg, leaving him with a double fracture of his jaw.

In addition to legal action being taken by performers against opponents, supporters are also now increasingly facing legal consequences for their unacceptable behaviour, such as running onto the pitch and attacking players. In February 2013, Wycombe goalkeeper Jordan Archer was attacked by a fan in the closing stages of his side's 1–0 win at Gillingham. A 17-year-old was arrested and charged with assault. Prior to this, in October 2012, Leeds fan Aaron Cawley was jailed for 16 weeks for attacking Sheffield Wednesday goalkeeper Chris Kirkland.

Performers may also interact with the law in a number of other ways, including contractual disputes. Performers are employees and as such should have the same employment rights as other workers. Their rights were greatly improved in 1995 by the **Bosman Ruling** which gave professional footballers within the EU the right to move freely to another employer (i.e. football club) at the end of their contract, and their existing club could not demand a transfer fee or retain the individual's playing licence. Players within the EU therefore have the right to work anywhere within the EU without restriction.

In terms of contracts with sponsors, a rare example of a brand suing an endorser was when Oakley brought an action against golfer Rory McIlroy when he left them without allowing them the 'first right of refusal' to sign a deal with Nike. Eventually it was resolved amicably without the need to go to court. Wayne Rooney's legal dispute with Proactive Sports Management, however, did go to court. The sports management company claimed it was owed commission by Rooney but the Court of Appeal ruled that the deal he signed as a 17-year-old was unenforceable and was a '**restraint of trade**'.

Memory tools

SOCCER is a good way of remembering a number of different reasons why sports performers might need assistance from the law during their sporting careers.

- S = Spectators attacking players
- O = Opponents being 'too violent'
- C = Contractual issues with sponsors
- C = Contractual issues with employers
- E = Equality of opportunities issues (e.g. racism)
- R = Refereeing negligence

KEY TERMS

Sports law: The laws, regulations and judicial decisions that govern sports and athletes who perform in them.

Damages: Individuals seeking legal redress and compensation for loss of earnings must prove that they have suffered an actual injury as the result of the deliberate harmful, reckless actions of an opponent.

Bosman Ruling: A ruling by the European Court of Justice which gave a professional football player the right to a free transfer at the end of their contract.

Restraint of trade: Action that interferes with free competition in a market. In sport, this might involve a clause in a contract which restricts a person's right to carry out their profession.

Figure 2 Wayne Rooney went to court to settle his legal dispute with Proactive Sports Management

STUDY HINT

You should aim to identify a number of different reasons why sports performers might need assistance from the law during their sporting careers.

CHECK YOUR UNDERSTANDING

Identify the reasons why sports performers may need protection from the law during their careers.

Uses of sports legislation in relation to officials (negligence)

Negligence is when someone (e.g. an official) fails to take reasonable care for another person to avoid any dangers that could cause them harm. Officials have a **duty of care** towards participants to make sure that all dangers around them are eliminated so they can participate in a contest in a safe environment. When they don't do 'everything possible' to keep participants safe, they may be seen as being 'negligent'; for example, allowing a match to be played on a dangerous surface that hasn't been checked prior to the match starting.

Negligence cases are being brought against officials at both professional and amateur levels of sport. For example, in rugby some court cases have highlighted the position whereby a referee can be found liable for injuries sustained by a player during the game. In the case of *Smoldon* v *Whitworth and Nolan*, a referee was found liable for serious injuries the claimant sustained following a scrum collapsing. In this case, it was found that the official was at fault due to the fact that he allowed a number of scrums to collapse during the course of the fractious match he was refereeing. The referee was found to have failed in following Rugby Football Board guidelines in relation to collapsed scrums. In this particular matter, it was found that the official had allowed two packs to come into the scrum too hard, leading to a scrum collapse on more than twenty occasions.

In the case of *Allport* v *Wilbraham*, a claim against a rugby referee failed. Allport, the claimant, was left paralysed from the neck down following a scrum collapse. He argued that the referee had failed to ensure that the scrum had been adequately controlled. In this case, the court preferred the evidence of the defendant (Wilbraham) and dismissed the claimant's claim for compensation.

Such cases illustrate that it is likely that there will continue to be litigation against referees and officials of sport in rugby, as well as in other sports, and they need to do everything in their power to ensure they are not negligent in the performance of their required duties.

Figure 3 Rugby officials need to be particularly vigilant at scrums

The uses of sports legislation in relation to coaches (duty of care)

In terms of sports coaches, the duty of care means they have a legal obligation to eliminate all the potential dangers and risks so that players can participate in a safe environment to ensure nobody gets hurt unnecessarily. For example, a coach could be sued for negligence if they allowed an indoor basketball session to take place on a wet sports hall floor. If a child then slipped and hurt themselves, the coach has failed in their duty of care to ensure participation in safe environment.

Coaches therefore need to be aware of their legal responsibilities, especially with respect to the advice they give sports performers and the way they manage and supervise participation in sport. Coaches have a legal responsibility to their athletes in a variety of different ways, including the following:

- **Health and safety:** Coaches are responsible for the health and safety of the performers and athletes in their care. They should have access to first aid facilities and have the means to contact emergency services should this be required. A coach could be deemed to be liable if evidence shows that normal standards and practices were not followed.

- **Protection from abuse:** Coaches have a responsibility to protect children from all forms of abuse, including emotional abuse (threats or taunting) and physical abuse (being hit by someone). All organisations (local sports clubs, local authorities etc.) should have a policy statement and guidelines regarding child abuse which a coach should adhere to.

- **Supplements:** Coaches have a legal and ethical responsibility to educate their athletes about drug use and abuse and provide general and appropriate advice on legal nutrition and supplements which can be used to enhance performance.

- **Duty of care**: It is widely accepted that in relation to children and young people, sports organisations and the individuals who work for them have a duty of care. When coaching young children, ensuring the participants' safety and welfare can be due to a *legal* duty of care or a *moral* duty of care. *Legally*, liability issues would only arise if an incident occurs and it can be demonstrated that the risk was foreseeable, but no action was taken to remedy it. In the sporting environment, when working with children and young people (e.g. at a sports club), coaches should ensure they follow a number of steps to demonstrate a reasonable standard of care. These include:
  - Keeping up-to-date contact details, medical details, registers of attendance.
  - Maintaining appropriate supervision ratios.
  - Ensuring that first aid provision is available at the club.
  - Ensuring that individuals regularly involved in coaching children have a current DBS clearance.
  - Ensuring they have undertaken an appropriate risk assessment for the activities being coached.

Morally, coaches have a responsibility for the safety and welfare of those under their control. Where children are involved, those in charge have to act '*in loco parentis*' which requires the coach to act as a reasonable parent would.

KEY TERMS

Duty of care applied to coaches: This requires coaches to take such measures as are 'reasonable' in the circumstances to ensure that individuals will be safe to participate in an activity.

In loco parentis: A Latin phrase which means 'in the place of a parent'. It is the authority parents assign to another responsible adult who will be taking care of their child (e.g. a sports coach at a sports club).

ACTIVITY

Using the information above and using **www.bowlschildprotect.co.uk/ Duty_of_Care.html**, identify four steps a sports coach should consider in order to demonstrate a reasonable standard in terms of a legal duty of care to children and young people.

The uses of sports legislation in relation to spectators (safety, hooliganism)

Earlier in this book we discussed the concerns surrounding spectator behaviour at sporting events. The **Taylor Report** on the Hillsborough tragedy was discussed in relation to solutions to try to curb the problem of football hooliganism which was at its height towards the end of the twentieth century. The focus now will be on how various examples of sports legislation have been used to improve safety at sports events and to try to control hooliganism in football.

Spectators at sports events must act within the law. They cannot invade playing surfaces or use racist chants without risking prosecution under various Public Order Acts. A variety of different Acts and pieces of legislation have been introduced since the mid-twentieth century to try to improve spectator safety at sporting events, as well as try to control the behaviour of fans so they act within the law. (As mentioned above, it is now illegal to trespass onto the field of play and chant in a racist manner towards players and opposition fans.) Some of these new laws are particularly applicable to the sport of football where clubs have a responsibility to ensure the health and safety of all spectators. A variety of different measures have been introduced to try to ensure safety and overcome hooliganism at sports events including football matches. These include the following:

- Removal of perimeter fences and terraces; all-seater stadia to replace the terraces.
- Control of alcohol sales on the way to grounds as well as in the grounds.
- Specified kick-off times imposed by police (e.g. in the case of a local derby, an early kick-off time can be imposed to decrease the likelihood of alcohol consumption).
- Increased security and police presence, intelligence gathering, improved police liaison between forces across the country and indeed the world.
- Tougher deterrents, e.g. banning orders, fines, imprisonment for offenders.

STUDY HINT

You should aim to be specific when describing measures taken to control crowd behaviour at football matches. It is not just a case of fining clubs, deducting points, segregating fans or banning alcohol.

Figure 4 Increased security presence in evidence

The various pieces of legislation that have emerged over the years to try to control fan behaviour at sporting events and improve safety can be considered as a 'timeline of crowd safety legislation'.

1 **Occupiers' Liability Act (1957):** This is considered to be the fundamental law governing spectator safety at sporting events. It states that an 'occupier' of a premises owes a common duty of care to their 'visitors'. An occupier is in charge of the premises, while the visitor is someone that is invited or permitted to be at the premises.

2 **Safety of Sports Grounds Act (1975):** This Act protects all spectators and covers all grounds in all sports.

3 **Sporting Events (Control of Alcohol etc.) Act (1985):** This law was introduced to ban possession of alcohol at a football match or on a journey to a match. It also empowered magistrates to impose conditions on licensed premises within sports grounds to ensure no alcohol can be sold by them during a match.

4 **Fire Safety and Safety of Place of Sport Act (1987):** A fire security certificate/licence needs to be gained from the local authority for an event to happen. The Act also sets the maximum number of spectators who will be safely allowed into a stand, as well as stating that stands have to be made from fire-proof materials.

5 **The Football Spectators Act (1989):** This allows banning orders to be put on individuals who have committed offences and the Act prevents them from attending sports events for a certain period of time at home and abroad.

6 **The Football Offences Act (1991):** This created three offences at football grounds to prevent the throwing of missiles, the chanting of racist remarks and trespassing onto the field of play.

ACTIVITY

Explain three key ways in which the various pieces of legislation identified have helped control and improve crowd behaviour and safety at football matches.

CHECK YOUR UNDERSTANDING

Identify the three offences banned at football matches included in the Football Offences Act (1991).

SUMMARY

After reading this chapter you should now have an understanding of a variety of legal examples and cases to help improve your ability to discuss the use of the law as applied to *performers* (when their career has been prematurely ended by a violent act on the field of play), *officials* (when they have been taken to court as a result of negligence and their failure to ensure a duty of care to participants involved in the sport of rugby), *coaches* (how they can ensure they do all they can to fulfil their duty of care requirements) and *spectators* of sport (how legislation has been introduced and applied to improve safety at spectator events, in football in particular).

PRACTICE QUESTIONS

1 Which of the following is an example of a sports coach ensuring they fulfil their 'duty of care'? (1 mark)

   a) Coaching basketball on a wet sports hall surface

   b) Coaching football on a frozen grass surface

   c) Coaching hockey on an uneven grass surface

   d) Coaching netball on a dry, clean sports hall surface

2 Identify the potential benefits of the law becoming more closely linked to the world of sport. (3 marks)

3 Explain how the law aims to protect spectators from hooliganism at football matches. (8 marks)

Chapter 6.7 Impact of commercialisation on physical activity and sport and the relationship between sport and the media

Chapter objectives

By the end of this chapter you should be able to:

● Understand and explain the positive and negative impact of commercialisation, sponsorship and the media in relation to the performer, coach, official, audience and sport.

The 'golden triangle'

This chapter focuses on how sport, commercialisation, sponsorship and the **media** are all strongly interlinked and mutually dependent on one another. For example, the media uses sport to gain viewers and readers. The media is itself used by businesses and sponsors for advertising purposes, promoting the company name and the products it sells. Businesses and sponsors pay the media for advertising time and space on TV, online, on the radio and in the newspapers; they also pay large sums to sports and sports performers to act as advertising mediums of their goods. Sports and sports performers are aware that they need to appear in the media to attract sponsorship, increase their profile and appeal to a wide audience. Sports performers need to be more professionally managed as a result of the increasingly commercialised nature of sport.

There is therefore a beneficial interlinking and interdependency between sport, commercialisation/sponsorship and the media, which has been called the 'golden triangle'.

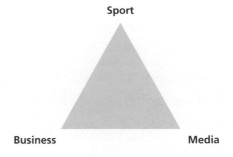

Figure 1 The 'golden triangle'

There are a number of advantages to elite sport as a result of the golden triangle, including the following:

- Increased income to the sport for allowing events to be televised. This can be spent at all levels of the sport – funding participation initiatives at grassroots level as well as providing finance to support elite athletes at the top of their profession.
- Increased promotion of the sport to gain more fans and increase its popularity.
- Increased sponsorship and income from business sources to pay for advertising at grounds and sporting events.
- Sports are organised and funded, which in turn improves the way they are run (i.e. in a more professional manner).
- Improved facilities benefit performer and spectator alike.

However, there are also a number of possible disadvantages to elite sport resulting from their links to the media and sponsorship. These include the following:

- Possibility of sensationalist media reporting which focuses too much on negative aspects of a sport.
- The media and sponsors can dictate kick-off times and scheduling of sports events, to the detriment of performers and fans.
- The media and sponsors can change the nature of a sporting activity (e.g. introducing more or longer breaks in play to allow for advertising).
- The media and sponsors only televise already popular, high profile sports.
- Sponsors and the media can be too demanding on elite performers and coaches (e.g. in relation to personal appearances and giving interviews).
- Sponsorship deals can increase the pressure to win or maintain lucrative contracts with companies willing to pay for an association with successful sports and sports performers.

The positive and negative impacts of the media on sport

The media uses sport to gain viewers or readers and to increase their income/advertising revenue. For the majority of people, the information and knowledge gained about sport is as a result of what they have seen or heard in the media (ranging from television, newspapers, magazines, radio, the internet and social media). The presence of the media as an influence in modern-day sport has turned it into a highly marketable commodity worth billions of pounds.

The best medium to view sport tends to be television as it can transmit instant live images directly to large numbers of people interested in watching. The late twentieth and early twenty-first centuries have seen the development of satellite TV channels (e.g. Sky Sports and BT Sport), with the use of sports channels being used strategically to increase subscribers willing to pay extra to watch a range of sports including football, cricket, rugby and golf. The increasing power and influence of the satellite TV companies such as Sky led to the government 'ring-fencing' certain sporting events to try to ensure the majority of fans were not deprived of the chance to watch them on free to access terrestrial TV. The 'OFCOM Code on Sports and Other Listed and Designated Events' provides a series of regulations which were issued by **OFCOM** and designed to protect the availability of major listed events in sport. The list of **ring-fenced** sporting events, however, has

KEY TERM

Media: An organised means of communication by which large numbers of people can be reached quickly.

CHECK YOUR UNDERSTANDING

Discuss the relationship between sport, sponsorship and the media.

KEY TERMS

OFCOM: The communications regulator in the UK (e.g. they regulate the television sector).

Ring-fenced: A number of sporting events at national and international level must be available for viewing on terrestrial or free-to-access TV rather than on satellite and subscription channels.

declined in recent years as satellite channels offer riches which the sporting authorities cannot refuse. For example, the England and Wales Cricket Board renegotiated England's home Test matches from Category A to Category B status which enabled them to sell exclusive broadcasting rights to Sky Sports from 2006 onwards. Category A events are those which must have live coverage via free-to-air channels (e.g. events such as the FA Cup Final and FIFA World Cup Finals), while Category B events consist of those which can be shown on pay-per-view as long as there is sufficient secondary coverage provided via highlights packages on free-to-air TV stations (e.g. events such as The Open Golf Championships and test cricket matches in England).

There are a number of reasons for the continued ring-fencing of certain major sporting events, including the following:

- To access the widest number and range of viewers.
- To avoid restricting coverage to subscription channels available only to those who can afford them.
- To increase geographical access to all viewers in all parts of the country to major sporting events.
- To enable viewing of certain events which are seen as part of our sporting heritage and culture.
- To enable access to sporting events which should be freely available to all to view (e.g. Olympic Games, Football World Cup, etc.).

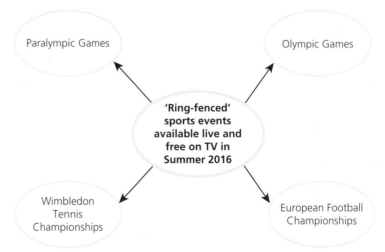

Figure 2 Ring-fencing

As mentioned at the beginning of this chapter, sport and the media can have a positive, mutually dependent relationship. Sports which have the following characteristics are particularly attractive to the media:

- They have high levels of skill for viewers to watch and admire which comes through a competitive, relatively well-matched competition.
- They are visually appealing and demonstrate physical challenge, lots of action-packed excitement and aggression (e.g. rugby).
- They are easily understood with relatively simple rule structures.
- The sport or sporting event is easy to televise and has a relatively short timescale which fits into viewers' busy schedules.
- They are seen as nationally relevant with easily identifiable personalities and role models. TV companies focus their coverage on sports like these, e.g. association football and golf.

ACTIVITY

Research and identify three sporting events which are ring-fenced for all to view on free-to-access terrestrial TV.

CHECK YOUR UNDERSTANDING

State three reasons why certain sporting events should continue to be 'ring-fenced'.

Certain sports are less attractive to the media (e.g. badminton, table tennis) as they are seen as being less popular with the viewing public and only have a limited target audience. These sports are seen as less exciting and less entertaining which makes it difficult for them to break into the male-dominated primetime slots, particularly when there are few well-known personalities in such sports. There is less commercial appeal to sponsors if sports are not receiving much coverage in the media, so a sport might remain relatively amateur in nature, with very few full-time professional opportunities available to performers, e.g. canoeing or shooting.

ACTIVITY
Research and identify three different ways in which cricket has changed and adapted to make it more attractive to TV coverage.

Table 1 The rise and rise of Premier League TV income

Time period	Total income	Income per year
1992–97 (5 years)	£253.5 million	£50.7 million
1997–2001 (4 years)	£848 million	£212 million
2001–2004 (3 years)	£1.56 billion	£520 million
2004–2007 (3 years)	£1.45 billion	£483 million
2007–2010 (3 years)	£2.53 billion	£843 million
2010–2013 (3 years)	£3.38 billion	£1.13 billion
2013–2016 (3 years)	£5.5 billion	£1.83 billion
2016–2019 (3 years)	£8.7 billion	£2.9 billion

Overall, the relationship between sport and the media can be viewed as being positive as well as potentially negative, as illustrated by the table below which identifies a number of advantages and disadvantages of media involvement in covering sport.

Table 2 identifies a number of possible negative effects of media coverage for a sport, including those which are linked to deviancy among sports performers.

CHECK YOUR UNDERSTANDING
Identify three possible disadvantages of media coverage for a sport.

Table 2 Advantages and disadvantages of media coverage for a sport

Advantages of media coverage	Disadvantages of media coverage
Increase the profile of the sport and individual performers within the sport.	National governing bodies/sports performers lose control to TV/sponsors. The traditional nature of a sport is lost; e.g. rule structures/timings of a sport are adapted to suit the demands of TV or sponsors.
Increased participation levels within a sport as a result of TV coverage which encourages others to take it up (e.g. cycling as a result of Tour de France or football as a result of World Cup coverage).	The media control the location of events, as well as kick-off times and, in some cases, playing seasons (e.g. Super League Rugby switched to a 'summer' game). There is sometimes too much sport on TV which can lead to possible boredom of spectators and/or lower attendance at events which are on TV.
More variations of a sport are developed to make it more 'media friendly', leading to more matches/fixtures for fans to watch (e.g. Twenty20 cricket).	There are inequalities of coverage – more popular sports such as football gain at the expense of minority sports such as squash. Certain prestigious events are now available only on satellite TV which requires a subscription payment, e.g. test cricket, golf's Ryder Cup, etc. This means there are fewer viewers for some sports due to the increasing control of SKY and BT Sport.
It generates higher levels of income and makes a sport more appealing to sponsors. It increases commercial opportunities, which further increases the financial gain of a sport or sports performers (e.g. golf, tennis, football).	Demands of media and sponsors negatively impact on high level performers (e.g. demands for interviews, personal appearances, etc.).
Increased standards in performance as well as behaviour as a result of an increased media focus.	The media can sometimes over-sensationalise or over-dramatise certain negative events in sport. A win-at-all-costs attitude develops due to high rewards on offer which leads to negative, deviant acts and players becoming poor role models (e.g. in football arguing with officials, diving to cheat and trying to win a penalty, etc.).
Rule changes lead to a speeding up of action/more excitement/entertainment in a sport (e.g. penalty shoot-outs).	More breaks in play (e.g. for adverts) can disrupt the spectator experience.

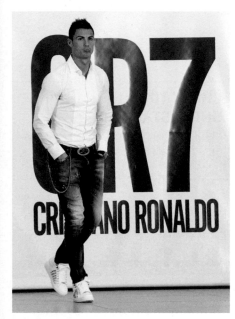

Figure 3 Cristiano Ronaldo is a high profile sports performer used to promote and sell various products

The positive and negative impact of commercialisation and sponsorship on sport

There are a number of reasons why sport is attractive to businesses. Businesses use television companies to promote and advertise their products. As sports coverage, through highlights packages and live broadcasts, attracts such vast audiences, there is a prime opportunity for businesses to reach large audiences.

Businesses give their support to elite teams and performers in a variety of different ways, including sponsorship, advertising contracts and product endorsements. Due to the following characteristics, sport becomes very attractive as a commercial enterprise:

- It has extensive media coverage.
- It gains large audiences, viewing figures and high levels of ticket sales.
- It links to professional/high profile sport.
- Players are contracted to perform with or endorse products.
- They offer extensive advertising, **merchandising** or sponsorship deals.
- Winning is important as it creates a link with success.
- The sport is media friendly/entertaining.

The **commercialisation** of sport has grown alongside the use of sport as part of the entertainment industry. Sports have become increasingly aware of their ability to make money from TV via the sale of rights to the highest bidder (e.g. Premier League football to Sky/BT Sport), as well as using this exposure to generate high levels of extra income from business and commerce. Televised sport offers companies an investment opportunity via sponsorship where financial input is made into sport from a company in order to better itself financially. This happens through:

- increased sales and promotion of a product
- increased brand awareness
- improved company image linked to the healthy image of sport
- opportunities to entertain clients via corporate hospitality
- decreasing the amount of tax a company pays as sponsorship is tax deductible.

At an individual level, certain sports performers are seen as more marketable in the modern-day sporting world than other performers. Why were companies more interested in David Beckham when he was at the height of his footballing prowess compared to his international and club team-mates Gary Neville and Paul Scholes? Why is Nike more interested in securing Rory McIlroy on a long-term **sponsorship** deal compared to his Irish golfing compatriot Graeme McDowell? Good looks and attractiveness to the public might have something to do with it, as well as the fact that individuals particularly in demand are at the very top of their profession. Ultimately sponsors want to invest in sports performers who will present a positive image of their product and help sell more of it!

This is certainly the case with golfer Rory McIlroy, who in 2015 made the top 50 of the Forbes Rich List of 'Highest Paid Celebrities' with his estimated $50 million earnings, consisting of over $30 million from product endorsements. A significant amount of his endorsement earnings were from a $250 million deal he signed with Nike in January 2013.

What makes Rory so appealing to a company such as Nike that they are willing to invest such a huge amount of money into him over a relatively long time period? Nike wants to be linked to success which Rory, as Number One in the world, certainly represents. The deal is linked to the expectation of continued success over a number of years, keeping Nike products in the public eye with McIlroy's continued media exposure across the world, as golf is a global sport with a high demographic. Golf is also a sport where there are opportunities for Rory to undertake promotional work as he is more in control of his schedules compared to a sport such as football. He looks good, is clean cut and well spoken, so he was seen as someone who could improve confidence in the Nike brand at a time when it was suffering from a number of scandals including Tiger Woods' private life and Lance Armstrong's doping.

Figure 4 Rory McIlroy

There are a number of potential positive and negative effects of sponsorship and commercial deals for elite sports performers and the sports they participate in, as outlined in the table below:

KEY TERM

High socio-economic demographic: A sport played or watched by individuals with high levels of disposable income.

Table 3 Positive and negative effects of sponsorship and commercial deals for elite sports performers

Positives	Negatives
Increased wages, prize money and extrinsic rewards.	Increased pressure to win and a win-at-all-costs attitude to maintain high level prize money, extrinsic rewards, wages, sponsorship deals, etc.
Increased availability of professional contracts where performers are able to devote themselves full time to sport, training harder and longer to improve performance.	An increase in 'deviant' behaviour due to increased pressure to win (e.g. performing when injured or over-training; taking illegal drugs; off-field drinking and gambling).
Performers are increasingly in the public eye and increasingly well known so they need to maintain discipline and behave appropriately to protect a positive image (e.g. on-field via fair play and sportsmanship; off-field via community and charitable work).	Performers are treated as commodities, bought and sold for economic reasons; sponsors become too demanding (e.g. via the requirement to make personal appearances at sponsorship events when they should be training).
Increased funding to pay for access to high quality training support and specialist equipment, etc.	Inequality of funding means performers in 'minority sports' (e.g. badminton, table tennis) miss out on funding and full-time professional opportunities.

The ethics of sport sponsorship

Elite sports performers, such as Jessica Ennis-Hill, and their agents sometimes need to consider the nature of a sponsor before deciding whether to accept a deal on offer or not. Should she sign a deal with a pay-loan company such as Wonga or agree to be sponsored by Santander instead, even if the rewards on offer are less? What should Jessica Ennis-Hill do if a fast-food company offers her a better deal than her Gatorade deal?

There are a number of possible reasons why an elite performer such as Jessica *should* consider the nature of a potential sponsor before deciding whether or not to accept a deal. As elite performers, they are role models and strongly influence the behaviour of others, so sponsorship from a junk-food company or product association with alcohol might not be considered as appropriate. Such products do not reflect the nature of sport which is more about health and fitness.

Performers have a social duty to others and need to carefully consider the ethical nature of any sponsorship deal to ensure it does not negatively affect their reputation and potentially endanger future commercial support (e.g. sportswear companies who are accused of the unethical manufacturing of goods might require careful consideration before a decision is reached on a potential deal).

Finally, the elite performer needs to look at the level of control a sponsor is potentially exerting on them before deciding whether or not to accept the deal (e.g. what are their demands for personal appearances, filming of commercials and so on?).

However, there are a variety of possible counter-arguments which can be used to explain why elite performers *should not* have to consider the nature of a potential sponsor before deciding whether or not to accept a deal. If a product is legal, elite performers have a right to accept a sponsorship deal if they so wish. It is unfair to expect elite performers to engage in a protest or statement when there are financial considerations at stake and their livelihood is at risk. Performers do not ask to be role models so they should be able to accept a sponsorship deal if they choose to do so. Indeed, they could argue that if they do not accept the sponsorship deal on offer, someone else will!

Memory tools

The reasons why an elite performer should consider the nature of a sponsorship deal before accepting it can be remembered via 'SPONSOR':

- S = Social duty to others
- P = Personal appearances demanded too much
- O = Opposed nature of the product to the reputation of the performer
- N = Negative impact on future sponsorship
- S = Support from sponsors is image dependent
- O = Opposed to the true nature of sport
- R = Role model for others

The increasing commercialisation of sports such as rugby, cricket and football has been viewed by many as a positive thing due to the increased excitement and entertainment generated. However, some view the growing influence of finance and commerce in sport as a negative development, with sponsors gaining too much control. The positive and negative effects of commercialisation and sponsorship on sport are outlined in the table below.

Table 4 Positive and negative effects of commercialisation and sponsorship on sport

Positive effects	Negative effects
Increased funding to a sport to provide improved facilities, equipment, coaching and Talent ID programmes to develop performers in that sport.	Sports might become over-reliant on the funding and income from commercial sources and experience problems if it is withdrawn.
Increased funding to provide technology at events to aid decision making from officials (i.e. reach correct decisions at important times of a sports event).	Money goes to already popular sports (i.e. there are inequalities of funding evident which mean sports like football, golf and tennis are highly attractive to sponsors, while sports such as hockey and trampolining are not).
Increased number of positive role models in a sport to inspire others to take part and increase participation rates in that sport.	The sport sometimes loses control (e.g. ticket allocations at major sports events go to corporate organisations/hospitality as opposed to the 'true fans').
Increased spectator interest and involvement (e.g. via wearing team kit/team colours).	Traditionalists might be against new competitions, rule changes or changes in a sports format to suit the demands of sponsors for more excitement and more breaks for adverts.
Increased number of events and competitions to help generate interest and promote a sport.	The location of events may be influenced by commercial considerations (e.g. American Football matches at Wembley Stadium to help the global appeal of the game).

The positive and negative impact of increased media coverage and commercialisation of elite sport for coaches and managers

Increased media coverage and associated commercialisation of sport not only influences performers, it can also positively and negatively impact on the coaches and managers who are in charge.

In terms of the positive effects, coaches and managers gain a much higher profile as a result of high levels of media coverage, which increases public awareness of their role. Such coverage has also led to increased salaries being on offer, particularly in high profile sports such as football. The increased funding received from sponsors and the sale of media rights, which is then invested into the sport, positively impacts coaches and managers because they are then able to invest some of this money into improving their playing squads, as well as support systems (e.g. training grounds and medical provision). Media coverage of sport also enables coaches to analyse their opponents more, as well as learn from other high level coaches.

On the negative side, coaches and managers are under intense pressure to be successful and win matches. There is a high level of public expectation to produce positive results and if not, managers can expect the sack relatively quickly. When the pressure is on, the expectation to deal with the media (which is often part of media deals such as that between the Premier League and Sky Sports) and answer their questions can be particularly difficult for managers. Inequalities of sponsorship and funding mean that coaches and managers in lower level clubs and minority sports find it harder to attract the best, high level performers to their clubs/sports, which means they are financially disadvantaged in relation to their higher profile colleagues.

The positive and negative impact of increased media coverage and commercialisation of elite sport for officials

Increasing media coverage and the commercialisation of sport have also impacted in both positive and negative ways on the referees and officials who take charge of sporting contests. The potential positives are outlined below:

- Increased profile of officials which increases public awareness of their important role in ensuring 'fairness' in sport.
- An increase in salary and possibility of full-time job opportunities as part of an elite group of match officials (e.g. in Premier League football).
- Increased funding to invest in support systems and training to improve standards of officiating; increased ability to learn from other officials.
- Increased funding to invest in technology to aid officials in their decision making.

On the other hand, there are also a number of possible negative outcomes of increased media coverage and commercialisation of sport on officials, such as the following:

- Increased pressure on officials to get decisions right (e.g. when TV channels including BT Sport have an ex-professional referee such as Howard Webb giving instant reviews of key decisions via TV replays).
- Increased expectation to respond to media enquiries and give interviews explaining their decisions.
- Risk of possible demotion or loss of job if a 'faulty decision' is highlighted in the media.
- Technology to aid officials in their decision making is not always available to them at lower levels of a sport.
- Officials may become too dependent on media technology when it is made available to them.

Memory tools

The negative impact of increased media coverage and commercialisation of sport for the official can be remembered via OFICAL:

- **O** = Over-use/over-dependency on technology
- **F** = Faulty decisions are highlighted
- **I** = Increased pressure to deal with media queries
- **CA** = Constant Analysis of decisions made
- **L** = Lack of availability of technology at lower levels of a sport

The positive and negative impact of increased media coverage and commercialisation of elite sport for the spectator/audience

There are a number of positive effects of media coverage and commercialisation of sport for the sporting experience of 'the audience', such as the following:

- Increased performance standards; players are of a higher standard and provide a high level of excitement and entertainment.
- Improved quality of facilities; larger, higher quality stadiums result from increased investment.
- Improved viewing experience via innovations such as changes in ball colour, creation of team merchandise to create team loyalty via the purchase and subsequent wearing of a team's kit.

- Increased access to watch sport; more opportunities to watch events live as more competitions, more events and more matches are taking place.
- More variations of a sport format develop which provide alternative viewing experiences.
- More funding is available to provide entertainment (e.g. cheer leaders/pop stars) at sports events.
- Rule changes introduced provide extra interest and extra excitement for the spectator, e.g. Twenty20 cricket.
- Increased funding for improved technology at a ground (e.g. video screens) and at home, e.g. interactive technology, HD coverage of sport and referee links.
- Increased excitement in the audience while awaiting the decisions of off-field officials, e.g. Hawkeye in tennis.
- Increased awareness of and knowledge of sport; creation of role models for fans to idolise.
- Increased elimination of negative aspects of sport (e.g. hooliganism).

There are a number of negative effects of media coverage and commercialisation of sport for the sporting experience of 'the audience', such as the following:

- Increased costs to watch sport, e.g. on pay-per-view satellite channels.
- Loss of the traditional nature of the sport.
- Increased number of breaks in play to accommodate adverts and decisions of officials.
- Fewer tickets available for the fans; more are allocated to sponsors and corporate hospitality.
- Changes in kick-off times to maximise viewing figures (i.e. scheduled at prime time), which is not always in the best interests of the long-distance travelling fan who wishes to watch it live.
- Minority sports receive less coverage; major sports dominate the TV schedules and might be 'over-exposed'.
- Links to 'team or player merchandise' are sometimes viewed negatively due to their high cost and regularity of change.

CHECK YOUR UNDERSTANDING
Explain how the increased level of media coverage of sport and sporting events has positively affected the audience.

SUMMARY
After reading this chapter you should have gained an awareness and understanding of the 'golden triangle', which illustrates the mutually beneficial links between sport, sponsorship and the media. Using a number of different examples from the world of sport applied to performers, coaches, officials and spectators, you should now understand the positive and negative ways in which commercialisation, sponsorship and the media can impact on them all in a variety of different ways.

PRACTICE QUESTIONS

1 Which of the following statements is a disadvantage of increased media coverage to an official? (1 mark)

   a) Increased availability of technology to aid decision making

   b) Increased profile and full-time job opportunities

   c) Increased pressure to get decisions right

   d) Increased salaries for those at the elite level

2 Discuss the impact of the 'golden triangle' on elite sport. (15 marks)

3 Define the term 'sponsorship' and identify how companies benefit from their involvement in sport. (4 marks)

4 Discuss whether an elite performer should consider the nature of a sponsor before accepting a sponsorship deal. (8 marks)

Chapter 6.8 The role of technology in physical activity and sport

Chapter objectives

By the end of this chapter you should be able to:

- Understand technology for sports analytics which involves the use of technology in data collection and an understanding of key terms such as quantitative and qualitative; objective and subjective; and validity and reliability of data.
- Understand the use of video and analysis programs.
- Explain testing and recording equipment in physical activity and sport, e.g. the metabolic cart for indirect calorimetry.
- Describe how GPS and motion-tracking software and hardware are being used in physical activity and sport.
- Explain how to maintain data integrity when using technology.
- Understand the functions of sports analytics (e.g. monitoring fitness for performance; aiding in skill and technique development; aiding in injury prevention via vibration and electrostimulation; undertaking game analysis; and use in Talent ID/scouting for talent).
- Explain the development of equipment and facilities in physical activity and sport, and their impact on participation and performance (e.g. via the impact of material technology on adapted equipment for the elderly and disabled; via facility development as a legacy of London 2012).
- Define the role of technology in sport and its positive and negative impacts on sport, the performer, the coach and the audience.

Use of technology in data collection

High quality **research** is vital to understanding all aspects of sport, exercise and health. When undertaking research and collecting information using technology, it is important that you are able to understand some important terms you might come across during your studies.

At the outset of this chapter, it is important that you are able to understand the term '**sports analytics**'. It is also useful to be able to relate such analytics to current examples of its usage in the world of elite sport, a number of which will be outlined later in this chapter. In cricket it can be used to study and give detailed averages and 'tendencies and potential weaknesses' of opponents, which bowlers can look to exploit.

Opta is a company that has statisticians gathering and analysing sporting data collected in order to create the best predictions of sporting outcomes as possible. Professional sports such as cricket and football have embraced companies such as Opta in their quest to fine-tune and optimise performance, give detailed analysis on opponents, as well as help

KEY TERMS

Research: A systematic process of investigation and study carried out with the aim of advancing knowledge.

Sports analytics: Studying data from sports performances to try to improve performance.

KEY TERMS

Quantitative data: Data that can be written down or measured precisely and numerically.

Qualitative data: Data that is descriptive and looks at the way people think or feel.

in the effective recruitment of new talent. For example, analysis of GPS information can tell which players in a game such as rugby or football cover the most distance during a game and at what speed. Training can then try to reproduce those distances and speeds to make it specific to the individual player.

There are a number of other terms identified in the specification for this area of the syllabus (the role of technology in performance evaluation and sport). These have previously been defined and introduced in Book 1, Chapter 7, which should be revisited as necessary to aid your understanding of the discussions in this chapter concerning the usage of different types of data to inform and educate sports performers, coaches and spectators alike.

Technology is being used in sport and physical activity to collect a variety of different types of data suitable for different requirements, aiming to ensure it is as reliable, valid and as objective as possible, as explained below.

Quantitative and qualitative research

Quantitative research is a formal, objective and systematic process used to gather quantitative data (i.e. factual information and numerical data). Most fitness tests used to analyse elite performers use quantitative data, e.g. the VO_2 max test on a treadmill.

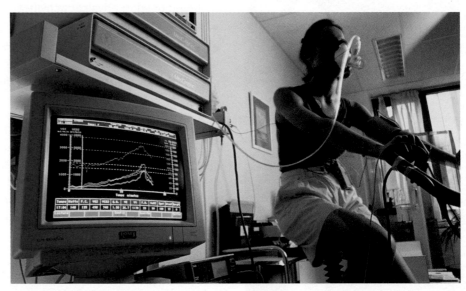

Figure 1 The VO_2 max test in action

Qualitative research is generally focused on words as opposed to numbers. The **qualitative data** collected is subjective as it looks at feelings, opinions and emotions, e.g. a group of coaches expressing an opinion when judging a gymnast performing a competitive routine.

Examples of areas where **quantitative data** could be gathered to try to prove a hypothesis include the following:

- In sport psychology, the potential positive link between motivational self-talk and its relationship to improving self-paced skills, e.g. a golf putt.
- In exercise psychology, research of a quantitative nature, e.g. on a numerical scale, could compare the relative effect of different environments on exercisers' moods: cycle trails in wooded areas vs cycling lanes in urban areas.

Qualitative research data is used to try to gain a better understanding of a participant's experiences. In sport psychology, qualitative methodology such as open-ended questions with focus groups can be used to explore the feelings of anxiety among elite athletes prior to performance at major sporting competitions. In exercise psychology, in-depth interviews could be used to help establish whether more frequent exercisers have a more accurate understanding of their injuries than less frequent exercisers. It is worth noting that qualitative data is sometimes less precise and can be less meaningful than quantitative data. It can also be very time consuming when collecting and analysing such data.

Objective and subjective

Objective data is information received based on facts. It is measurable and observable and therefore highly suitable and meaningful for decision making when feeding back to sports performers; e.g. in a performance analysis of a swimmer at the EIS.

Subjective data is information based on personal opinions, assumptions, interpretations, emotions and beliefs. With an emphasis on personal opinions, it is seen as less suitable and meaningful when feeding back to performers; e.g. when a parent is talking to their child at half-time during a football match, giving them their opinion on their performance in the first half!

KEY TERMS

Objective data: Fact-based information which is measurable and usable (e.g. the level achieved on the multi-stage fitness test which links to a VO_2 max score).

Subjective data: Based on personal opinion, which is less measurable and often less usable!

ACTIVITY

A netball coach tries out two different players in the position of Centre in pre-season matches, with a view to selecting one of them to start the first competitive league game of the season. They both play two out of the four pre-season games against similar levels of opposition. Give examples of valid, objective data which is quantitative in nature that you would advise the netball coach to collect to help inform them when making their decision.

Validity and reliability

Data collection when using technology should be both valid as well as reliable.

Validity

Validity refers to the degree to which the data collected actually measures what it claims to measure. To assess the validity of data collection, an important question to ask is:

● Does the data collected measure exactly what it sets out to do?

Reliability

Reliability is when the data collected is consistent and similar results are achieved when the data collection process is repeated at a later date. In quantitative research, reliability can be one researcher conducting the same test (e.g. skinfold measurements) on the same individual on a number of occasions and getting the same or very similar results. Alternatively, it can be different researchers conducting the same test on the same individual and getting the same or very similar results.

In qualitative research, reliability relates to the same researcher placing results into the same categories on different occasions, or different researchers placing results into the same or similar categories.

Reliability can be affected by errors occurring when researchers do not know how to use equipment correctly, e.g. in the use of skinfold calipers

STUDY HINT

Validity can also relate to the extent to which inferences, conclusions and decisions made on the basis of data are appropriate and meaningful.

KEY TERMS

Validity: An indication of whether the data collected actually measures what it claims to measure.

Reliability: Refers to the degree to which data collection is consistent and stable over time.

when assessing body composition. Accuracy can also be affected by poorly maintained equipment, e.g. weighing devices giving initial incorrect readings which affect calculations, e.g. body mass index (BMI).

> **ACTIVITY**
>
> To help understand the basis of reliability of information received, think about standing on a set of weighing scales which should be well maintained to ensure meaningful data is obtained.
> When would the scales be considered
> **a)** reliable
> **b)** unreliable?

The validity of data is requisite to data reliability. If data is not valid, then reliability is questionable. In other words, if data collected is *not* valid, there is little or no point in discussing reliability because data validity is required before reliability can be considered in any reasonable way.

Video and analysis programs

Coaches and athletes are using video, DVD or digital technology as a medium more and more to analyse individual technique as well as team performances. At an individual level, video analysis can also be used to analyse gait and biomechanical aspects of performance, with any information gained also being potentially helpful in injury rehabilitation. (See Chapter 5, Book 1 for more detailed coverage of biomechanics in sport.)

Video motion analysis usually involves a high-speed camera and a computer with software, allowing frame-by-frame playback of the footage on video. It is useful in the individual analysis of technical performance (e.g. to identify and correct problems with an athlete's technique such as the angle of release when throwing a shot; or ball release velocity and arc of travel when fielding or throwing in cricket; or the head and body position when taking a shot at goal in football). Such analysis can take place either immediately after performance, e.g. at the side of a track) or it can be undertaken in a more controlled laboratory environment.

The process of motion analysis has developed into two distinct sport science disciplines:

- **Notational match analysis:** Used to record aspects of individual/ team performance. Notational analysis takes place through the study of movement patterns, strategy and tactics in a variety of different sports. It is used by coaches and sport scientists to gather objective data on the performance of athletes.

- **Biomechanics:** Used to analyse the sporting impact of body movements. It involves quantitative-based study and analysis of sports activities. (It is sometimes called kinematics – the study of the motion of bodies with respect to time, displacement, velocity and speed of movement.)

The two disciplines use similar methods to collect data and both rely on IT for data analysis. But the main thing they have in common is

KEY TERM

Video motion analysis: A technique used to get information about moving objects from video.

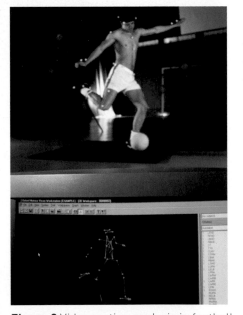

Figure 2 Video motion analysis in football

the use of **measured observation** (i.e. **quantitative analysis**) during or after an event to **quantify performance** in an accurate, reliable and valid way.

An English Institute of Sport (EIS) report has shown that, on average, athletes and coaches can only recall about 30 per cent of performance correctly – so **performance analysis (PA)** can help us with the other 70 per cent (i.e. tell the athlete what actually happened, as opposed to what they think happened!).

Performance analysis is now acknowledged as an important aid to performance enhancement at all levels and failure to use it might result in poor immediate decisions being made (e.g. in competition), as well as in the longer term in relation to an athlete's training programme.

There are a variety of PA techniques used by coaches and sport scientists to provide them with task, performance and physiological data. Within a training environment, immediate visual feedback software is useful to provide images pre- and post-feedback for the athlete and coach to compare to. (See Chapter 2.2, Book 1 for further information on the principles and theories of learning and performance.)

In a competitive environment, the coach and performer might look at the stats of their opponent(s) before discussing the data, alongside any other past experiences against such opposition, to come up with a game-plan to win! In this case, they would look to use particular strategies and tactics to outwit their opponents.

KEY TERM

Performance analysis (PA): The provision of objective feedback to performers trying to get a positive change in performance. (Feedback can be gained on a variety of performance indicators including the number of passes made; distance run in kilometres; number of shots attempted, etc.)

CHECK YOUR UNDERSTANDING

Identify three potential problems a sports coach might have if they choose not to use video analysis programs, but rely instead on their own observation and analysis skills.

STUDY HINT

The main purpose of motion analysis is to improve individual and/or team performance, as well as analyse opposition patterns of play to gain a tactical advantage.

ACTIVITY

Visit one of the following links to find out more about PA/motion analysis software used in sport.
- **Dartfish:** www.dartfish.com
  This is video software which enables individuals to view, edit and analyse videos of technique, e.g. running style; high jump performance in athletics, etc.
- **Upmygame:** www.upmygame.com
  This is a video analysis app you can use to connect with top coaches which gives you access to drills and practices.
- **Prozone:** www.prozonesports.com
  Prozone can be used to analyse and improve player performance via use of high-definition cameras which provide detailed performer/team analysis in football.

STUDY HINT

If you have access to motion analysis software at your school, college or sports club, it might be useful with your coursework to analyse in detail your technique or performance (in the role of performer) or the technique or performance of someone else (in the role of a coach).

With rapid advances in IT and digital photography, PA is increasingly being used by the world's top sports performers and coaches to maximise performance. PA has to prove its use as an accurate, valid and reliable record of performance by gaining systematic observations that can be analysed, with a view to bringing about positive change in performance. Examples of its use include notational match analysis to record individual and team performance; e.g. in basketball, to record the ratio of shots taken to baskets scored, and in netball, for identification of strengths and weaknesses of an individual player to provide a technical focus for future training sessions.

ACTIVITY

Choose an invasion game where opponents are in direct competition with one another (e.g. hockey, netball, rugby, football, basketball, etc.) and attempt to design and complete your own simple player analysis. Focus on one player involved in the match and gather data on one aspect of skill or technique (e.g. passing) used in the activity selected.

You can look at the number of passes made in a set time period. This can then be expressed as a ratio or percentage of successful passes during the time observed.

CHECK YOUR UNDERSTANDING

Imagine you are a basketball coach and you have the following shooting data available on your main two offensive players. This information can be used to help feed back to the players concerned, as well as inform future shooting strategies.

1 Use the data below to explain which player (i.e. Player 1 or Player 2) has been the most successful at shooting.
2 What other additional information would you need to consider when making your judgement on the relative shooting capabilities of Player 1 and Player 2?
3 How could you use the data to inform your offensive players' shooting strategies in their next match?

Basketball shooting data

	No. of lay-ups attempted	No. of lay-ups scored	No. of set shots in key attempted	No. of set shots in key scored	No. of 3-point shooting attempts	No. of successful 3-point shots
Player 1	5	5	4	3	4	1
Player 2	5	4	5	3	4	1

Testing and recording equipment

The metabolic cart for indirect calorimetry

A **metabolic cart** is an electronic medical tool used to measure the body's metabolism through the amount of heat produced when the body is at rest. The metabolic cart uses a process called **calorimetry** to get this measurement. The result can help tell medics more about a person's overall health condition. The various parts of the device, which include a computer system, monitor and breathing tubes, are typically mounted together on a mobile push-cart, hence the name, so that it can easily be moved from one room to another.

KEY TERMS

Metabolic cart: A device which works by attaching headgear to a subject while the person breathes a specific amount of oxygen over a period of time.

Calorimetry: The measurement of the heat and energy eliminated or stored in any system.

Indirect calorimetry is a technique where the headgear from the cart is attached to a subject while they breathe for a specific amount of time. The subject's inspired and expired gas flows, volumes and concentrations of O_2 and CO_2 are all continually measured. These measurements are then translated into a heat equivalent. It is a non-invasive technique and is regarded as being relatively accurate.

The two figures (concentrations of O_2 and CO_2) will provide the result for the metabolic cart, which is generally measured as **resting energy expenditure (REE)**. The REE for a patient can vary quite a bit. The results can change according to a range of conditions. Between individuals, the REE changes with regard to a person's overall weight or height to weight ratio. Age and gender can also influence the result of this test. In addition, the chemistry of the body in response to various drugs will change the outcome.

Therefore due to average differences in size, it is lower in women when compared to men. Smoking and drugs such as amphetamines can both increase someone's REE.

Figure 3 A metabolic cart in use

CHECK YOUR UNDERSTANDING
Identify different reasons for individual variations in an individual's REE over a period of time.

Indirect calorimetry and use of a metabolic cart can therefore help individuals:

- To determine their energy requirements and response to nutrition over time.
- To calculate energy expenditure, which allows determination of nutritional requirements/calorific needs.
- Who are classified or potentially classified as obese.
- In the calculation of their REE, which helps medics determine the amount of food and nutrition needed.

Possible difficulties or sources of error affecting validity and reliability using indirect calorimetry via a metabolic cart include:

- Inaccuracies from air leaks.
- Possible inaccuracies from measurement or recording errors.
- Difficult to use on children.
- Overfeeding or underfeeding may occur, based on results received.
- Single snapshots are worse than 'average results/studies' over a longer period of time.
- The process actually measures consumption, not needs.

Memory tools

Possible sources of error when using a metabolic cart can be remembered via 'LOSE':

- **L** = Leakage of air
- **O** = Overfeeding or underfeeding may occur post-results
- **S** = Single snapshots are not as good as average results over longer time periods
- **E** = Errors in taking measurements may occur

KEY TERMS

Software and hardware: Computer **software** is any set of machine-readable instructions which direct a computer's processor to perform specific operations. Computer **hardware** is the physical component of computers.

GPS (Global Positioning System): A space-based navigation system that provides location and time information.

'G' forces: Forces acting on the body as a result of acceleration or gravity (e.g. the G-load/force of an American football 'hit' on an opponent).

ACTIVITY

Think about and write down three pieces of information a rugby coach might receive from a GPS tracking system during training or matches.

CHECK YOUR UNDERSTANDING

Identify four different ways in which GPS data can help to improve player performance.

Use of GPS and motion-tracking software and hardware

GPS software tracking systems are very useful when helping coaches to monitor players during matches, as well as in training. Such systems give coaches a vast amount of information immediately, at the touch of a button on a computer! They track the speed, distance and direction of the individuals.

GPS can also provide data which helps improve performance via monitoring success rates in technical performance. In high contact sports (rugby, for example), it can measure the impact in **'G' forces**. It can also help coaches to make objective decisions about possible replacements/substitutions. This can help decrease the risk of injury, as GPS can help gauge a performer's fatigue level. If a performer is unfortunate enough to be recovering from injury, GPS can be used to manage workload during their rehabilitation.

GPS technology has recently entered into the world of football and many believe it will become increasingly popular in the coming years. For footballers to stay competitive and reach their goals, they have to work harder than their competition. This can be made easier for them by using GPS tracking. In essence, the GPS tracking of players today is used to gather meaningful data on different aspects of a player's performance. GPS tracking of players allows the measurement and monitoring of players' speed and distance performed during a game or a training session. GPS tracking is also used to measure a player's heart rate, pace, recovery time and the amount of dynamic acceleration. A number of reasons can therefore be given for using GPS technology for player performance tracking, such as:

- Makes better use of training time to ensure training meets game demands.
- Improves the tactical analysis undertaken at a club.
- Helps a coach compare player performance and potentially 'pick the best players' for the team based on GPS data.
- Helps to get injured players successfully through rehab at a faster rate.

In addition to the use of GPS to aid elite performer development, GPS technology has recently developed to enable athletes at all levels to benefit from it. **Strava** is just one example of how elite and non-elite athletes alike can improve their performance via GPS technologies becoming more readily available.

Such GPS tracking apps via smartphones or dedicated GPS devices involve lots of athletes from all over the world who alone or together are working hard and are determined to achieve their best. It helps people to connect, compare and compete with one another, lets individuals track their swims, rides and runs and helps them analyse and quantify their performance and use the data to provide motivation to try to improve their performance.

Figure 4 Tracking performance via GPS technology

Monitoring data integrity

The overall intent of **data integrity** is to ensure data is entered into the system and recorded exactly as intended, and when it is retrieved later, it should be the same as when it was originally recorded.

Data integrity can be compromised in a number of ways through:

- Human error when data is entered.
- Errors occurring when data is transmitted from one computer to another.
- Software bugs or viruses.
- Hardware malfunctions such as disk crashes.

Ways to minimise threats to data integrity include:

- Regularly backing up data.
- Controlling access to data and protecting against malicious intent via security mechanisms.
- Designing interfaces which prevent the input of invalid data; taking care when entering data.
- Using error detection and correction software when transmitting data.
- Not leaving a computer unattended for others to access.

An understanding of the functions of sports analytics

When asking the question, 'Why sports analytics?', the answer to many is fairly obvious: the effective use of sports analytics can help an individual and/or team increase their chances of success and win more frequently and more consistently. The focus should therefore be more about 'how' sports analytics can be used to gather new, meaningful statistical information on player performance and/or game details. Then, to consider 'how' can it be synthesised and summarised into key points which help improve the efficiency and effectiveness of performance for those involved in sport or physical activity.

Use of analytics in the monitoring of fitness for performance

Analysing data and assessing fitness levels is common in high level sport and is becoming more common in lower levels of performance. One function of sports analytics is to use them to gain information to help in monitoring fitness for performance, whether this be for individual recreational purposes (e.g. monitoring heart rate or amount of calories being burnt when training for a marathon) or for elite sport purposes (e.g. elite marathon runners monitoring key aspects of performance such as distance covered in training, pace of running, sleep statistics, calorie input and output, as well as heart rate monitoring before, during and post-exercise). There are a number of **smart wearable fitness and sports devices** available to aid such performers in their quest to improve performance based on the key information it provides.

> **ACTIVITY**
>
> Research how a smart wearable fitness/sport device can help in performance monitoring and improvement (e.g. Adidas MiCoach; Adidas MiCoach Smart Run or via www.wareable.com/fitness-trackers/the-best-fitness-tracker).

> **CHECK YOUR UNDERSTANDING**
> Identify three ways to ensure data integrity is maintained.

KEY TERM

Smart wearable fitness and sports device: Device that is worn or attached to a performer's body while in use to provide instant feedback on aspects of performance such as distance covered, heart rate, etc.

Figure 5 A smart wearable fitness/sports device

Use of analytics in skill and technique development

Sports analytics can be a highly valuable tool in aiding the skill and technique development of elite performers.

The use of video and analysis programs to improve skills and techniques has been covered in detail earlier in this chapter. An analytics program called Dartfish was mentioned as one example of how technology can be used to capture, create, analyse and share video content on sports performance. The software available via Dartfish combines technical, tactical and statistical information to provide information which can be used to improve skills and techniques on the spot or identify areas for improvement in future training sessions. It is particularly useful in sports and activities where visual feedback will be beneficial for the performer and coach.

Use of analytics in injury prevention (e.g. vibration and electrostimulation)

Vibration technology can be used for various purposes including exercise recovery, injury prevention and rehabilitation. Application of vibration therapy can be made both directly (i.e. applied to the affected area) and indirectly (transferred to the whole body or body part affected).

Advocates of vibration therapy claim there are a number of possible health benefits which can be gained from both whole body and localised vibration therapy. These include:

- improving bone density
- increasing muscle mass/increased muscle power
- improving circulation
- reducing joint pain
- reducing back pain
- alleviating stress
- boosting metabolism
- an overall reduction in pain/delayed onset of muscle soreness (DOMS)
- maintenance of cartilage integrity where weight-bearing activities are difficult to undertake.

All of these benefits help to prevent future injuries.

Sports performers are no strangers to 'sore muscles' which can negatively impact on training and performance. **Electrostimulation** can provide a number of positive effects for sports performers which include an increase in strength and power, as well as improving recovery time from training by expelling the lactic acid after a workout is over. It can also stimulate the muscles and help promote blood flow during a warm-up.

Electrostimulation works by providing a gentle external electrocution of the muscles to stimulate them. This is a more natural process than it sounds as electrostimulation actually reproduces what an individual brain does to the nerves and muscles when they are voluntarily contracted. The only difference is the electrodes, which are attached to a person's skin, send small shocks or impulses to the muscles without affecting the central nervous system (CNS) or the brain.

KEY TERM

Vibration technology: Vibration training/therapy is also known as whole body vibration (WBV) and an example of its usage involves the use of vibration plates to induce exercise effects in the body.

CHECK YOUR UNDERSTANDING

Identify three possible benefits to health of using vibration therapy technology.

KEY TERM

Electrostimulation: The production of muscle contraction using electrical impulses.

Many professional athletes now use electrostimulation devices to assist them in their rehabilitation from injury, as well as recovery from training sessions. When applied for rehabilitation purposes, electrostimulation can be used in physical therapy in the prevention of muscle atrophy which can occur from disuse, e.g. after musculoskeletal injuries where damage to bones, joints, muscles, ligaments and tendons occurs. They are also used by athletes to help prepare for competitions as an aid to develop strength through the ability to train harder. Like any other 'electrical device', it is important not to over-use electrostimulation as long-term exposure is viewed as highly ineffective. Saturation is indeed possible, and if an individual's muscles get stimulated for too long, they can get exhausted and stop contracting. Use of electrostimulation therefore needs to be carefully planned and integrated into a training programme in order for it to be effective as a training aid.

Electrostimulation can aid in the prevention of injuries in the following ways:

- By strengthening and toning the muscles to help prevent injury (e.g. it can strengthen the muscle groups of the legs to give stability and help prevent injury or recurring injuries to the knees and ankles).

- By helping to prevent losses in fitness levels via application to specific muscle groups which maintains muscle tone during periods of inactivity.

- By assisting in rehabilitation through the gradual strengthening of injured or weakened muscles via small incremental increases in workload on the muscles (i.e. by inducing stronger muscular contractions) as part of rehab.

- By helping to get rid of lactic acid after a training session or competition, as well as decreasing muscle tension and potential injury by providing a relaxing effect to muscles.

Use of analytics in game analysis

As mentioned earlier in this chapter, analytics can be used in sport, e.g. in team games such as netball and basketball, to gather quantitative data, including player performance metrics which measure the amount of court covered during matches by individual players. Elite level sport has embraced the role of technology and sports analytics in providing them with valuable information on player performance, either on the pitch or on the court. Use has increasingly been made of video and data, captured and displayed on iPads, which is then used to give real-time analysis and feedback to coaches during games, which ultimately aims to give them an edge over the opposition.

On the field or court during games of football and netball, for example, sports analytics can also be used to measure the performance of individual performers which can help improve player performance and fitness after they have finished. Use of small GPS receivers can help measure aspects such as distance covered in games, as well as top speeds reached and/or acceleration speeds achieved by individual performers during matches. The information received from games can help coaches and physios fine-tune training programmes and optimise rest and recovery times.

The data gained via sports analytics can also assist coaches when looking at tactics, formations and substitutions during games. Access to precise data allows coaches to compare an individual player's performance to their 'normal play', as well as match team tactics to the squad available to them. It is important to appreciate that as the technology available for game analysis develops further, there is more of a need to be selective and choose the information to capture which is most relevant. Quality of information is more important than quantity of information.

Figure 6 Analytics in football

Use of analytics in Talent ID/scouting

Sports analytics can be used to provide qualitative data on individual performers in a range of different sports, e.g. through written scouting reports commenting on opposition players and/or feedback from players being watched with a view to recruiting them onto a Talent ID programme.

Technology can be used in 'pathway analytics' as a method of systematically profiling and benchmarking the effectiveness of performance pathways across Olympic and Paralympic sports. Talent ID programmes have developed over the years, linking to the specific technical, physiological and psychological requirements of different sports, for example, Tall and Talented requires technically gifted sports performers to be above a certain height for sports such as basketball and rowing. The data gathered on potential recruits needs to be systematically gathered and analysed so it can be used as effectively as possible in identifying the best, most talented athletes who are the 'most likely' to succeed at elite level.

The development of equipment and facilities in physical activity and sport

Adapted equipment for the elderly and disabled

Technology and innovation are two key words for those who work in the world of adapted sports equipment. In the twenty-first century, mobility limitations resulting from age or disability no longer need to constitute a barrier to participation in sport and physical activity.

Assistive or adapted technology in sport is an area of technology in which design is on the increase. New devices are being created to help elderly and disabled sports enthusiasts to participate at recreational level, as well as create highly advanced equipment for elite Paralympians. In athletics, adaptive equipment such as specially designed wheelchairs is used on the track, and in the field, throwing frames for the shot put and discus.

Assistive devices can therefore enable training and exercise, as well as providing the opportunity for participation in sport. Other examples of assistive or adapted devices include lightweight wheelchairs for basketball, tennis and road-racing, and cross-country sit skis which allow skiers to sit down and push themselves along a set course.

Wheelchairs are an important assistive technology in sport which can be individually designed and adapted to meet the specific requirements of different sports. Sports such as tennis and basketball require lightweight frames to enable fast-paced movements, sharp turns and lots of agility. But contact sports such as rugby require chairs with strong reinforced frames and impact/foot protection. Racing chairs are designed with bucket seats, angled wheels for improved stability and a T-frame with a third wheel in front, allowing precision steering, as well as improving balance.

Examples of adapted equipment designed to encourage physical activity in the elderly include:

- *Finger extension exerciser*: This is used to help with hand and wrist movements.
- *Low impact pedal exercise machine*: This gives the opportunity for elderly individuals to participate in low impact exercise to stimulate circulation and help to try to maintain muscle tone.
- *Exercise balance beam*: This can be used to help maintain/improve balance, co-ordination and mobility.
- *Technologically advanced wheelchair design*: This helps elderly individuals who are confined to wheelchairs to continue to be mobile and involved in adapted activities such as wheelchair athletics.

Prosthetic devices have been designed and developed to meet a number of athletic purposes. For example, prosthetic leg devices (e.g. the Springlite prosthesis device) have been designed to assist athletes in running via improved gait efficiency. Prosthetic legs have also been designed for use in cycle racing. The introduction of new materials for prosthetic devices, such as carbon flex-fibre, and new developments in wheelchair technology are positively impacting the performance in many sports.

Technology and facility development – the Olympic legacy (surfaces/multi-use)

'Places people play' is an initiative being delivered by Sport England in partnership with the British Olympic Association. This initiative aims to deliver on the Olympic and Paralympic legacy promise to increase sports participation by providing sports facilities for the local community to access and use. 'Iconic Facilities' is part of this initiative, designed to transform the places people use to play sport in towns, cities and villages across the country. The Iconic Facilities fund directs funds into a small number of 'Best Practice' strategic facility projects designed to increase mass participation in sport across England. Best practice is based on high

ACTIVITY

Research and identify three key differences between wheelchair designs for wheelchair rugby players compared to wheelchair tennis players.

Figure 7 Lightweight wheelchairs for road racing

KEY TERM

3G surfaces: Third-generation artificial synthetic grass pitches.

CHECK YOUR UNDERSTANDING
Discuss the benefits to sport of technological developments in artificial surfaces.

quality design and long-term sustainability of a facility which delivers multi-sport provision with a focus on sporting activities that have high participant numbers.

There have been a number of technological developments in surfaces which are suitable for such multi-sport provision, with **3G surfaces** increasingly being used. The rubber infill in 3G surfaces gives the artificial grass surface playing characteristics similar to those of natural grass.

3G artificial grass is a sand and rubber infilled sports synthetic surface which is ideal for sports such as hockey, football and rugby. It allows high levels of use in a wide variety of sports and its benefits include the fact that it can be played on more frequently and for longer than natural grass. Synthetic grass also gives consistent conditions, unlike natural grass which can become very worn and unpredictable. While there have been a number of benefits to artificial surfaces being designed and used in sport, one of the main problems in sports like football is that some do not reflect the true bounce of grass. In addition, they have been criticised for being too rigid, leading to joint or ligament injuries. The more recent 3G/4G surfaces have gone some way to rectifying such problems with even fully competitive games of rugby now being played on an artificial surface. Rugby Super League team Widnes Vikings have re-embraced artificial turf at their home stadium in Hallam, as have Saracens Rugby Union at Allianz Park.

Advances in technology have also led to the development of multi-use games areas (MUGAS). A specific surface for each sport would be ideal, but often too expensive and impractical in terms of space for many local authorities, schools and sports clubs. MUGAS, made of artificial grass, are often the best solution to providing multi-sport opportunities and increasing participation in sport and physical activity helps the 'Places people play' initiative deliver on its promise.

In addition to the multi-sport legacy provision, specialist facilities have been developed in certain high participation sports such as cycling. The Lee Valley VeloPark is part of the Olympic legacy development of new sports facilities for cycling which includes a road cycle circuit which can be lit to enable night-time use and competition, as well as a skills training area with jumps, grade reversals and level changes.

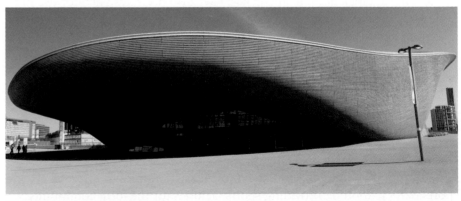

Figure 8 Lee Valley VeloPark

An understanding of the role of technology in sport and its positive and negative impacts on sport, the performer, the coach and the audience

Sport

Technology has the potential to optimise performance in a sport and achieve a combination of 'marginal gains', which ultimately lead to gaining a small competitive edge over opponents, which can often be the difference between winning and losing.

Team Sky Principal Sir Dave Brailsford is a high profile proponent of 'marginal gains' in his specialist sport of cycling. When he was in charge of British Cycling at London 2012, attention to detail even included the development of heated trousers to help a cyclist's muscle temperature during periods of inactivity. The trousers were developed by Loughborough University working with Adidas to come up with clothing which was scientifically proven to improve the performance of cyclists.

(For further information, see www.lboro.ac.uk/research/our-research/case-studies/improvingathleteperformancethroughsportsclothing.)

Technology can also have a positive impact on sport by helping to increase participation and make it more inclusive. The development of adapted equipment such as carbon fibre prosthetic blades and lightweight wheelchairs described earlier in this chapter has certainly increased access to sport for people with disabilities. We have also covered how technology can benefit a sport by increasing the quality of surfaces it is played on, as well as providing meaningful data via GPS systems which can help in the short- and long-term development of players.

> ### STUDY HINT
> When discussing the impact of technology on sport, you should aim to clearly identify and talk about both positive and negative effects.

There are also possible negative implications of using technology for sport, including the following:

- It can be misleading. Pure data can be misleading at times, e.g. if a performer has not covered many metres in a game, but the tactics and game context are such that it does not require them to do so.

- It can be expensive so inequalities might exist in terms of access to the latest technology available in a sport, e.g. only the wealthiest countries and teams are able to succeed. Some might argue that the high costs of technological advancements in sport might be invested better in participation initiatives as opposed to a few elite performers.

- It can lead to paralysis by analysis. Players and coaches might become too reliant on data to inform their decision making and unable to react creatively and instantly to on-field problems or issues as they occur.

- It can have a placebo effect. Are athletes simply gaining increased confidence by using equipment even though it may have limited scientific proof to support it? Is technology acting as a sporting placebo, increasing a player's confidence?

The performer

There are a number of potential benefits of technology for sports performers, which include the following:

- *Improved clothing/footwear.* This can lead to improved performances; for example, bodysuits used by athletes have helped sprinters increase their speed. Their use in swimming was a little more controversial as they led to some dramatic performance improvements with several world records being broken in a short space of time following their introduction. Swimsuits such as the LZR Racer from Speedo used fabrics such as polyurethane to reduce drag and compress the muscles to apparently create a sensation of buoyancy, giving performers wearing them an advantage in races.

- *Improved sports equipment.* This can aid skill/technique development (e.g. modern-day footballs have been designed to allow more swing and curve than before). Technological developments in golf have allowed manufacturers to build lighter clubs to increase swing speeds and enable golfers to hit golf balls a lot further and with more control than before. Clubs can now be personalised and designed to meet the individual needs of a golfer. Aerodynamics has improved through driver head designs decreasing wind resistance and increasing club head speed. In addition, today's wearable technology appeals to many performers, including golfers, as it is more compact, non-intrusive and highly intuitive than ever before. Golfers wear devices such as **Game Golf** while playing in practice rounds to get an in-depth analysis of their strengths and weaknesses on the course.

- *Improved protective equipment* (e.g. cricket helmets to withstand ever increasing fast paced deliveries).

- *Improved recovery from training* (e.g. via **compression clothing**).

- *Improved recovery from injury and better rehabilitation* (e.g. oxygen tents).

- *Detailed scientific analysis of performance via GPS data* to provide meaningful technical and physiological feedback to performers and coaches.

- *Increased knowledge of diet and sports supplements* (e.g. carbo-loading; sports energy drinks).

- *Advancements in drug-testing technology* to keep up with performers taking illegal performance-enhancing substances.

- *Improved sleep enabling appropriate rest and recovery* from training or competition. Sleep is important for physiological recovery as well as an individual's reaction time. Players at some professional clubs (e.g. in football) who are poor sleepers are given wristbands (e.g. the Fatigue Science Readiband), which use movement sensors to assess sleep quality.

KEY TERMS

Game Golf: A lightweight GPS tracking device which captures accurate shot locations and calculates club performance during a round of golf.

Compression clothing: Items such as elasticated leggings, socks or shirts worn to promote recovery by improving circulation. They can decrease the pain suffered from muscle soreness/stiffness and decrease the time for muscle repair.

Figure 9 Compression clothing

CHECK YOUR UNDERSTANDING

Identify three benefits of wearing compression clothing for athletes.

ACTIVITY

Visit **www.pgatour.com/changing-game/2014/09/02/wearable-technology.html** and describe a wearable technology which is being used to help golfers monitor and improve performance:
i) technologically
ii) psychologically
iii) physically.

There are a number of potential negative effects of technology for the sports performer, including the following:

- It can lead to injury or over-aggression; e.g. from bladed boots; or due to the use of protective equipment which makes some performers feel invincible or less inhibited.

- It can lead to cheating as drugs are taken by athletes who believe they will get away with it (e.g. taking effective masking agents or taking a newly developed performance-enhancing substance for which there is no test).

- It can be expensive and unaffordable for some, which leads to potential inequalities and unfair advantages if the technology is not available to all.

- The availability of technological advancements aiding performance might be dependent on an individual or team sponsor, which might positively or negatively impact the chances of success. The use of modern technologies in sport may mean that competition at the very highest level is only affordable to the leading top athletes due to the high costs of specialised sports equipment.

  In cycling, Team Sky and its associated sponsorship deals have funded very high level investment in the latest technology, giving them an advantage over their rival teams who have considerably lower levels of funding/sponsorship. An example of an award-winning partnership is that between Team Sky and Jaguar, where the investment and shared expertise in design and engineering have enhanced Team Sky performances, leading to a number of Tour de France titles for their riders Sir Bradley Wiggins and Chris Froome.

CHECK YOUR UNDERSTANDING

Identify three potential negative impacts of technology for sports performers.

The coach

As previously discussed, the impact of sports analytics and technology on sports performers can be highly informative as they aid in the detailed analysis of performance for coaches. Video analysis of matches enables an assessment of player performance tactically, technically and physiologically. For example, an in-depth technical analysis can be instantly gained through such programs as Dartfish and Prozone. The detailed information gained can help a coach develop more focused training programmes designed to improve on any weaknesses identified. While technology has its positives, it can prove a hindrance if there is an over-emphasis on performance analysis data. Use of computers is also a possible negative as they are open to potential hacking which might lead to information on weak links in a team being passed on and exploited by the opposition.

The audience/spectator

On the audience side, statistical enthusiasts can visit many websites to find out various pieces of information on their favourite teams and players. The data collected in different ways can be organised to make it more easily understandable and digestible to fans and spectators, who can gain improved knowledge about the physical, technical and tactical aspects of performance in a sport.

Advancements in technology have certainly impacted in positive ways on the audience. Officials are now 'mic'd-up' (e.g. in rugby) so the audience can hear what is being said on the field of play. This increases involvement and excitement in the audience and enhances their viewing experience. Increased interest and excitement are also gained by the audience as a result of technology being employed to aid officials in their decision making (e.g. use of Hawkeye in tennis).

The increasing use of technology to aid officials in their decision making has a number of advantages for an audience watching sporting events, such as:

- It ensures the right decisions are reached with less frustration at incorrect decisions.

- It helps officials communicate with one another and the players, which the audience can sometimes hear (e.g. in rugby matches).

- Increased accuracy of timing and distances achieved, which are quickly communicated to the audience (e.g. via big screens in the stadium).

- Increased excitement in the audience while they await decisions (e.g. Hawkeye at the Wimbledon Tennis Championships).

However, there are also some disadvantages of officiating technology as far as the audience is concerned. For example:

- A loss of respect in the crowd for the official as the 'final decision maker'.
- Costs limit the use of technology at events which can give an inconsistent experience to spectators, as well as performers.
- Breaks in play can be disruptive for spectators if they take too long or there is an over-reliance on technology which leads the official to over-use it. For example, in the opening 2015 World Cup fixture when England played Fiji, the referee Jaco Peyper was criticised for his over-reliance on the TMO, which seriously slowed down the action and negatively impacted on the viewing experience.

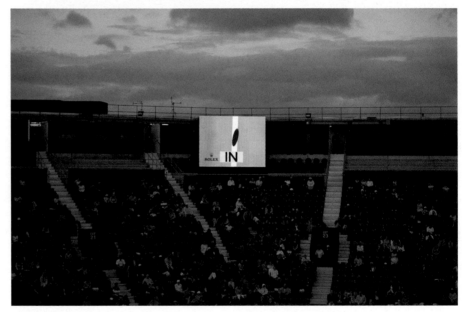

Figure 10 The crowd watch a Hawkeye decision at Wimbledon

A question is sometimes asked whether or not modern TV broadcasting technologies can give the same level of quality spectating experience as actually attending the sports event.

In some ways you could argue that it does, due to developments in high quality sound and picture technology which gives users an impressive view of the sport. The introduction of digital TV allows for highly individualised experiences. Viewers can choose the way they experience sport by selecting camera angles or watching more than one match at a time on a split screen. In many ways, the inclusion of expert commentary and close-up visuals can be said to give the TV audience a heightened experience of sport. Action replays and freeze-frames allow increasingly detailed analysis of key incidents to take place, which inform and educate the viewing public.

However, viewers' experiences are largely shaped by the commentators and expert pundits who might give biased views with little room for those of an alternative nature. TV viewing can also be said to lack the 'real atmosphere', with little sense of being a part of the spectacle or playing a role within the contest. In addition, when watching sport on TV at home, there is very little interaction with other fans, which for many is a key part of their audience experience!

CHECK YOUR UNDERSTANDING
Identify three ways in which broadcasting technology has positively impacted on the audience in sport.

SUMMARY

As a result of studying this chapter, you should be able to explain, using practical examples in sport and physical activity, how technology such as video and analysis programs, as well as GPS and motion-tracking software, can all be used to help collect data to inform and improve performance. You should also understand how such data can be collected to ensure objectivity, validity and reliability.

In addition, you should understand how a metabolic cart can be used to measure a person's calorimetry at rest and how such a measurement can be used to help gain an understanding of an individual's overall level of health and fitness.

Various functions of sports analytics have been explored so you can use practical examples of a range of technological developments to help explain the value of analysing data to improve fitness and technique, prevent injury and identify talent. You should also now understand the importance of adapted or assistive technology in enabling increased access to sport by people with disabilities and the elderly. Advancements in artificial multi-use surfaces have been discussed so you should now have an awareness of how such facility provision has improved access to sport as a positive legacy of London 2012. Finally, you should be able to debate the positives and negatives of technology on sport linked to a variety of different sporting examples.

PRACTICE QUESTIONS

1 Which of the following is a negative aspect of technology when used to aid officials in their decision making? (1 mark)

   a) Increased performer confidence in the correct decisions being made.

   b) Increased disruption to a sporting event as a result of lots of referee referrals.

   c) Increased excitement in the crowd as decisions are awaited on the big screen.

   d) Increased accuracy of timings or measurements taken.

2 Identify two types of adaptive equipment used in the sport of athletics. (2 marks)

3 State the disadvantages to the sporting event of the increased use of technology to help officials in their decision making. (3 marks)

4 Modern technological products are becoming an increasingly important part of modern-day twenty-first century sport.

   Outline the advantages on performance in sport of using such technology. (8 marks)

5 How have sports spectators benefited from advancements in technology? (3 marks)

Chapter 7.1 Tackling the A-level examination

As a student of AQA A-level Physical Education, you will know that preparing for your examinations in the correct manner is crucial to your success. Before starting to revise, you should familiarise yourself with the structure of the A-level papers and what skills you are likely to need when sitting Paper 1 and Paper 2. Even if you have completed the AS qualification, you should study the unique differences within the A-level papers.

Structure of the papers

There are two papers for AQA A-level Physical Education, which both involve a mixture of different question types:

- Multiple-choice questions
- Short answer questions
- Extended answer questions.

As both papers are two hours long and include 105 marks, you have just over one minute per mark. Remember to spend the appropriate amount of time on your answer, based on how many marks the question asks for. Remember that your examination is worth 70 per cent of your final mark, so you do not want to rush and should manage your time to ensure that you can answer all of the questions on the paper.

The 105 marks in each paper are structured into three sections that all contain multiple-choice, short answer and extended answer questions.

Paper 1: Factors affecting participation in physical activity and sport

Contains three sections:

Section A: Applied anatomy and physiology

Section B: Skill acquisition

Section C: Sport and society

Questions are as follows:

- Section A: multiple-choice, short answer and extended writing (35 marks)
- Section B: multiple-choice, short answer and extended writing (35 marks)
- Section C: multiple-choice, short answer and extended writing (35 marks)

Paper 2: Factors affecting optimal performance in physical activity and sport

Contains three sections:

Section A: Exercise physiology and biomechanics

Section B: Sports psychology

Section C: Sport and society and technology in sport

Questions are as follows:

- Section A: multiple-choice, short answer and extended writing (35 marks)
- Section B: multiple-choice, short answer and extended writing (35 marks)
- Section C: multiple-choice, short answer and extended writing (35 marks)

It is important that you remember to bring black pens and a calculator into the examinations. As the examination may include data or some simple mathematical calculations, a calculator is a requirement.

Multiple-choice questions

These will involve a series of options, which have a 'lozenge' to colour in at the end of each option.

For example, if you were asked to 'Define the term *residual volume*', you would select the definition by colouring in the circle at the end of the correct answer, as shown below.

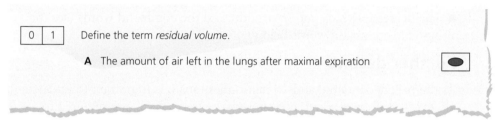

Figure 1 An example of a completed multiple-choice question

Remember, it is easy to fall into the trap of rushing in such questions, so be careful to stick to your plan and take time to think through which answer is correct. You do not want to be left with 'dead time': time left at the end of the examination staring into space!

Short answer questions

These do not necessarily allow you to bullet point the answer. If a question asks you, for example, to discuss, you will need to explain in detail both sides of an argument. Remember, it is only the command words of 'give', 'state', 'name' and 'identify' that allow you to simply list your answers. See the guide to command words below.

Extended questions

Each of the three sections within both papers will include **extended questions** which require you to write your answers in continuous prose, i.e. sentences and paragraphs. The extended questions included will be of different lengths so an appropriate amount of time should be taken to reflect the number of marks. For example, an 8-mark question would not need as extensive an answer as a 15-mark question.

The following points are strongly advisable (irrespective of the length of an extended question) and should be noted:

1. Start by reading the question … and then read it again.
2. It is important to make sure that you have understood the question before starting to answer.
3. Follow the tips below (in Further tips and advice) regarding the use of Time, Topic, Command and Context.

4 Think about making a small plan before starting to ensure that your answer will have a suitable structure and flow.

5 Remember that the extended questions require extended answers. There is a large space available as you are expected to develop your answers. Keep asking yourself: 'Have I explained that point in enough detail?'

6 The amount of space available has been given to you intentionally. It is completely possible that a focused and appropriate answer will take up the majority of that space.

When writing your extended answer, it is important to focus on several points:

- The level of your knowledge.
- The accuracy of what you are writing.
- The detail included in your answer.
- How the knowledge you have demonstrated has been applied to the question.
- The degree to which the language you have used has made use of correct terminology.
- The degree to which you have addressed the command words (see the guide to command words below).

Further details

As the papers contain 8 and 15 mark questions it is important to understand how these will be marked. For an 8-mark question you are required to:

- Show your knowledge
- Apply that knowledge to the question
- Analyse or evaluate as appropriate to produce reasoned conclusions.

It may be beneficial to use the following rhyme as a prompt:

'Knowledge … apply … say why'

For example, the top 'band of marks' you can achieve requires you to:

- Use appropriate terminology and language
- Show that the knowledge you have is detailed
- Produce a focused, structured and well reasoned answer
- Make analytical or evaluative links between your points.

There is no set number of points that you must make, but you must fully expand on each point, apply it and explain in a clear way how it is appropriate to the question.

As an example, if a question required you to identify which muscle fibre types are predominantly responsible for the effective performance of certain athletes, the bullet points above are appropriate to answer this question in continuous prose:

- Show your knowledge of the fibre types used by the athletes in the question *by describing the structure and function of the different types of muscle fibres.*
- Apply that knowledge to the question, showing why these are the main type/s used *by linking the different types of muscle fibres to different activities or different aspects of an activity.*
- Analyse or evaluate as appropriate to produce reasoned conclusions- fully examining why these fibre types produce effective performance *by describing how effective the use of different muscle fibres are to the activity described.*

The 15-mark questions follow a very similar format to the 8-mark questions, however there will potentially be more to say and more to link together. The 15-mark questions will still examine how well you:

- Show your knowledge (although 15 mark questions will require more breadth and/ or depth of knowledge)
- Apply that knowledge to the question
- Analyse or evaluate as appropriate to produce reasoned conclusions-showing how the varying factors are linked.

As an example, if a question asked you to evaluate the reasons for taking erythropoietin (EPO), beta blockers or anabolic steroids as an athlete, a suitable process to answer the question would be:

- Show your knowledge of the three drug types *by describing the physiological and psychological effects of the different drugs.*
- Apply that knowledge to explain who would be most likely to take such drugs *by identifying what type of performer might take a particular drug and how that might benefit their performance.*
- Evaluate the reasons for taking such drugs, i.e. what would they actually hope to achieve from taking them and how effective are they.

In a similar fashion to the 8-mark questions, there is no set number of points that you must make, but you must fully expand on each point, apply it and explain it a clear way how it is appropriate to the question.

Command words

When answering questions, it is vital to take your time to understand what the question is actually asking you. The following list gives an accurate explanation of what each potential command word actually means.

- **Analyse:** Break down into component parts. Separate information into components and identify their characteristics.
- **Apply:** Using the information given, put it into effect in a recognised way.
- **Assess:** Make an informed and/or accurate judgement.
- **Calculate:** Complete a calculation to work out the eventual value of something.
- **Comment:** Look at the information provided to present an informed opinion.
- **Compare:** Identify similarities and or differences.
- **Complete:** To finish or complete a task by adding to the information already given.
- **Consider:** Often used to test analysis and evaluation. Involves reviewing and responding to information that is given.
- **Contrast:** To identify differences between things.
- **Define:** Provide or specify a meaning or definition.
- **Describe:** To set out the characteristics of something.
- **Discuss:** To give both sides of an argument. To present key points about different ideas or strengths and weaknesses of an idea.
- **Evaluate:** To judge the 'worth' of something from available evidence.
- **Explain:** To set out purposes or reasons in detail.
- **Give:** Simply providing an answer from knowledge/recall.
- **Identify:** To simply name.

- **Interpret:** To use the information given and translate it into a recognisable form.
- **Justify:** To support a case or idea with evidence.
- **Label:** Providing appropriate names on a diagram.
- **Name:** Identify using a recognised technical term/give a name.
- **Outline:** Set out the main characteristics.
- **Plot:** Mark/plot on a graph.
- **State:** To express clearly and briefly.
- **Sketch:** Draw roughly/approximately.
- **Suggest:** Present a possible or plausible case/solution.

Revision ideas

There is no one, tested way to revise that works for everyone. You must find your own method but remember to replicate examination conditions, in that:

- You cannot bring notes in.
- You are under time pressure.

Mind maps

Mind maps or spider diagrams can be great way to build up your ability to recall information without having the benefit of your notes. Simply, choose a specific topic area, and without your notes, write down what you can remember. When you feel you cannot remember any further information, consult your notes then start again.

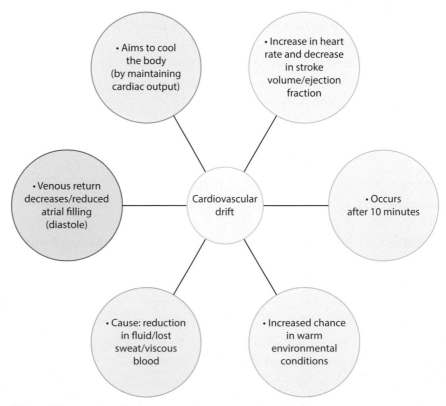

Figure 2 A sample mind map

Previous examination questions

It may be helpful to study previous examination questions. The examination board produces sample assessment materials and mark schemes, which can be of great benefit to you to test yourself on the types of questions that could appear in the paper. Remember that the specification before 2016 also contains a wealth of questions and mark schemes, which are still relevant today. Try to test your knowledge under the actual timed conditions you will face in the paper.

Revision cards

Revision cards are a great way to re-write your notes in a small, concise but manageable format. Create topic cards with the main points to remember or create questions on one side with the answers on the other.

Study buddies

Study buddies can be great in that you can ask each other questions and learn from each other. It is often a good idea to use past examination questions to both try and then compare each other's answers. You can download old AQA questions from their website.

Further tips and advice

As a definitive plan for exams, it may be an idea to adopt the principle of Time, Topic, Command, Context (TTCC). In simple terms, this involves going through four stages when answering questions:

1 **Time:** Look at the number of marks and calculate how long you will need to take to think and plan, then write, your answer.

2 **Topic:** Once you know how long you have got, read the question to work out what the topic area being examined is. This may involve reading the question several times.

3 **Command:** Check that you have seen and highlighted or underlined the main command word/s within the question so that you know what is being asked. For example, if you see 'Explain', it means you need to give detail and set out reasons.

4 **Context:** Read the question again (and again, if necessary) to work out the context – i.e. what is it actually asking me to do.

If you were looking at the following question, the four stages of TTCC can be applied.

Question: Explain what happens to tidal volume and residual volume as a result of the onset of exercise. (2 marks)

● **T**: 2 marks = think about how the marks correspond to the time you need to spend on this question

● **T**: The topic is tidal volume and residual (lung volumes)

● **C**: The command word is explain – give detail/ set out reasons

● **C**: The context is to explain in detail and give reasons as to what happens to tidal volume and residual volume if you start exercise, providing at least two points (one for each). As explain is the command word, it would not be enough to state that tidal volume increases – this needs to be explained.

It is also important never to leave questions out altogether. It is worth making an educated guess even if you do not know the exact answer.

Chapter 7.2 Tackling the non-examined assessment (NEA)

As a student studying A-level Physical Education, you will be required to carry out a non-examined assessment. You may well call this the 'practical' part of the course but it is officially called the non-examined assessment (NEA).

This part of the course is worth 30 per cent of your mark and will be assessed by the teaching staff in your school or college, although moderation of marks will be carried out by external AQA staff.

The maximum number of marks you can score for the NEA is 90.

Practical task: One role and one activity

As a student, you will assume one role. The potential options are **performer** or **coach**. Whether you choose to perform or coach your chosen activity, it must come from the agreed activity list, as stated in the table below. You will notice that each activity has three areas of assessment, i.e. three 'things' you will be assessed in.

Table 1 Official activity list

Activity	Relevant comments	Assessment 1	Assessment 2	Assessment 3
Amateur boxing		Attacking skills	Defensive skills	Tactics & strategies
Association Football	Cannot be 5-a-side or futsal	Attacking skills	Defensive skills	Tactics & strategies
Athletics		Event 1	Event 2	Tactics & strategies
Badminton		Attacking skills	Defensive skills	Tactics & strategies
Basketball		Attacking skills	Defensive skills	Tactics & strategies
Camogie		Attacking skills	Defensive skills	Tactics & strategies
Canoeing (Flat water) (White water)		Event/race 1 Downstream skills	Event/ race 2 Upstream skills	Tactics & strategies
Cricket		Attacking skills	Defensive skills	Tactics & strategies
Cycling	Track or road cycling only	Attacking skills	Defensive skills	Tactics & strategies
Dance		Dance 1	Dance 2	Choreography
Diving	Platform diving	Attacking skills	Defensive skills	Tactics & strategies
Gaelic football		Attacking skills	Defensive skills	Tactics & strategies
Golf		Short irons (7- wedges), putting	Long irons (Driver-6 iron)	Tactics & strategies
Gymnastics	Floor routines and apparatus only	Piece of equipment 1	Piece of equipment 2	Tactics & strategies
Handball		Attacking skills	Defensive skills	Tactics & strategies
Hockey	Must be field hockey, not ice hockey or roller hockey	Attacking skills	Defensive skills	Tactics & strategies
Equestrian		Flatwork	Jumping	Tactics & strategies
Hurling		Attacking skills	Defensive skills	Tactics & strategies

Activity	Relevant comments	Assessment 1	Assessment 2	Assessment 3
Kayaking (Flat water) (White water)		Event/race 1 Downstream skills	Event/ race 2 Upstream skills	Tactics & strategies
Lacrosse		Attacking skills	Defensive skills	Tactics & strategies
Netball		Attacking skills	Defensive skills	Tactics & strategies
Rock climbing	Can be indoor or outdoor	Climb 1	Climb 2	Tactics & strategies
Rowing		Bow side	Stroke side	Tactics & strategies
Rugby League	Cannot be tag rugby	Attacking skills	Defensive skills	Tactics & strategies
Rugby Union	Can be assessed as sevens or 15-a-side. Cannot be tag rugby	Attacking skills	Defensive skills	Tactics & strategies
Sculling		Race 1	Race 2	Tactics & strategies
Skiing	Outdoor/indoor on snow. Must not be dry slopes	Race 1	Race 2	Tactics & strategies
Snowboarding	Outdoor/indoor on snow. Must not be dry slopes	Race 1	Race 2	Tactics & strategies
Squash		Attacking skills	Defensive skills	Tactics & strategies
Swimming	Not synchronised swimming	Race 1	Race 2	Tactics & strategies
Table tennis		Attacking skills	Defensive skills	Tactics & strategies
Tennis		Attacking skills	Defensive skills	Tactics & strategies
Trampolining		Compulsory routine	Voluntary routine	Tactics & strategies
Volleyball		Attacking skills	Defensive skills	Tactics & strategies
Specialist activity	**(Certified learning need)**	**Assessment 1**	**Assessment 2**	**Assessment 3**
Blind cricket		Batting skills	Bowling/fielding skills	Tactics & strategies
Boccia		Throws at the jack	Blocking throws	Tactics & strategies
Goal ball		Attacking skills	Defensive skills	Tactics & strategies
Powerchair football		Attacking skills	Defensive skills	Tactics & strategies
Polybat		Attacking skills	Defensive skills	Tactics & strategies
Table cricket		Batting skills	Fielding skills	Tactics & strategies
Wheelchair basketball		Attacking skills	Defensive skills	Tactics & strategies
Wheelchair football		Attacking skills	Defensive skills	Tactics & strategies
Wheelchair rugby		Attacking skills	Defensive skills	Tactics & strategies

STUDY HINT

If you have already done AS, you can use the same or a different activity for your A-level.

Perform or coach?

It may or may not be an easy decision for you, but it is important to understand how you will be assessed if you choose to be a performer or a coach.

Figure 1 Perform or coach?

There are several common features that you must take into account when choosing whether to perform or coach.

- The performance (or coaching) *must* be done in a fully recognised version of the activity, e.g. an 11-a-side football match.
- There are two exceptions to this:
  - Climbing – the chosen climbs must have natural features that appropriately challenge the climber.
  - Dance – the chosen dances must simply be performed in a formal environment in front of an audience, e.g. dance show.
- Your actual performance or coaching will be worth 45 of the 90 marks available.
- The other 45 marks will come from completing an Analysis and Evaluation task (analysing and evaluating your performance, *or* analysing and evaluating the performance of the person you have coached). Alternatively, you can choose to analyse another person if you so wish – one of your peers, for example.

The performance role

As a performer, you must perform in the full recognised version of your sport. Remember, if you choose to climb, you are 'competing against a suitably challenging environment'; and if you are a dancer, your dances must be completed in a formal environment, e.g. a dance show.

Your practical performance is scored out of 45. Each area of assessment is scored out of 15. For example, a footballer can score:

- Area of assessment 1: 15 marks (attacking skills)
- Area of assessment 2: 15 marks (defensive skills)
- Area of assessment 3: 15 marks (tactics and strategies)

In relation to the example we have provided above, football has set skills listed in the specification. These skills are divided into core skills and advanced skills. This is the same for all activities. Part of your assessment will focus on your ability to use advanced skills.

For football, these are listed as:

Outfield player:

- Receiving the ball using chest and head to control the ball.
- Passing – use of inside and outside of dominant foot.
- Use of non-dominant foot for short and long passes.
- Use of inside of non-dominant foot.
- Dribbling – use of inside and outside of non-dominant foot.
- Shooting – volley.
- Use of inside and outside of dominant foot to add spin, swerve or dip.
- Short and long range with non-dominant foot.

For area of assessment 3, tactics and strategies refer to:

- The tactics or strategies you use when performing, e.g. to play a certain position, to mark tight, to favour an attacking option, to select a certain route (climbing), to use a certain breathing rate (swimming), etc.
- The success of how you use tactics or strategies to outwit opponents (if necessary).
- The success or otherwise of the tactic/strategy you use in a fully competitive context.

Remember that the specification states core and advanced tactics and strategies that you should be able to demonstrate. Thus for the football example above, the advanced tactics and strategies include:

- jockeying
- ability to play in two or more roles in a variety of formations (e.g. CDM role in 4–4–2 and CB in back four)
- interception of pass
- zonal marking.

Areas of assessment 1 and 2

The assessment of areas of assessment 1 and 2 can be summarised by:

- How well you perform suitable core and advanced skills in a full competitive context.
- How accurate and/or successful you are in applying these core and advanced skills.
- The level of competition you are performing at.
- The level of appropriate fitness you have for your activity.
- The level of psychological control you have for your activity.

Area of assessment 3

The area of assessment 3 can be summarised by:

- The level of motivation/commitment you have within your activity.
- Your understanding and application of rules within your activity.
- Your ability to use core and advanced strategies/tactics or the ability to compose/choreograph routines for your activity (NB the level of competition is considered).
- The number of errors you make when applying tactics and strategies.
- If you use choreography, the use of motifs, heights and use of space (so as to engage with the audience).
- The use of different skills and techniques as a result of the choices made with reference to tactics/strategies or choreography.

Recording evidence

It can be difficult capturing footage of yourself performing at your best. If you are asked by your teacher to do so, please remember a few simple rules:

- You should be seen performing at the highest level possible.
- Don't forget it must be the full recognised version of the activity, e.g. 5-a-side football will not do!
- It must be clear and the person watching it must be able to actually see you!
- One competitive performance should be enough but you may need to use different competitive contexts. Although editing should be kept to a minimum so that passages of play can be seen, any irrelevant breaks in play can be edited out.
- Team sports require a 'player cam' approach, i.e. the camera should follow you but also be on a wide enough setting to see what is going on in the game.
- The mark awarded will not be based purely on the level you are performing at. For example, even if you are an international performer, there must be an appropriate amount of evidence of you actually performing.

Figure 2 Attacking

Figure 3 Defending

Figure 4 Applying tactics and strategies

Figure 5 Watch the performer(s) performing in a fully competitive context. **Analyse** their strengths and weaknesses in relation to chosen core and advanced skills.

Figure 6 Remove the performer(s) from the competitive context to **modify** the weaknesses using appropriate drills, intervention or communication.

Figure 7 Refinement occurs when the performer is put into the full competitive context again.

- It is sometimes advisable to include 'voice over' on top of the footage. For example, in a game of rugby there may be 30 bodies covered in mud! In this case, it will help your cause if you commentate as to where you are and what you are doing.
- For the person assessing you, some activities are easier than others to work out the tactics and strategies you are using. It may be obvious to see a badminton performer is deliberately using drop shots to drive their opponent forwards; however, in an activity such as golf, it may be better to explain your tactics or strategy to the camera prior to playing the shot.

The coaching role

If you decide to choose the coaching role, you are still opting to work in an environment whereby the performer you are coaching is performing in a fully recognised and competitive version of their activity, e.g. it cannot be a small-sided hockey match. Similar to the performance role, it is acceptable that climbers are climbing an appropriately challenging rock face and dancers are performing in a formal context, e.g. a dance show.

The key to being a successful coach at A-level is your ability to improve (refine) the skill level and performance of the person or people you are coaching. This process will follow three distinctive stages: see Figures 5, 6 and 7.

As you can see above, the process of coaching involves analysis, modification and refinement of chosen core and advanced skills. However, other variables are also taken into account by your teacher when awarding marks:

- Your ability to communicate with the performer(s).
- Your ability to use appropriate terminology, language or terms.
- How well the person/people understand you when you coach.
- Your choice of appropriate drills or technical intervention to cause refinement.
- The timing of your intervention, e.g. when to provide analysis.

The areas of assessment for a coach

Your coaching is scored out of 45. Each area of assessment is scored out of 15:

- Area of assessment 1: 15 marks (coaching of attacking skills or equivalent)
- Area of assessment 2: 15 marks (coaching of defensive skills or equivalent)
- Area of assessment 3: 15 marks (coaching appropriate tactics and strategies or equivalent)

Similar to the performance role, for coaches there is a set list of what constitutes an attacking core skill and an attacking advanced skill. The key to being a successful coach is that you follow the suggested format:

- The coach is expected to analyse the performance of an individual within a fully competitive/performance context to identify one skill to be developed to enhance performance.
- The coach then delivers a planned progressive session to modify the chosen skill so that performance of this skill is refined.
- This process should be repeated for each of the areas of assessment (one skill from area of assessment 1; one skill from area of assessment 2; and one skill from area of assessment 3).
- The coach will complete this process on a chosen core skill and one advanced skill from each area of assessment

Area of assessment 3

For area of assessment 3, coaching tactics and strategies refer to:

- Coaching the tactics or strategies the performer uses, e.g. they may be too attacking and require coaching to develop the defensive side of their game. A swimmer may need coaching to develop an appropriate breathing rate to maximise their potential to win the race, etc.
- Coaching appropriate tactics or strategies to allow the performer(s) to outwit opponents.
- Coaching the performer(s) to maximise their opportunities for success.
- The coach must remember to select a core skill and an advanced skill to coach.

Analysis and evaluation task

Whether you choose to be a performer or a coach, half of your NEA mark comes from submitting an analysis and evaluation task. The task is worth 45 marks, meaning that your final NEA mark will be made up of:

- Practical performance/coaching – 45 marks
- Analysis and evaluation task – 45 marks

The task is split into two components: analysis (20 marks) and evaluation (25 marks).

As a student, you will be required to analyse and evaluate, using appropriate theoretical content from the specification. This analysis and evaluation will be about one performer (you or another person) performing from one activity from the specification.

Just to make it clear:

- You can analyse and evaluate your own performance (or the person you have coached), **or**
- The performance of another person.

In producing the task, you can complete it in one of two ways. It is possible to submit:

- A written piece of work, **or**
- A mixture of written work (e.g. essay style/PowerPoint slides, etc.) **and** additional verbal explanation (e.g. providing more detail on the PowerPoint to explain it further).

Analysis (20 marks)

Performers

You have to analyse how well you or another person has performed in a fully competitive context, e.g. 11-a-side game of football. The activity being performed must be an activity included in the activity list (see Table 1).

Coaches

You have to analyse how well the person you have coached or another person has performed in a fully competitive context, e.g. 11-a-side game of football. The activity being performed must be an activity included in the activity list (see Table 1).

You have to identify one weakness from areas of assessment 2 and 3 only. As an example, a netball player will have to choose a weakness in their defensive play (e.g. goalkeeper rebounding) and a weakness in their tactics and strategies (e.g. goalkeeper being over ambitious, passing straight into the centre third). However, if you would prefer to outline more than one weakness for each area of assessment, this is also acceptable, e.g. poor start and leg technique in swimming. However, if you choose to do this, remember that you will need to discuss how to improve one of these weaknesses in your evaluation.

Here are some activity-specific examples of what these weaknesses may be. However, you can choose whatever you like as long as the defensive weakness is a skill and the tactic/strategy was used within the performance

Table 2

Activity	Area of assessment 2: Weakness example	Area of assessment 3: Weakness example
Rugby	Defensive weakness: Front on tackle	Tactical/strategic weakness: Over-use of kicking for territory
Hockey	Defensive weakness: Jab tackle	Tactical/strategic weakness: Playing as a winger, I attack but seldom carry out defensive duties/track back
Badminton	Defensive weakness: Defensive overhead clear	Tactical/strategic weakness: Over use of drop shot with poor disguise (became predictable)
Horse riding	Ride 2 with jumping: Poor jumping technique	Tactical/strategic weakness: Inappropriate choice of line in to fences
Swimming	Race 2: Poor start	Tactical/strategic weakness: Ineffective pacing
Dance	Dance 2: Poor travel/elevation	Choreography: Poor design/linkage of moves
Sculling	Race two: Poor catch during stroke	Tactical/strategic weakness: Ineffective and tiring stroke rate

In choosing a weakness or weaknesses for area of assessment 2, remember that the weakness must be a skill. This is very important as your understanding of the technique used and the impact that this weak technique has had on performance will form part of your assessment.

Although no word count is put on your weaknesses, you should aim to identify what the detail behind the weakness was concisely, i.e. don't waffle!

A potential structure for your analysis is shown below:

Table 3 Analysis section: Weakness 1 (Space for writing should be amended accordingly.)

Person being analysed	Activity performed
Area of assessment 2:	**Weakness identified:**
Background information (e.g. – where appropriate, who was performing/against who/when/what was happening at the time/what was the score/how had they been performing, etc.)	
Technical explanation of the weakness and the impact this weakness had on the performance:	

Table 4 Analysis section: Weakness 2 (Space for writing should be amended accordingly.)

Person being analysed	Activity performed
Area of assessment 3:	**Weakness identified:**
Background information (e.g. – where appropriate, who was performing/against who/when/what was happening at the time/what was the score/how had they been performing, etc.)	
Explanation of the tactical/strategic/choreography weakness and the impact this weakness had on the performance:	

Major points to consider about your analysis:

- Make sure your area of assessment 2 weakness is a skill – e.g. tackling. This will allow you to fully explain the technique that was used and what was incorrect about it.

- Look to use technical terms relevant to the activity being analysed.

- Mention as many aspects of the technique as you can, e.g. you will need to mention many body parts! Where were your or their eyes looking? What angle was the top half of your or their body at? What were your/ their arms/hands doing? How flexed was your/their hip? Was the angle at your/their knee correct? What were your/their feet doing, e.g. plantar-flexed?

- It is not enough to just provide a detailed account of technique used. You must also explain the *impact* that the poor technique has had on the performance. An example of this is briefly shown for poor defensive net play in badminton:

As my net play was clearly ineffective, my shots became predictable and I found that my opponent seemed to know I was going to drop the shuttle short. Anticipating my shot, he was often able to flick the shuttle with a flat trajectory to the back of the court, making it hard for me to move quickly enough to the back. Although played as a defensive shot, I often found that the net shot simply allowed my opponent to have time to choose to move me across the court near to the net, or move me back. On one occasion in the second game, I played a defensive net shot after my opponent had played a drop shot, however he appeared to anticipate this and simply flicked the shuttle across the court with disguise, winning the point. I then became worried about my use of the net shot and started to hit the shuttle high which played into my opponent's strength – his smash.

- In analysing your weakness, you could consider making reference to an elite named performer who you feel uses the perfect technique. Some comparison to this person may help you to fully explain the weakness/es that you have.

Evaluation: 25 marks

For the weaknesses you have identified, you must suggest appropriate causes and corrective measures which have to come from the theoretical content within the specification.

For example, if your area of assessment 2 weakness was tackling in rugby, you need to choose an appropriate aspect of the course which explains why that weakness exists and an appropriate theoretical area to correct the weakness.

- **For example:** Poor tackling in rugby.
- **Possible cause:** Over-arousal.
- **Possible corrective measure**: Cognitive stress management techniques.

Remember: Any relevant aspects of the theoretical content can be used.

NB If, for example, in area of assessment 2, you have highlighted more than one weakness, the cause and corrective measure that you discuss should relate to only one of those weaknesses. For example, a football player may have analysed some weakness within their tackling and defensive heading; they should therefore identify a theoretical cause and corrective measure for one of these, i.e. the tackle **or** the defensive header.

You have some options when completing the evaluation:

- You may choose just one theoretical area for the cause/corrective measure (to show how well you understand that aspect of the theory); **or**
- You may make reference to more than one relevant theoretical area for your cause/corrective measure (to show your knowledge across several areas and how they link together).

Figure 8 Poor tackling in rugby

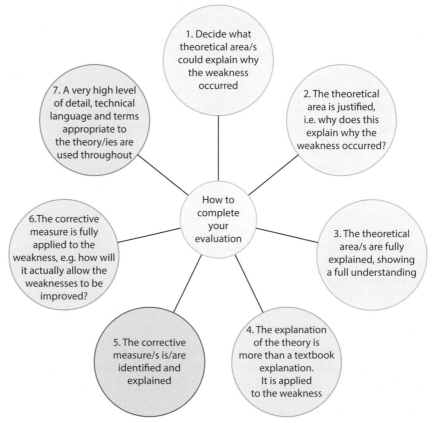

Figure 9 The key criteria you must meet in order to complete your evaluation effectively

A potential structure for your evaluation is shown below:

Table 5 Evaluation section: Weakness 1 (Space for writing should be amended accordingly.)

Person being analysed	Activity performed
Area of assessment 2:	Weakness identified:
Theoretical cause for the weakness identified: Topic	
Topic identified to act as a corrective measure:	
Explanation:	

Table 6 Evaluation section: Weakness 2 (Space for writing should be amended accordingly.)

Person being analysed	Activity performed
Area of assessment 3:	Weakness identified:
Theoretical cause for the weakness identified: Topic	
Topic identified to act as a corrective measure:	
Explanation:	

Final checklist:

1 Choose which activity you are going to do from the list.
2 Choose which role you will undertake: performer or coach.
3 Liaise with your teacher about how you will be assessed and how evidence will be gathered.
4 Carry out your performance or coaching.

5 Complete your analysis and evaluation task on yourself, who you coached or another person.

6 You will need one weakness (or more) from your area of assessment 2 and another for area of assessment 3.

7 Make sure the weaknesses allow you to demonstrate your knowledge of technique for area of assessment 2.

8 Choose appropriate parts of the theoretical course which explain why the weaknesses existed (The causes).

9 Choose appropriate parts of the theoretical course to explain how to correct the weaknesses (The corrective measures).

In conclusion, your analysis and evaluation task is your chance to show that you understand the technique used when performing and the impact poor technique has on performance. It also allows you to demonstrate your knowledge of tactics and strategies or choreography while linking the knowledge you have gained from the theoretical side of the course to the identified weaknesses.

Good luck!

Answers

Extended questions banded marking

The following descriptors are for questions that are marked using 'banded' marking. The examiner will decide in which band to place the answer, based on set criteria, the assessment objectives and the indicative content contained in the question. A mark will then be awarded from within the band in which the answer has been placed. The band criteria, assessment objectives and mark allocations are given below. Indicative content is given in each extended question answer.

In addition to the bands, the answer is assessed in accordance with the assessment objectives that are outlined in the specification.

These are:

AO1 Demonstrate knowledge and understanding of factors that underpin performance and involvement in sport.

AO2 Apply knowledge and understanding of the factors that underpin performance and involvement in sport.

AO3 Analyse and evaluate the factors that underpin performance and involvement in physical activity and sport.

● For 8-mark questions, the division of marks is AO1 = 2, AO2 = 3, AO3 = 3.

● For 15-mark questions, the division of marks is AO1 = 4 AO2 = 5, AO3 = 6.

These assessment objectives are reflected in the band descriptors given below.

8-mark questions

Level	Marks	Description
4	7–8	● Knowledge is comprehensive, well detailed and shows very good breadth and depth. ● Evaluation is consistent and shows links between method and impact on performance. ● Relevant terminology is used and the answer is clear, coherent and focused with good reasoning.
3	5–6	● Knowledge is accurate and well detailed with evidence of breadth and depth. ● Evaluation is made between method and impact. ● Relevant terminology is used and the answer has some reasoning and is clear, coherent and focused.
2	3–4	● Knowledge is generally accurate with some detail and breadth and depth of knowledge is sometimes evident. ● Limited evaluation is made between method and impact. ● Some relevant terminology is used and the answer has some reasoning, clarity and coherence.
1	1–2	● Knowledge is limited and breadth and depth of knowledge is not evident. ● No evaluation is made between method and impact on performance. ● Some relevant terminology is used and answer lacks clarity and coherence.

Mark scheme for 15-mark questions

Level	Marks	Description
5	13–15	● Knowledge is extensive, accurate, well detailed, relevant and shows breadth and depth. ● Analysis and evaluation are comprehensive and consistent with links between relevant factors and impact. ● Relevant terminology is used with a high level of reasoning, clarity, relevance and focus.
4	10–12	● Knowledge is comprehensive, accurate, generally well detailed and shows evidence of breadth and depth. ● Analysis and evaluation are consistent with links between relevant factors and impact. ● Relevant terminology is used with good reasoning and shows clarity, relevance and focus.
3	7–9	● Knowledge is generally accurate, well detailed and shows evidence of breadth and depth. ● Analysis and evaluation are consistent with some links between relevant factors and impact. ● Relevant terminology is used with some reasoning and mostly shows clarity, relevance and focus.

4	4–6	• Knowledge is generally accurate with some detailed and evidence of breadth and depth is sometimes evident.
		• Analysis and evaluation are limited with limited links between relevant factors and impact.
		• Relevant terminology is sometimes used with some reasoning but lacking clarity, relevance and focus.
1	1–3	• Knowledge is limited with limited or little depth and breadth.
		• Analysis and evaluation not evident with no links between relevant factors and impact.
		• Relevant terminology is sometimes used but the answer lacks clarity and coherence.
	0	• No relevant content.

Chapter 1.1 Energy systems

Answers to Check your understanding questions

(p.4)

The aerobic system has three stages, one of which is the 'Krebs cycle'. Describe how energy is produced during the 'Krebs cycle'.

- Pyruvic acid splits into two acetyl groups
- These are then transported to Krebs cycle by co-enzyme A
- The acetyl group combines with oxaloacetic acid
- Citric acid is formed
- Hydrogen is removed from the citric acid
- And taken to the electron transport chain
- Carbon dioxide is produced and removed
- Fatty acids also combine with acetyl co-enzyme A
- Beta oxidation takes place
- Two ATP molecules are produced

(p.6)

Name the main energy system being used in the 100 m and explain how this system provides energy for the working muscles.

- Anaerobic/no O_2
- Creatine kinase is the enzyme:
  - that breaks down the PC that is stored in the muscles into creatine and phosphate
- Energy is used/released for ATP synthesis
- Aerobic energy is needed for recovery.

Name the main energy system being used in the 400 m and explain how this system provides energy for the working muscles.

- Anaerobic glycolytic system
- Takes place in the sarcoplasm of the muscle cell
- Where oxygen is not available.
- Glycogen is broken down into pyruvic acid
- Then the pyruvic acid is then further broken down into lactic acid
- Two ATP are re-synthesised

(p.7)

Analyse the relative contributions of different energy systems in a game of basketball compared to a game of football.

- An answer that includes analysis of game intensity.
- Basketball is played at a higher intensity than football.
- More anaerobic than football.
- It has a smaller playing area and all the players have to cover the full court.
- There are time-outs in the game to help with recovery.

(p.10)

Use the graph on the right to work out how much PC has been restored at one minute.

- Approximately 75 per cent

(p.12)

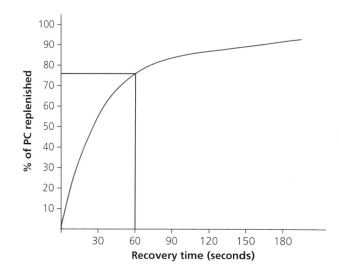

At the end of an 800 m swim, the swimmer will be out of breath and will continue to breathe heavily even though they have come to a complete rest. Explain why this breathlessness occurs.

- EPOC: excess post-exercise oxygen consumption
- Aerobic energy is needed
- Requires oxygen to:
  - Restore PC/ATP
  - Re-saturate myoglobin with oxygen
  - Remove lactate/lactic acid
- Also temperature and metabolic rate remain high
- Energy is needed for a high heart rate and breathing rate.

(p.14)

As part of their training programme, an elite 400 m runner uses interval training. The table below shows their time for six 400 m sprints, where each sprint was followed by a 60-second recovery period:

First run	Second run	Third run	Fourth run	Fifth run	Sixth run
52.4s	52.8s	53.1s	53.4s	53.6s	54.2s

During this training session, the athlete would have reached their lactate threshold. What do you understand by the term lactate threshold and how would the majority of the athlete's energy be supplied during the periods of activity?

Lactate threshold:
- The point at which lactic acid/lactate rapidly starts to accumulate in the blood

Energy supply:
- Energy provided by the lactic acid system
- Glycolysis occurs
- Where glucose is broken down into pyruvic acid

(p.15)

State and explain three structural/physiological characteristics that can lead to an improvement in VO$_2$ max.

Any of the following with an explanation as to how they can improve VO$_2$ max:

- Increased maximum cardiac output
- Increased stroke volume/ejection fraction/cardiac hypertrophy
- Greater heart rate range
- Less oxygen being used for heart muscle so more available to muscles
- Increased levels of haemoglobin and red blood cell count
- Increased stores of glycogen and triglycerides
- Increased myoglobin content
- Increased capillarisation around the muscles
- Increased number and size of mitochondria
- Increased surface area of alveoli
- Increased lactate tolerance
- Reduced body fat – VO_2 max decreases as the percentage of body fat increases
- Slow twitch hypertrophy.

(p.19)

The results from the respiratory exchange ratio (RER) can be used to check that training is effective. Can you explain the term respiratory exchange ratio?

The respiratory exchange ratio (RER) is the ratio of carbon dioxide produced **compared** to oxygen consumed.

Answers to Activities

(p.4)

Test your knowledge and try to draw your own diagram, starting with glucose in the top left-hand corner and ending with the electron transport chain in the bottom right-hand corner. Then add the stages to summarise aerobic energy metabolism.

Hard to give an answer to this as there will be many different versions. Overview in Figure 7, Summary of ATP re-synthesis from the complete breakdown of glycogen, highlights the key words to be placed in their diagram.

Can you think of four different sporting examples when the ATP–PC system would be the predominant method of re-synthesising ATP?

Examples that are high intensity lasting less than 10 seconds, for example:

- 100 m
- long jump
- running out for a centre pass in netball.

Can you think of three different sporting examples when the anaerobic glycolytic system would be the predominant method of re-synthesising ATP?

Examples that are high intensity lasting longer than 10 seconds, for example:

- 400 m
- a gymnastics floor routine
- 100 m freestyle race.

(p.7)

Into which box would you place the following athletics events on this continuum?

- 100 m
- 400 m
- 1500 m
- Marathon

Answer:

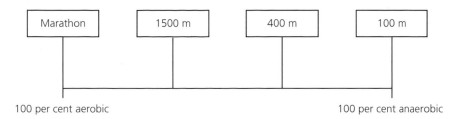

Copy and complete the table below by giving examples from a game of your choice to show when each of the three energy systems will be used.

Name of game	ATP–PC system	Anaerobic glycolytic system	Aerobic system
A named game – not dance/athletics/swimming, etc. as these are not games!	Any example that is high intensity lasting less than 10 seconds	Any example that is high intensity lasting longer than 10 seconds	Any example that is low intensity lasting less longer than a minute

(p.10)

Can you think of an example in a team game where it is possible to delay play for up to a minute to allow for significant restoration of PC stores?

Any idea to delay play, e.g. tying a shoelace, kicking a ball hard over the side line so it takes time to retrieve it, checking the strings of a tennis racket.

(p.11)

Can you put the following labels in the correct position?
- Oxygen consumption during exercise
- Oxygen deficit
- Fast replenishment stage
- Slow replenishment stage

Answer:

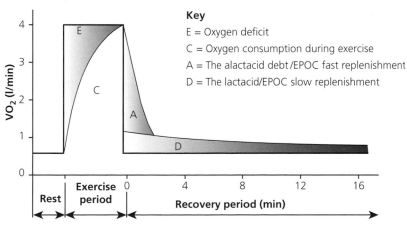

Key
E = Oxygen deficit
C = Oxygen consumption during exercise
A = The alactacid debt/EPOC fast replenishment
D = The lactacid/EPOC slow replenishment

(p.12)

Copy the following diagram and see if you can summarise the functions of the fast and slow components of EPOC:

Answer:

```
                    ┌──────────┐
                    │   EPOC   │
                    └──────────┘
                   ↙            ↘
┌─────────────────────┐    ┌──────────────────────────┐
│ Fast component:     │    │ Slow component:          │
│ • Restores ATP and PC│   │ • Removes lactic acid    │
│ • Re-saturates       │   │ • Meets the demand for   │
│   myoglobin          │   │   extra oxygen to keep   │
│   with oxygen        │   │   breathing and          │
│                     │    │   heart rate high        │
│                     │    │ • Maintains the increase │
│                     │    │   in temperature         │
└─────────────────────┘    └──────────────────────────┘
```

(p.14)

The graphs in Figures 12a and 12b show changes in oxygen uptake (VO_2) and lactate levels of an average performer and an elite performer. There are noticeable differences between the two graphs. Can you find them and explain why?

1   The oxygen uptake line goes higher because the elite performer has a higher VO_2 max.

2   The lactate line goes higher because the elite performer produces or can tolerate more lactate.

3   The elite performer produces hardly any lactate, even when running.

4   The lactate threshold occurs at a higher percentage of the oxygen consumption – more like 75–80 per cent for the elite performer.

Answers to Practice questions

(p.22)

1   Elite athletes may use the results from lactate sampling to ensure that their training is effective. Explain the term lactate sampling.

- Taking blood samples (to measure the level of lactic acid).
- Ensures training is at the correct intensity/monitor improvements over time.
- Provides accurate/objective measure.
- Measures OBLA/lactate threshold/occurs at 4 mmols.

2   Michael Johnson holds the world record for the 400 m with a time of 43.18 seconds. Explain how the majority of energy was provided during the race.

- Anaerobic/no O_2
- PFK is the enzyme that is responsible for:
  - glycolysis
  - here, glucose/glycogen/carbohydrate/ is broken down to pyruvate/pyruvic acid
- Pyruvate/pyruvic acid is then converted to lactate/lactic acid
- Two ATP produced.

3   At the end of a team game, players may experience EPOC. Define EPOC and give the functions of the fast component of EPOC and explain how these functions are achieved.

EPOC:

- Excess post-exercise oxygen consumption

Fast component:

- restoration of ATP and PC
- re-saturation of myoglobin with oxygen

Achieved:

- restoration of phosphocreatine takes up to 3 minutes for 100 per cent; 30 seconds for 50 per cent
- 2–3 litres of oxygen consumed
- myoglobin replenishment takes up to 2 minutes
- uses 0.5 litres of oxygen

4 **Explain the factors that can affect lactate threshold.**
- Exercise intensity – in high intensity exercise, fast twitch fibres are used which use glycogen as a fuel; when glycogen is broken down to form pyruvic acid, lactic acid is formed.
- Muscle fibre type – slow twitch fibres produce less lactate than fast twitch fibres.
- Rate of blood lactate removal – if lactate production increases then lactate will start to accumulate in the blood.
- Training – allows muscle to improve their capacity for aerobic respiration through adaptations, e.g. increase in myoglobin. This avoids the use of the lactic acid system.

5 **Elite athletes spend considerable time developing their fitness, using a variety of methods, in order to produce peak performance.**
   a) **Explain why some athletes, such as marathon runners, may choose to spend time training at altitude.**
   b) **What are the potential problems associated with altitude training?**

a)
- Improved endurance/stamina/aerobic capacity/VO_2 max
- Reduced concentration/partial pressure of oxygen at altitude
- Compensation through increased red blood cells/haemoglobin
- Erythropoietin
- Enhanced oxygen-carrying capacity (on return to sea level)

b)
- Reduced PO_2 – training very hard
- Loss of fitness/detraining effect
- Increased lactate production/accumulation
- Altitude sickness/weeks to acclimatise
- Solution – live at altitude and train at sea level
- Other physiological: blood viscosity/psychological/social/environmental factors.

6 **The triathlon is an athletic event that involves performers undertaking a long distance swim, immediately followed by a cycle race and then finally a run of several kilometres. Name the main energy system being used throughout the race and explain how this system provides energy for the working muscles. At the end of the race, the triathlete will be out of breath and will continue to breathe heavily even though they have come to a complete rest. Explain why this breathlessness occurs.**

AO1 – Knowledge Identified as the aerobic system and/or EPOC using simple statements

AO2 – Application of the aerobic system and/or how EPOC works

AO3 – Analysis/Evaluation Linked explanation of the correct method of energy production in relation to the triathlete and importance of EPOC

Points that need addressing:
- Aerobic/with oxygen

ATP regenerated during three stages:

Stage one: glycolysis
- Glycogen is converted to glucose and broken down to pyruvic acid
- By the enzyme PFK
- Occurs in the sarcoplasm

Stage two: Krebs cycle

- Occurs in the matrix of the mitochondria
- Acetyl CoA/Citric acid is oxidised
- CO_2 is the bi-product
- Hydrogen is formed
- 2 ATP are re-synthesised
- Following beta oxidation fats can enter krebs cycle

Stage three: electron transport chain

- Occurs in the cristae of the mitochondria
- water formed
- 34 ATP are re-synthesised

Aerobic system relevant for a triathlete because:

- More ATP can be produced -36 ATP
- There are no fatiguing by-products (carbon dioxide and water)
- Lots of glycogen and triglyceride stores so exercise can last for a long time.
- EPOC/Excess Post-Exercise Oxygen Consumption
- Aerobic energy is needed
- Requires oxygen/ O_2
- Restoration of PC/ATP/Phosphagens
- Re-saturation of myoglobin with oxygen
- Lactate/lactic acid breakdown/removal

Importance of a cool down to keep:

- High temperature/high metabolic rate
- Energy for high heart rate/breathing rate

Explanation of how these functions are achieved

- restoration of phophocreatine takes up to three minutes for 100 per cent /30 seconds for 50 per cent
- 2–3 litres of oxygen consumed
- myoglobin replenishment takes up to 2 minutes
- uses 0.5 litres of oxygen
- can oxidize lactic acid
- to carbon dioxide and water
- converted to glycogen/glucose
- stored in the muscles and liver
- converted to protein
- sweated/urinated

Chapter 2.1 Information processing

Answers to Check your understanding questions

(p.30)

1 What is information processing?

Taking account of the sporting environment to make decisions prior to a response.

2 What do you understand by the term 'Display'?

The sporting environment.

3 **Name two external senses used in sport and give an example of how each might be used.**

- Hearing – hearing the sound of the ball touching the bat in cricket or similar.
- Vision – seeing the flight of the ball.

4 **Name three internal senses, or proprioceptors, used in information processing and give examples of how each might be used.**

- Touch: the feel of the racket in the hand when doing a drop shot in badminton.
- Balance: used by the gymnast on the balance beam.
- Kinesthesis: the position of the limbs when doing a spin during a dive from the high board.

5 **What is selective attention?**

A method of filtering relevant from irrelevant information gathered by the senses.

6 **Name three advantages to a sports performer of using selective attention.**

- Faster decisions
- Prevents overload of the memory system
- Helps to focus on an aspect of the task.

7 **What does DCR mean?**

Detection, comparison and recognition.

(p.35)

1 **Draw a diagram to show the structure of the working memory.**

As Figure 9, page 31.

2 **Name three features of the long-term memory.**

- It lasts a lifetime.
- Stores motor programmes.
- Sends and receives information from the working memory.

3 **What is the first role of the working memory?**

To pick up *relevant* information from the environment.

4 **What are the four components of the working memory?**

1 The central executive
2 The phonological loop
3 The visuospatial sketchpad
4 The episodic buffer.

(p.38)

1 **What is a schema?**

- An adapted motor programme.
- A set of concepts that can be adapted to the situation.

2 **What is the function of recall schema?**

To initiate movement.

3 **What is the function of recognition schema?**

To control movement.

(p.43)

1 **Define the terms reaction time, movement time and response time.**

- Reaction time = Onset of stimulus to onset of movement

- Movement time = Start to completion of task
- Response time = Onset of stimulus to completion of task

2 What is the relationship between reaction time, movement time and response time?

Response time = Reaction time + Movement time

3 What is the difference between a simple reaction time and a choice reaction time?

- Simple reaction time is a reaction to one specific stimulus.
- Choice reaction time is a reaction to several stimuli and/or numerous options in response.

4 What does Hick's law tell us?

The more choices, the longer the reaction time.

5 What does the single channel hypothesis suggest?

Only one stimulus can be processed at any one time.

6 What is anticipation?

Pre-judging a stimulus.

7 Name two types of anticipation.

- Spatial
- Temporal.

Answers to Activities

(p.24)

Think of a sporting arena such as the one pictured (in Figure 2). Make a list of the items of information that are available from this environment when you play sport.

Answers might include information such as the crowd, the ball, the opponents, the officials.

(p.25)

Give examples from a sport of your choice of the senses you would use and the items of information you would pick up as you performed or played that sport.

Examples might include:

- Using sight to pick up the position of an opponent when marking in a team game.
- Using kinesthesis to detect the position of the limbs during the clean and jerk in weightlifting.

(p.27)

Consider a game or event that you recently took part in. Think of some of the decisions you made during that game or event. What information did you use to make those decisions and what information was not needed? Try to list the relevant and irrelevant information.

Student's own answer. Information might include player positions, which pass to make or equivalent.

(p.28)

Make a list of the types of feedback and describe each type.

- Positive feedback – encouragement
- Negative feedback – error correction
- Extrinsic feedback – from an outside source
- Intrinsic feedback – from within
- Knowledge of results – concerns the outcome
- Knowledge of performance – about technique

(p.29)

The features of information processing occur in a specific order. Look again at the main points of each of the processes involved in information processing and see if you can place them in the order you think they would occur. List each process in order from first to last.

Here are the terms to place in order:

- Environment
- Effector mechanism
- Translatory mechanism
- Feedback data
- Display
- Muscular system output data
- The sensory organs
- Perceptual mechanism (includes selective attention).

Your answer to the above activity is important, since the order you have described leads to an information processing model. Did your order look like the one below?

Information-processing model

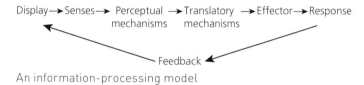

An information-processing model

(p.30)

Look at the diagram of the Whiting model. Where do you think selective attention might occur?

There are numerous arrows going into perception but only one coming out, due to selective attention!

Some questions to think about from the Whiting model are given below. Consider and discuss with your fellow students.

Why are there numerous arrows going from the effector mechanisms into the muscular system?

More than one muscle used.

Why are there numerous arrows going into the perceptual mechanisms but only one arrow going out?

Selective attention is used.

Why do you think the central mechanisms are included in the model?

Because the mechanisms in the top part of the diagram occur within the body systems. Those features of the model in the bottom half can occur externally.

(p.37)

Consider the skill of a rugby pass.

Some of the points coaches might highlight when using this skill are:

1 Judging the distance needed to make that pass reach the team mate so that they do not have to slow down when catching the ball.
2 The recipient of the pass reaching out to catch the ball.
3 Scanning the pitch to see players who are available for the pass.
4 Weighting the pass using strong or soft hands to make sure it reaches the intended target.

State which of these coaching points are appropriate for use in the parts of a schema.

Which of the coaching points could be relevant for use in:

- the initial conditions
- response specifications
- sensory consequences
- the response outcome?

Now consider the skill of a javelin throw and these four coaching points:

1   The assessment of the number of steps to be taken in the run-up from the start of the throw.
2   The distance thrown.
3   The grip on the javelin during the throw.
4   The foot placement before the run-up starts.

Which coaching points would be relevant for use in initial conditions and response specifications (the recall schema)? Which would be relevant in the sensory consequences and the recognition schema?

Answer (rugby pass):

- Initial conditions: 3
- Response specifications: 1
- Sensory consequences: 4
- Response outcome: 2

Answer (javelin throw):

Recall schema:

- Initial conditions: 4
- Response specifications: 1

Recognition schema:

- Sensory consequences: 3
- Response outcome: 2

(p.38)

Think back to the concepts used during information processing. Which of these concepts could be used by a sports performer during reaction time?

- Picking up information from the senses.
- Using selective attention to identify the stimulus.
- Making a decision using the memory, perceptual and translatory mechanisms.
- Sending an impulse by the effector mechanism.

(All done before movement!)

(p.39)

Figure 17 relates to a 100 m sprint. Consider the definitions of reaction time, movement time and response time and see if you can relate them to the skill of catching a ball hit by the batter in a game of rounders.

- Reaction time would be picking up the flight of the ball as it leaves the bat until just before the first movement to go towards the ball.
- Movement time would be from making the first step towards the ball and catching the ball in the hands.
- Response time would be from picking up the stimulus of the flight of the ball until the catch is made.

Answers to Practice questions

(p.44)

1   An impulse carried from the brain to the muscles that initiates movement best describes which of the following processes?

Answer: c) Effector mechanism

2   Games players use information processing to make decisions. Explain the types of sensory information used in team games.

> *Choose four from:*
> - Vision/sight
> - Audition/hearing
> - Equilibrium/balance
> - Touch
> - Kinesthesis

3   Effective sports performers use a process called selective attention.
    Using an example from sport, explain the term selective attention and evaluate the effectiveness of this process in helping a sports performer to make decisions.

Question 3 is marked using the extended question banded marking criteria given at the end of this section.

Indicative content includes:

- Filters relevant information from irrelevant
- Suitable example
- Prevents information overload
- Allows player to focus on specific aspects of the task
- Helps working memory system which has limited capacity
- Speeds up decision making
- Improves reaction time
- Can be improved by specific practice to help skill development
- May be hindered by poor or changing environment, e.g. can't see ball!

4   During a tennis match, the ball hits the top of the net during a rally and the receiver has to adjust their response. This causes a delay before the final response can be made. Explain why this delay occurs.

> *Choose three from:*
> - Only one piece of information can be processed at a time
> - Called the single channel hypothesis
> - One signal must be cleared before another one can be responded to
> - Causes a delay in responding to the second stimulus
> - Psychological refractory period
> - Second stimulus arrives before first one is processed

5   Consider the sporting situations of an athlete at the start of a 100 m race waiting for the starter's signal and a games player in midfield about to make a pass.
    a) Which performer do you think would have the faster reaction time? Explain your choice.
    b) What strategies could the athlete use to achieve a faster response time?

Part a)

> *Choose four from:*
> - 100 m start should have fastest reaction
> - Simple reaction time: one option

- Choice reaction time: more than one option
- Hick's law
- More choices: increased response
- Graph
- Athlete affected by anticipation
- Games player may be affected by psychological refractory period

Part b)

Choose three from:

- Concentration/pay attention/selective attention
- Practise reacting to gun/grooving the response
- Improve physical fitness
- Be at optimal arousal level/motivation
- Anticipation of the gun
- Mental practice

6 **During sporting performance it may be necessary to process information using the memory system. What are the features and functions of the working memory?**

Question 3 is marked using the extended banded marking criteria given at the end of this section.

Indicative content:

Uses four stages:

1) Central executive controls information from the senses coming into the working memory.

2) Phonological loop – deals with hearing and helps produce a memory trace.

3) Visuospatial sketchpad – deals with movement and kinesthesis.

4) Episodic buffer – programmes and sorts information to be sent to the LTM.

- Has a short time span, around 30 seconds
- Has a limited capacity, around 5–9 items
- Produces memory trace to initiate motor programme/movement
- Deals with the present
- Information must be rehearsed or it is lost.

7 **A schema consists of 'recall' and 'recognition' components. Which of the following statements are features of recall schema?**

Answer: a) Occurs before the action and initiates movement.

8 **Schmidt's schema theory is based on four sources of information, called parameters, which are used to modify motor programmes. Explain these four sources of information.**

Four from:

- (Knowledge of) initial conditions/initial set up/environmental conditions.
- (Knowledge of) response specifications/response demands/what is needed.
- Sensory consequences/kinesthesis/knowledge of performance/feel of movement.
- Movement outcomes/knowledge of results/KR.

9 **How can a coach organise practices to enable a schema to develop?**

Choose four from:

- Practice to be varied/avoid blocked or massed practice/examples.
- Should include plenty of information.
- Should have feedback.
- Should be realistic to the game/activity.

- Should include transferable elements.
- Should become more challenging/ more difficult.

10 **Explain the relationship between reaction time, movement time and response time, and explain the strategies a coach or player could use to improve response time, showing how effective such strategies may be.** (15 marks)

Indicative content

Reaction time: onset of stimulus to onset of movement

Movement time: start to completion of task

Response time: onset of stimulus to completion of task

Response time = reaction time + movement time

Strategies	Effectiveness
Mental practice	must be in a calm environment
Train to the stimulus	must be realistic
Focus concentrate	depends on performer ability
Make stimulus intense	depends on the equipment e.g. bright ball
Improve fitness	depends on existing fitness levels and appropriate method
Anticipation	good if correct; if incorrect, causes delay.

Chapter 3.1 Injury prevention and the rehabilitation of injury

Answers to Check your understanding questions

(p.52)

How can hyperbaric chambers aid injury rehabilitation?

- The chamber is pressurised.
- Pressure increases the amount of oxygen that can be breathed in.
- This means more oxygen can be diffused to the injured area.
- The excess oxygen dissolves into the blood plasma, where it can:
  - reduce swelling; and
  - stimulate white blood cell activity; and
  - increase the blood supply at the injury site.

(p.53)

How would you treat a muscle strain?

RICE = Rest, Ice, Compression, Elevation

(p.55)

How does an ice bath help a performer to recover?

- Involves sitting in ice-cold water for between 5–20 minutes.
- Causes blood vessels to tighten/decreases metabolic activity/vasoconstriction.
- Restricting blood flow to the area.
- Reduces swelling/tissue breakdown/aids muscle repair.
- After leaving the ice bath, area is flooded with new blood/vasodilation.
- Fresh oxygen removes lactic acid (when out of the ice bath).

Answers to Activities

(p.49)

Can you think of another sport and identify what protective clothing is necessary?

Lots of possibilities; for example:

- American football – shoulder pads
- Ice hockey – pads, helmet, gloves

Using your own sport or activity, design an appropriate warm-up.

Whatever the sport, answer must include the three stages: pulse raiser, stretching and movement patterns.

(p.50)

Can you think of some other active stretches?

Hamstring stretch

Quadriceps stretch

Can you think of some other passive stretches?

Gastrocnemius (calf) stretch

Adductor (groin) stretch

(p.51)

Can you think of some other exercises where you use your body weight as the resistance?

Press-ups, sit-ups, squats, etc.

Answers to Practice questions

(p.56)

1   **The use of ice baths and cryotherapy can aid recovery. Analyse which of these methods you think is the most effective and give reasons why.**

Both methods use the same principle of using cold temperatures to aid recovery:

- Through vasoconstriction of the blood vessels.
- Therefore reducing inflammation and blood flow and getting rid of waste products such as lactic acid.
- The value of ice baths is that anyone can use one (you can do it at home).
- Cryotherapy chambers are only available to elite athletes.

- Cryotherapy is less time consuming.
- The body returns back to normal quicker.

2 **What is the difference between an acute injury and a chronic injury? Use examples when you explain your answer.**
- An acute injury occurs suddenly during exercise or competition.
- Pain is felt straight away and is often severe.
- A chronic injury occurs after playing sport or exercise for a long time.
- They are often called overuse injuries.
- Suitable examples of each.

3 **How can hydrotherapy help sports rehabilitation?**
- Hydrotherapy takes place in warm water.
- It improves blood circulation, relieves pain, relaxes muscles.
- The buoyancy of the water helps to support body weight.
- This reduces the load on joints.
- Allows for more exercise than is permitted on land.
- Exercise is done against the resistance of the water to strengthen the injured area.

4 **Why is sleep important for improved recovery?**
- More sleep is needed following a heavy exercise programme.
- A deep sleep rebuilds the damage done to muscle cells.
- Deep sleep: where blood is directed towards the muscles to restore energy.
- 8+ hours as a guide for an elite athlete.

Chapter 4.1 Linear motion

Answers to Check your understanding questions

(p.68)

Using arrows, draw the forces acting on the following bodies. Think carefully about the point of application, the size and direction of the force.

(p.70)

Can you explain how an athlete uses positive impulse during their sprint?
- Positive impulse is used for acceleration at the start of the race.
- The athlete applies more force with their quadriceps as they extend their knee/gluteals as they extend their hips/gastrocnemius as they push off the blocks.
- To create greater momentum.
- If the net impulse is positive then acceleration occurs.
- Positive impulse graph drawn.

Answers to Activities

(p.59)

Work out the displacement from the following components of the triathlon:

- Swim = 1.5 km
- Bike ride = 0 km
- Run = 200 m

(p.60)

Calculate the average speed and the average velocities for the components of a triathlon.

Distance	Time	Displacement	Average speed m/s	Average velocity m/s
1.5 km swim	30 mins 30 secs	1.5 km	0.82	0.82
40 km cycle	90 mins	0.0	7.41	0.0
10 km run	45 mins	0.2 km	3.7	0.07

(p.61)

Now try to explain what is happening in this distance–time graph which is a combination of the above:

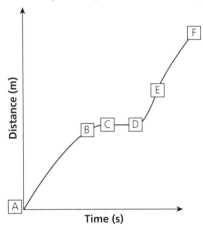

- A–B = constant speed
- B–C = deceleration
- C–D = no motion
- D–E acceleration
- E–F constant speed

(p.62)

Can you think of three examples in any team game where acceleration is an important quantity?

- To lose a player
- To beat an opponent
- To get to the ball first
- To create momentum

The table below gives the 10 m split times and velocity for an elite 100 m sprinter.

10 m splits	Time (s)	Time for each split (s)	Velocity (m/s)
10	1.87	1.72 (reaction time was 0.15)	5.8
20	2.89	1.02	9.8
30	3.81	0.92	10.9
40	4.68	0.87	11.5
50	5.52	0.84	11.9

10 m splits	Time (s)	Time for each split (s)	Velocity (m/s)
60	6.36	0.84	11.9
70	7.20	0.84	11.9
80	8.05	0.85	11.8
90	8.91	0.86	11.6
100	9.77	0.86	11.6

From this table, calculate the sprinter's acceleration:

- from 10 m to 20 m
- from 20 m to 30 m.

From 10 m to 20 m:

$$\text{Acceleration} = \frac{\text{Change in velocity (m/s)}}{\text{Time taken (s)}}$$

Change in velocity = Final velocity – Initial velocity

$$\frac{9.8 - 5.8}{1.02} \qquad \frac{4}{1.02}$$

$$= 3.92 \text{ m/s}^2$$

From 20 m to 30 m:

$$\frac{10.9 - 9.8}{0.92} \qquad \frac{1.1}{0.92}$$

$$= 1.19 \text{ m/s}^2$$

(p.63)

Complete the blanks in the table below.

Performer	Mass (kg)	Velocity (m/s)	Momentum (kgm/s)
100 m sprinter	80	11.9	952
Prop	120	9	**1080**
Centre forward	70	10.5	735
Middle distance runner	65	9.5	617.5

Copy the table below and complete the missing information and use it as a revision guide.

Measurements used in linear motion

Measurement	Definition	Unit of measurement	How to calculate? (if relevant)
Mass	Mass is the quantity of matter the body possesses.	kg	
Distance	Distance is measured in metres and is the path a body takes as it moves from the starting to the finishing position.	m	
Speed	Speed is a measurement in metres/second of the body's movement per unit of time with no reference to direction.	m/s	$\dfrac{\text{Distance covered (m)}}{\text{Time taken (s)}}$
Weight	Weight is the force on a given mass due to gravity.	N	
Acceleration	Rate of change of velocity.	m/s²	$\dfrac{\text{Change in velocity (m/s)}}{\text{Time (s)}}$
Displacement	Displacement is measured in metres and is the shortest route in a straight line between the starting and finishing position.	m or km	$\dfrac{\text{Displacement (m)}}{\text{Time taken (s)}}$
Velocity	The rate of change of displacement.	m/s	
Momentum	Momentum is the product of the mass and velocity of an object.	kgm/s	Momentum (kgm/s) = Mass (kg) × Velocity (m/s)

(p.65)

Can you think of sporting examples where maximising friction is important and explain how greater friction is achieved?

Any answer that takes account of the surface characteristics of the two bodies in contact and the temperature of the two surfaces in contact.

Answers to Practice questions

(p.71)

1   Sketch two vector diagrams representing the differing resultant forces for a long jumper and for a high jumper during take-off.

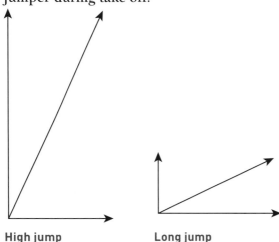

High jump   **Long jump**

2   Ice hockey is often regarded as a very physical game, with many collisions occurring during normal play. A stationary ice-hockey puck was struck with an ice hockey stick and travelled across the ice until it struck and rebounded from a wall.
    The diagram below shows the changes in horizontal linear velocity experienced by the puck. Assume that air resistance and friction on the ice are negligible, and describe and explain the horizontal motion of the puck associated with each of the periods of time identified as P, Q, R, S and T.

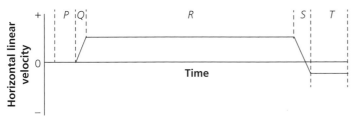

P:
- Puck stationary/at rest on the ice
- No external forces acting

Q:
- Time when stick in contact with puck/force applied by stick
- Puck changing velocity/accelerating
- In direction of force applied by stick

R:
- Puck travelling with constant (horizontal) velocity
- No external forces acting on the puck/friction free

S:
- Time when puck hits wall
- Puck decelerates (caused by force applied by the wall)
- Eventually travels in opposite direction/rebounds off the wall

T:
- Puck moving across ice with constant negative horizontal linear velocity
- No forces acting
- Reduced velocity (due to energy absorbed by impact)

3 The graph below shows a velocity–time graph for an elite 100 m sprinter.
Use the graph to work out the velocity of the sprinter after 3 seconds and give a period of time when the sprinter's acceleration was the greatest.

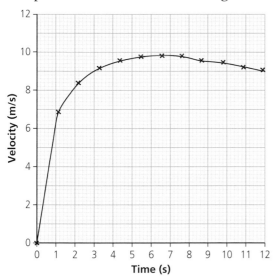

- Velocity: 9.1 m/s (accept 9.0–9.2).
- Greatest acceleration: 0–1 seconds.

4 What is happening to the sprinter between 6 and 11 seconds?

Deceleration/decrease in velocity. (Slowing down is not sufficient.)

5 The acceleration that a performer achieves when sprinting is related to impulse. What do you understand by the term impulse, and how can the athlete use impulse during their sprint?
- Impulse is force *times* time
- Relates to a change in momentum
- Positive impulse is needed for acceleration
- Negative impulse occurs when the foot lands/braking action
- Net impulse is positive which equals acceleration
- Graph annotated.

Chapter 4.2 Angular motion

Answers to Check your understanding questions

(p.75)

Explain, using Newton's first law of angular motion, how a performer can alter their state of rotation.

Any example where a rotating body turns around its axis until an external torque changes the spin, e.g. landing on the trampoline after performing a double somersault. The performer continues to rotate until they land on the trampoline bed and then the trampoline exerts an external torque which changes their angular motion.

(p.78)

Why do you think a diver may want to increase their moment of inertia just before they enter the water?

The diver needs to control their entry into the water so they need to reduce the rate of their spin. Increasing their moment of inertia will achieve this as they spread their body out away from the axis of rotation.

Answers to Activities

(p.73)

Can you think of three sporting examples when a force is applied outside the centre of mass of an object or body to cause rotation to occur?

Any rotational movement such as:

● Free kick in football so the ball swerves around the wall.
● Back spin on a netball shot.
● Top spin in tennis.

Can you think of examples from the shoulder joint for each axis of rotation?

● Transverse – flexion.
● Sagittal axis – abduction.
● Longitudinal axis – horizontal abduction.

(p.76)

Using Figure 5, calculate the angular velocity and angular acceleration of the gymnast to get from position X to position Y if the time taken is 0.6s.

$Angular\ velocity = \dfrac{1.9}{0.6} = 3.16\ rads/sec$

$Angular\ acceleration = \dfrac{3.16}{0.6} = 5.2\ rads/sec$

Answers to Practice questions

(p.79)

1 Coaches use biomechanical analysis to help optimise performance. The diagram below is incomplete. When complete, it should show three curves representing the following parameters during a backward tucked somersault:
   ● angular momentum
   ● moment of inertia
   ● angular velocity.
   Add the missing curve and label all three curves.

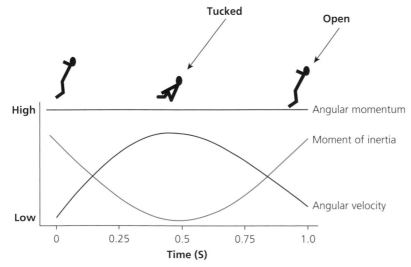

2   Explain Newton's first law of motion in relation to a dancer spinning.

- Newton's first law states that that a body will continue to turn about its axis of rotation with constant angular momentum unless an external force is exerted upon it.
- Therefore the dancer will continue to spin:
  - with constant angular momentum
  - unless an external force acts on her.

3   How does the gymnast alter her speed of rotation by changing her body shape?

Points that need addressing:

- Transverse axis
- During rotations angular momentum remains constant
- Angular momentum = moment of inertia x angular velocity
- Angular momentum-quantity of motion/rotation
- Moment of inertia - spread/distribution of mass around axis/reluctance to rotate;
- Angular velocity = speed of rotation
- Change in moment of inertia leads to change in angular velocity/spin of rotation
- Moment of inertia and angular velocity are inversely proportional
- Brings arms/legs closer to axis of rotation leads to
- increase in angular velocity/speed of rotation/spin
- Arms/legs further from axis of rotation leads to decrease in angular velocity/speed of spin

Chapter 4.3 Projectile motion

Answers to Activities

(p.80)

Can you think of other examples in sport when the human body becomes a projectile?

Examples include: diving header in football; gymnast tumbling routine; trampolining; high jump; high board diving.

(p.83)

Can you identify the flight path of a golf ball, football and shot put and explain why they follow this flight path?

Object	Flight path	Why?
Golf ball	Distorted parabola	Sheer distance it travels means that it is in the air for longer so air resistance has a greater effect. It is also very light.
Football	Slightly distorted parabola	Bigger cross-sectional area so more air resistance.
Shot put	True parabola	High weight and low air resistance.

Answers to Practice questions

(p.84)

1   In a game of badminton the performer hits the shuttle into the air and it then becomes a projectile. Explain how the various forces act to affect the badminton shuttle *during* its flight.

- The badminton shuttle follows a non-parabolic flight path.
- The shape of the shuttle means air resistance is the larger force.
- Air resistance acts on the horizontal components.
- Gravity acts on the vertical components.

2 Name three factors that affect the distance a shot put travels.

- Angle of release
- Velocity of release
- Height of release

3 Draw a diagram to show the flight path of a shot put and on your diagram label and explain the changing vertical and horizontal vectors at the following points:
- the point of release
- the highest point of flight
- the point immediately before landing.

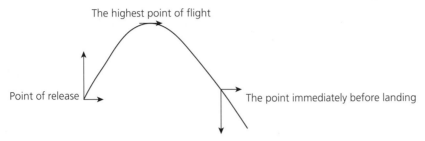

- A large positive vertical component on release as the shot travels up away from the athlete.
- No vertical component at the highest flight point.
- Larger negative vertical component before landing due to the effects of gravity.

Chapter 4.4 Fluid mechanics

Answers to Check your understanding questions

(p.87)

Explain how increasing the cross-sectional area of a moving body can increase drag.

A greater cross-sectional area means there is no streamlining, so air resistance will have a bigger effect on a moving body!

(p.88)

Describe how the javelin makes use of an upward lift force.

When the javelin is released at an angle, the air that travels over the top of the javelin has to travel a longer distance than the air underneath. So the air above the javelin travels at a faster velocity, which creates a lower pressure. This lower pressure above the javelin creates an upward lift force and allows the javelin to stay in the air for longer and travel further.

Answers to Activities

(p.87)

Can you think of some other examples in sport where the shape and surface characteristics of a moving body can increase or decrease drag?

- Golf: Dimples in a golf ball create more air resistance.
- 100 m start: At the start, the athletes stay low. Being upright will increase air resistance.

(p.88)

Try to explain what would happen if the angle of attack for the discus was 90°.

This angle of attack is too great and there will be a greater measure of drag. This means there will be a reduction in lift so the discus will not travel as far.

Answers to Practice questions

(p.89)

1 Identify what is meant by a drag force and, giving an example from sport, explain how the effects of a drag force can be reduced.
   - Drag force is a force that acts in opposition to motion.
   - Therefore it has a negative effect on velocity.

   Suitable example:
   - A cyclist will streamline their body position to reduce their cross-sectional area by crouching low over the handlebars, rather than sitting upright.
   - This will increase their velocity.

2 Identify and explain two factors that can increase or decrease drag.
   - Velocity – the faster something travels increases drag.
   - Cross-sectional area – a larger cross-sectional increases drag; or the reverse.
   - The surface characteristics of a moving body – a more streamlined, aerodynamic shape reduces drag.

3 Explain the Bernoulli principle in relation to a downward lift force for a racing car.
   - The Bernoulli principle is where air molecules exert less pressure the faster they travel and more pressure when they travel slower.
   - In a racing car, the spoiler is angled so the lift force can act in a downward direction to push the car into the track.
   - This happens because the air that travels over the top of the car travels a shorter distance (due to the angle of the spoiler) than the air underneath.
   - This results in the air above the car travelling at a slower velocity which therefore creates a higher pressure.
   - This higher pressure above the car creates a downward lift force and allows the tyres of the car to maintain a firm grip on the track.

Chapter 5.1 Psychological factors that can influence an individual in physical activities

Answers to Check your understanding questions

(p.94)

1 List three characteristics of a performer who displays approach behaviour.

Three from: confident, task persistent, likes feedback and evaluation, takes risks, welcomes challenge, attributes success internally

2 List three characteristics of a performer who shows the need to avoid failure.

Three from: gives up easily, avoids feedback, takes easy options, protects self-esteem.

3 What is achievement motivation?
   - Drive for success minus fear of failure

4 Name three things that influence the level of achievement motivation.
   - *Personality*: either NACH or NAF
   - Combined with the *probability of success*
   - And the *incentive value* of the task

5   **Suggest three things a coach could do to develop the need to achieve.**
- Set goals that are realistic yet challenging.
- Set task-related goals not just outcome goals.
- Allow success.
- Use reinforcement.
- Improve confidence.

(p.102)

1   **What is the difference between self-confidence and self-efficacy?**
- Self-confidence is a general belief in ability.
- Self-efficacy is a belief in ability for a specific situation.

2   **What is sporting trait confidence?**
The belief in the ability to do well in a range of sports.

3   **What is sporting state confidence?**
The belief in the ability to do well in one sporting moment.

4   **List the four factors that contribute to the level of self-efficacy.**
- Performance accomplishments
- Vicarious experience
- Verbal persuasion
- Emotional arousal

5   **Name some strategies to improve performance accomplishments.**
- Set goals
- Make them more challenging when achieved
- Allow success
- Point out past success
- Set goals on performance not outcome.

(p.106)

1   **What is the difference between a prescribed leader and an emergent leader?**
A prescribed leader is appointed from outside the group; an emergent leader is appointed from within.

2   **Name three qualities of a leader.** Three from:
- Charisma
- Empathy
- Communication skills
- Motivator
- Experience
- Knowledge
- Organised
- Inspirational

3   **What is the difference between a person approach and a task approach to leadership?**
The person approach concerns group relationships.
The task approach is concerned with results and beating others.

4   **What is the laissez-faire style of leadership?**

When the leader has very little input into group actions.

5   **In a situation where the group is experienced, has respect for the leader and is clear in its goals, what style of leadership would you use?**

Autocratic: no need to consult in this situation. For an experienced group, the laissez-faire style could be used.

6   **Name some features of the group that could affect the style of leadership used.**

- Group size
- Age
- Gender
- Experience
- Ability

(p.111)

1   **What is a stressor?**

A cause of stress.

2   **Give three examples of a stressor.**

- Fear of failure
- Injury
- Increased competition – the big game
- Strong opposition.

3   **Name two different responses to a stressor.**

Negative or stress, positive or eustress.

4   **Name three methods of cognitive stress management.** Three from:

- Positive-self talk
- Thought stopping
- Imagery
- Visualisation
- Attentional control.

5   **Name three methods of somatic stress control.** Three from:

- Biofeedback
- Progressive muscle relaxation
- Centring
- Goal setting.

6   **What are the four styles of attentional control?**

- Broad/external
- Broad/internal
- Narrow/external
- Narrow/internal.

7   **What is the difference between attentional narrowing and attentional wastage?**

Narrowing is when the ability to process cues is reduced with increased arousal. Wastage is when important cues are missed.

(p.115)

1 Why is using correct attributions so important in sport?

Correct attribution increases task persistence, motivation and confidence.

2 Name two external and unstable attributes.

- Luck
- Referee decision

3 Name two internal and unstable attributes.

- Effort
- Amount of practice

4 What could happen if internal stable reasons are given for failure?

Learned helplessness.

5 What is attribution retraining?

Changing internal and stable reasons for failure to external and unstable reasons.

6 What is mastery orientation?

Giving internal and stable reasons for success, showing confidence and thinking success can be repeated.

Answers to Activities

(p.91)

Consider the characteristics of a player with the need to avoid failure. Discuss with a classmate why you think they would play against someone much better than them or someone much worse.

A need to avoid failure personality plays against either a much better or much worse opponent because in either case they protect their pride and self-esteem. They can beat the worse opponent and they are not expected to win against the best, so no loss of pride either way!

(p.93)

Look carefully at the graph shown in Figure 4. Make a copy of the graph and show in your copy two points on the line of the graph: one where you think a need to achieve performer will be and one where you think a need to avoid failure performer would be.

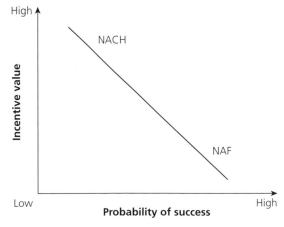

(p.94)

Use examples to show how a coach could allow success during practice.

A passing drill in basketball could be performed without opposition at first and once the skill has been mastered, the drill could then be developed to include opponents or conditioned games

Basketball player doing a pass: this drill could be started without opposition to allow success.

(p.96)

Using a sporting example, explain how you would increase the confidence of a sports performer using Vealey's model.

Student's own answer: answers ensure the approach to the task is positive, ensure the task is within the performer's ability and give positive evaluations of the outcome.

(p.100)

Study the four factors that affect the self-efficacy of the performer.

Below are some strategies that would help coaches improve the self-efficacy of a performer. Write them in the correct boxes below.

- Realistic challenging goals
- Encouragement
- Attainable role models
- Coach one on one
- Attribute success internally
- Set goals on performance not outcome
- Avoid social comparison
- Use rewards
- Point out past successful performances
- Mental practice.

1 Performance accomplishments	2 Vicarious experience
Set realistic goals	Show role attainable role models
Set goals on performance not outcome	
Point out past successful performances	
3 Verbal persuasion	**4 Emotional Arousal**
Avoid social comparison	Use mental practice visualisation or imagery
Coach one on one	
Use rewards	
Give reinforcement and praise	
Attribute success internally	

(p.102)

Can you suggest some examples from sport of prescribed and emergent leaders?

Any relevant answers: e.g. Jose Mourinho – prescribed to Manchester United; Steph Houghton – emerged as England football captain.

(p.103)

Consider the qualities of a leader discussed above and give some examples from sport when you think those qualities were clearly shown.

Any personal example.

(p.105)

How could the influence of the leader and the group affect the choice of leadership style?

The leader's characteristics influence the choice of leadership style since a leader with empathy, for example, would use that quality to listen to the group; while a leader with good communication skills would be prepared to spell out their tactics in training to the group. The experience of the leader is also important, since a leader with experience of their sport would wish to pass on such knowledge, while a less experienced leader would perhaps wish to consult with the group. Using their experience, the leader may have developed a style that they prefer to use.

The features of the group affect the choice of leadership style. With a group of females, the use of empathy and consultation would be the best choice, while males might prefer a more authoritarian approach to their training. With an able group, the coach could allow some flexibility and allow the group to use their experience to decide what they want to work on. Beginners might need to be told what to do. The age of the group is important; an older group may have some experience and knowledge to add to a discussion, while a younger group may welcome being told new information.

(p.106)

Study the list of factors that influence the choice of leadership style. For each of the factors, give a justification of the correct choice of style to suit that specific influence. Use the table below to give your answer. An example has been done for you.

Influence	Example/Explanation
Situation: Time available Danger Type of task/sport	**If lots of time is available, use the democratic style. If no time is available, use the autocratic style. In dangerous situations, use the autocratic style. The democratic style can be used in a safe environment.** With an individual sport, a democratic style might be appropriate. In team training, autocratic instruction would be better.
Leader: Characteristics Experience	A leader with the characteristic of empathy, for example, would prefer a democratic approach. Experienced leaders may wish to pass on advice in an authoritarian way.
Group: Group size Gender Age Experience	• For large groups, use the autocratic style. • For males, use the autocratic approach. • For an older age group, use the autocratic approach. • For beginners, use the autocratic approach.

(p.107)

Consider the different stressors outlined above. For each stressor, try to think of an example from a game or performance when that stressor happened to you. How did it make you feel and how did you overcome it?

Student's own answer.

(p.109)

Think back to a game or performance in which you did really well. Try to recall some of the good things you did in the game and how you felt after the event. Did your recollections bring positive thoughts?

Student's own answer.

(p.113)

Here is a list of attributes that might be used by players and coaches to explain the reasons for winning or losing.

Look at the model in Figure 32, make a copy of it and then see if you can place the attributes listed in the correct area of the diagram.

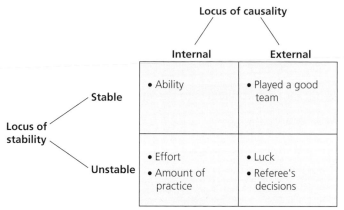

Locus of causality

	Internal	**External**
Stable	• Ability	• Played a good team
Unstable	• Effort • Amount of practice	• Luck • Referee's decisions

Locus of stability

Answers to Practice questions

(p.116)

1   In terms of attribution theory, a coach should use Weiner's model of attribution to blame losing a game on factors that are:

Answer: c) unstable and external or b) stable and external

2   Setting goals to improve confidence might help mostly to promote which of these four influences that are said, according to the psychologist Bandura, to affect self-efficacy?

Answer: c) performance accomplishments

3   Games players should be motivated when they approach competitive situations.
   i)   Explain the influences that might determine a player's level of achievement motivation.
   ii) How could a coach improve the approach behaviour of players in their charge?

i)   Four from:
   ● Interaction of situation and personality
   ● Situation – incentive value
   ● Measured against degree of difficulty
   ● Past experience of task
   ● Personality – Need to achieve; or avoid failure
   ● Confidence

ii) Four from:
   ● Setting achievable goals
   ● Allowing success
   ● Reinforcement
   ● Improving self-efficacy
   ● Attributing success internally

4   A good leader can influence the outcomes of sports performance.
   i)   Outline the characteristics of a good leader and explain the difference between a prescribed and an emergent leader.
   ii) What do you understand by the autocratic style of leadership and when, according to Fiedler, should this style be best used?

i) Two from:
- Experience
- Charisma
- Inspirational
- Good motivator
- Good communicator
- Empathy or equivalent.

Prescribed is appointed from outside the group

Emergent is appointed from within the group

ii) An autocratic style of leadership is when the leader makes decisions and dictates to the group. The autocratic style should be used in a most favourable situation with:
- Clear task
- Motivation
- Respect for leader
- Group harmony
- High group ability

And in a least favourable situation when:
- No respect for leader
- Task unclear
- Low motivation
- Low ability
- Danger
- Group lack harmony

Questions 5 and 6 are marked using the banded marking criteria for extended questions given on page 221. The indicative content is included here.

5 **Sports performers may benefit from high levels of confidence or self-efficacy. Using Bandura's model, explain how the influence of vicarious experience and emotional arousal affect the level of self-efficacy of a sports performer and show how these two influences could be improved. (8 marks)**

Indicative content:
- Vicarious experience – seeing others do the task
- Demonstration
- Role models
- Video
- Must be of similar ability/age
- Performer must have capability of doing the task
- Allow success
- Emotional arousal – the interpretation of the level of nerves
- Increased anxiety arousal may affect performance.
- Controlled by mental practice
- Cognitive stress management
- Visualisation
- Imagery

6 **In the build-up to and during a tennis match, a player may experience increased levels of stress. Discuss and evaluate the techniques a coach or player could use to reduce the effects of cognitive stress. (15 marks)**

Indicative content:

Cognitive stress management is psychological.

Thought stopping:

- Using a cued action trigger to stop negatives
- Pre-rehearsed
- Depends on prior learning of cued action

Positive self-talk:

- Replacing negatives with positives
- Example
- Must focus on positive not negative
- Imagery
- Re-creating experiences of successful actions
- Or emotions
- Must be successful
- Depends on ability to recall and recreate

Visualisation:

- Re-living a vision of successful action
- Image from practice is locked in and taken to real event
- Must be successful in practice and in image

Mental practice:

- Sequence pictured in the mind without movement
- Order is important
- Must have memory capacity to recall sequence

Attentional control:

- Four styles
- Must use correct style for the situation to reduce stress
- Psychological skills training. Can practise above techniques

Chapter 6.1 Concepts of physical activity and sport

Answers to Check your understanding questions

(p.119)

Explain the benefits to society of increasing participation in physical recreation.

Three from:

- Increased health and fitness decreases strain on the NHS and lowers obesity rates.
- Increased social integration as individuals from different social communities join clubs and socially interact.
- Increased employment/economic benefits result from more people using facilities and buying equipment to participate.
- A more positive use of free time increases social control and decreases crime statistics in a more socially inclusive society.
- Increased skill levels at the 'participation' stage leads to more individuals potentially progressing through to 'elite level'.

State the characteristics of sport.

Three from:

- It is serious/competitive.
- It has set rules/strict rules (e.g. set time limits; set boundaries).
- It involves use of specialist equipment/set kit.
- Officials appointed by national governing bodies are present to enforce the rules.
- Strategies and tactics are involved to try to outwit opponents.
- Rewards are received as a result of 'success', e.g. extrinsic rewards such as medals/trophies.
- High skill levels/high prowess are visible in sporting performance.
- High levels of commitment/strict training are involved.

(p.120)

Lots of people take part in sport to increase their health and fitness.

Identify two functions of taking part in sport for an individual.

For individuals sport helps as it:

- Increases their self-confidence as a result of skill improvement and success.
- Provides more opportunities to communicate/socialise/work as part of a team/make friends at sports clubs.
- Develop positive sporting attitudes, e.g. fair play/sportsmanship.

(p.122)

OAA form a part of a school's overall PE programme.

Identify the benefits of participating in OAA such as climbing.

There are a number of functions of outdoor education for young people including:

- Learning to appreciate and engage with the natural environment.
- Learning to develop new physical skills/survival skills (e.g. abseiling, climbing).
- Increased self-esteem.
- Increased health and fitness.
- Increased co-operation; improvement in social skills/leadership skills.
- Increased cognitive skills; decision-making; leadership skills.
- Increased awareness of conservation skills.
- Increased commitment to active leisure.
- Experience challenge/excitement/adrenaline rush/perceived risk.

(p.124)

Identify three similarities and three differences between PE and physical recreation.

Similarities:

- Both develop physical skills.
- Both develop health and fitness.
- Both help individuals achieve intrinsic benefits/have fun.

Differences:

Physical recreation	Physical Education
Voluntary/choice	Compulsory
In a person's free time	In school time
Informal/relaxed	Formal teaching and learning
Participants control activity themselves; self- regulated	Teacher in charge
Participation level	Foundation level
Simple/limited organisational structure	Highly structured

Identify four differences between school sport and National Curriculum PE.

National Curriculum PE	School sport
In lesson time; curriculum time	In free time; extra-curricular
Compulsory	Element of choice; voluntary involvement
For all	For the chosen few; elitist
Emphasis on taking part	Emphasis on winning; competitive
Teacher-led	Coaches involved
Wide variety of activities experienced	Specialisms develop

Answers to Activities

(p.117)

Identify whether or not you would consider the following as leisure time activities.

a) Working part-time at Burger King.

b) Going to the gym to keep fit after work.

c) Sending your friends a message on Facebook about going out.

d) Attendance at your A-level PE lessons.

a) No it is work, therefore not free time.

b) Yes, it is something you might choose to do in your free time.

c) Yes, it is something you might choose to do in your free time.

d) No, it is something you have to do! It is obligated and therefore not free time!

(p.118)

State three characteristics of running as physical recreation.

● Choice/choosing to go running/jogging

● To relax/enjoy a run/jog

● At your own pace

● In your free time/after work

● How long you run/jog: the route taken can be changed as the participant wishes depending on how you feel.

(p.119)

Identify how taking part in tennis can meet three characteristics of sport.

Three from:

- Strict rules apply, e.g. set court area
- Umpires/officials enforce the rules
- High skill levels are involved, e.g. volleying/serving
- Strategies and tactics are used to outwit an opponent
- Extrinsic rewards are available for winning a match/tournament
- It is competitive
- Specialist equipment is used
- Commitment/serious training is involved

(p.122)

Give examples of how outdoor education can be used to develop:

- **physical skills**
- **social skills**
- **cognitive skills**
- **increase health and fitness.**

Suggested examples:

- Skiing, climbing, canoeing, caving: *physical skills*
- Working as a team; taking turns to lead on a mountain walk: *social skills*
- Deciding which route to take when mountain biking/mountain walking, etc.: *involves decision making/ development of cognitive skills*
- *Increased health and fitness*: as a result of exertions taking part in orienteering, climbing, mountain biking, etc.

Using examples, identify three ways in which perceived risk can be experienced as part of a school's PE programme

Three ways perceived risk can be experienced:

- As a challenge that stimulates a sense of danger/adventure/gives an adrenaline rush.
- For beginners/inexperienced performers in a safe environment.
- With danger minimised via stringent safety measures/use of expert instruction (e.g. wearing a safety harness when climbing).

(p.123)

Identify three differences in running when it is performed as physical recreation compared to running when it is performed as a sporting activity.

Three ways running as physical recreation compares to running as sport:

Running as physical recreation	Running as sport
Available to all/voluntary/choice	More selective/obligation/for some an occupation
Emphasis on taking part/participation focus	Emphasis on winning/serious/competitive
Limited/varied effort/commitment required	Involves a high level of effort/commitment, e.g. to training
Rules can be modified, e.g. timings, distances	Set rules/distances apply
Self-officiated/self-regulated	External officials enforce rules
Mainly intrinsic rewards	Extrinsic rewards available for success, e.g. winning trophies/medals
Varied skill/fitness levels	Higher skill/fitness levels
Basic equipment/clothing used/worn	High-tech equipment/clothing used/worn

Answers to Practice questions

(p.125)

1 **Which of the following statements best describes the characteristics of sport?**

Answer: d) The performance level of the development continuum with an emphasis on winning.

2 **What are the functions of physical recreation for the individual?**

Three from:

- It increases health and fitness and helps in the development of physical skills.
- It provides a challenge, sense of achievement, and increases confidence.
- It can act as a stress relief from work, and helps individuals to relax.
- It helps people to socialise and meet up with friends.
- It provides people with a sense of fun/enjoyment.
- It helps ensure participation in physical activity for as many years as possible, well into later life.

3 **Identify the benefits of participating in sport to society.**

Three from:

- Decrease strain on the NHS/lower levels of obesity as health and fitness improves.
- Increased social control/lower levels of crime as individuals make more positive use of free time.
- Increased social integration/equality of opportunity via increased participation in sport together by different socio-economic groups/ethnic groups.
- Increased national pride as a result of increased standards of performances/successes of national teams.
- Economic benefits/increased employment/benefits of regeneration due to money invested/spent on sport, e.g. as a performer/spectator/consumer.

4 **Outline the functions of National Curriculum PE in schools today.**

Four from:

- Development of positive attitudes to lead to healthy lifestyles; increase in health and fitness.
- Increased participation in a variety of activities, developing physical skills/competencies.
- Develop personal and social skills; teamwork; communication; leadership; co-operation.
- Develop positive ethics; morality; sportsmanship.
- Experience and engage in competitive sports and activities outside school through community links, and/or links to sports clubs.
- Improve problem solving, decision making, cognitive skills, creativity; develop strategies and tactics in a range of activities.
- Increase the skills of self-analysis; learn how to plan, perform and evaluate; learn how to recognise improvements/own successes; increase self-esteem.
- Encourage lifelong participation; create a sporting habit for life.

5 **Identify the problems schools face in offering OAA within their school PE programmes.**

Three from:

- Lack of time (e.g. time in the curriculum).
- Lack of money (e.g. high costs of specialist equipment).
- Lack of qualified/motivated staff.
- Location of school (e.g. lack of access/long distance to travel to specialist facilities).
- Health and safety concerns.

6   **Using an example, explain what is meant by perceived risk.**

Climbing/abseiling or other suitable example:

- Gaining a sense of danger; the individual thinks the activity is 'risky'.
- A sense of excitement is experienced; the individual has an adrenaline rush.
- But the situation is controlled (e.g. via wearing a safety harness/ropes attached).
- It is encouraged by 'activity leaders'.
- And is appropriate for the 'less experienced'.

7   **Cycling has enjoyed a recent increase in participation among all ability levels.**
     Compare cycling when it is performed as a physical recreation activity with cycling when it is performed as a sporting activity.

Four from:

Cycling as physical recreation	Cycling as sport
Available to all/voluntary/choice	More selective/obligation/for some an occupation
Emphasis on taking part/participation focus	Emphasis on winning/serious/competitive
Limited/varied effort/commitment required	Involves a high level of effort/commitment, e.g. to training
Rules can be modified, e.g. flexible time, distances involved	Set rules apply, e.g. strict timings, set distances
Self-officiated/self-regulated	External officials enforce rules
Mainly intrinsic rewards	Extrinsic rewards available for success, e.g. winning trophies/medals
Varied skill/fitness levels	Higher skill/fitness levels
Basic equipment/clothing used/worn	High-tech equipment/clothing used/worn

8   **Explain the potential benefits to society of increased participation in sport and physical recreation.**

- Increased health and fitness leads to a decrease in heart disease/obesity and less strain overall on the NHS.
- People spending more money on buying equipment/using facilities results in economic benefits/increased employment opportunities/benefits to the sport and leisure industry.
- Increased skill levels can result in a more employable/highly skilled population and increase the morale of that population.
- More positive use of free time keeps people occupied in acceptable activities and results in increased social control/lower crime statistics.
- Increased equality of opportunity in society/a wider participation base feeds through to the performance level and potentially increases the chances of success at elite levels.
- Increased success at elite level leads to an increase in national pride.
- Increased social interaction results in a better community/increased community morale/increased social integration.

Chapter 6.2 Development of elite performers in sport

Answers to Check your understanding questions

(p.128)

Identify the social and cultural factors which encourage the development of elite performers and improve the chance of UK athletes winning medals at the Olympics.

Social and cultural factors to include:

- Level of media coverage/status of sport/role models to aspire to.
- Equal opportunities policies/anti-discriminatory practice/sports equity.
- A positive educational experience, e.g. at school/FE college/university.

- Access to specialist clubs to develop sporting talents (e.g. via high quality facilities; top level coaching).
- Support from family/friends/peers.
- Social class/socio-economic status.

(p.129)

Describe the role of UK Sport in elite performer development.

- Works on a strategy to increase sporting excellence in the UK.
- Manages/distributes National Lottery/World Class Programme funding/Athlete Personal Awards.
- Promotes ethical behaviour at the highest level.
- Works to attract major sporting events to the UK, e.g. via Gold Events Series.
- Manages the UK's sporting relationships with other countries, e.g. via International Voice Programme.
- Talent ID role.
- Helps sports performers develop a positive lifestyle suitable for elite sport; provides Performance Lifestyle Advice, e.g. via EIS.
- Funds/supports the work of the National Institutes of Sport.
- Supports the development of elite level coaches, e.g. via World Class Coaches.

(p.131)

The home nations of England, Northern Ireland, Scotland and Wales all have National Institutes of Sport. Identify five ways in which these National Institutes are aiding the development of the UK's elite athletes.

1 S = Sport science (e.g. biomechanics/performance analysis) and sport medicine support (e.g. medical screening/podiatry)
2 P = Performance Lifestyle Programmes are provided.
3 O = Organisations work in partnership (e.g. EIS and UK Sport).
4 R = Research and innovation (providing the latest advances in technology).
5 T = Top quality facilities to train in; and high level coaches are provided.

(p.132)

Identify four ways in which a national governing body can help to ensure the development of elite performers.

1 Via Talent ID programmes/regional scouts.
2 By providing funding; by making decisions on funding/distributing funding, e.g. UK Sport WCPP funding/Athlete Personal Awards.
3 By liaising with other organisations involved in elite performer development, e.g. UK Sport/EIS and providing Talent Identification Programmes.
4 By providing high quality coaching/top class facilities to train in, e.g. via National Centres such as the FA's centre in Burton.
5 By providing Performance Lifestyle support.
6 By increasing the numbers participating in the sport and potentially increasing the talent pool.
7 By providing structured levels of competition.
8 By providing development squads from local through regional and onto national levels.
9 By successful submission and implementation of their Whole Sport Plan.
10 By developing and applying equal opportunities policies.

(p.135)

Identify three key objectives UK Sport aims to achieve through its Gold Event Series.

1   Supporting high performance success.
2   Creating high profile opportunities for people to engage in sport.
3   Use and demonstrate the legacy of London 2012 and Glasgow 2014.
4   Drive positive economic and social impacts for the UK.

(p.136)

Describe the four key phases of UK Sport's Talent recruitment programmes.

● Campaigns start with a 'talent search' which can involve the general public and/or the sports community.

● Interested athletes are invited to submit an application form to UK Sport for them to consider.

● Successful applicants are invited to Phase 1 testing, hosted at venues around the home nations. Phase 1 involves performing a range of different fitness and skill tests linked to the sport.

● Results from Phase 1 tests influence progression onto Phases 2+3 which further assess an athlete's suitability for a sport via medical screening, performance lifestyle workshops and psychological/behavioural assessments.

Answers to Activities

(p.127)

Identify three physical and three psychological qualities you feel are necessary for an individual to develop as an elite performer.

Three physical qualities from:

● High level of ability

● High level of skill

● High level of fitness

● Correct body type/somatotype.

Three psychological qualities from:

● High level of motivation/commitment to training/self-discipline

● High level of self-confidence/high level of self-efficacy

● Ability to control arousal

● Ability to accept feedback

● Mentally tough/high pain tolerance.

(p.130)

Visit www.eis2win.co.uk/pages/Physiology.aspx and identify three ways in which exercise physiology services are improving elite performers at the EIS.

● It can enable advice to be given to athletes/coaches on how their preparation/training is influencing competition performance.

● Work in the lab can help evaluate training as it happens, allowing the athlete and coach to objectively monitor what impact a particular training session has had on the body.

● Physiology can improve an athlete's performance by giving important objective information which can help coaches to adapt training programmes to maximise their desired outcome.

(p.132)

Research British Rowing's Rowability and Indoor Rowing schemes (e.g. via Sport England or British Rowing websites) and identify which groups in society they are particularly aimed at.

- **Rowability:** A new programme aimed at helping more disabled people into rowing.
- **Indoor Rowing:** A scheme introduced to increase the chance to row in gyms and give youngsters a positive first experience of indoor rowing through school games competition formats.

Identify and explain four different elements of the RYA England Talent Programme.

- Developing the existing network of Volvo RYA Champion Clubs which identify and nurture young talented sailors in their early years in the sport.
- Enhancing partnerships with Junior Class Associations to provide junior racing and training programmes and optimal race training environments.
- The creation of 6–10 regional high performance clubs.
- Creation of training squads and support at regional and England national junior level.
- Exposing young talented sailors to appropriate international regatta experience.
- Support to develop the coaches working with young talented sailors.

(p.134)

Identify three features of an EIS Performance Pathway Health Check (PHC).

- The PHC is an important diagnostic tool supporting summer and winter Olympic and Paralympic sports.
- It provides a review of a sport's current systems and practices when supporting the development of potential medal winners in their sport.
- It includes a review of the sport's long-term vision and strategy for elite development.
- It includes a consideration of the coaching and training environments a sport has in place to develop elite performers.

Answers to Practice questions

(p.137)

1 **Which of the following is a national governing body of sport?**

Answer: c) British Cycling

2 **What are the personal qualities necessary for an individual to progress toward elite level sport performance?**

Three from:

- Long term commitment/motivated to achieve/self-discipline
- Mentally tough/determined/prepared for self-sacrifice
- High pain tolerance
- High levels of confidence/self-efficacy
- High levels of natural ability/highly skilled
- High levels of physical fitness

3 **UK Sport plays a key role in co-ordinating Talent ID programmes to help achieve its aim of developing elite performers.**
Identify the characteristics of an effective Talent ID programme.

Four from:

- There is a simplicity of administration and record keeping, evident with clear/appropriate division of roles. Performers can be assessed via a clear database.
- Talent identification monitoring systems are used that are built on good practice and use appropriate tests.

- Well-structured competitive programmes and development squads are provided at various levels appropriate to participants' current level of performance and provide a structured route through to elite level.
- Specialist/high quality training facilities to support progression are provided; testing facilities are of a high standard.
- Funding is allocated to young up-and-coming performers at different stages of their development.
- Talent spotting is undertaken via high quality coaches/high quality talent scouts.
- There is high level provision of support services (e.g. sports scientists, physiotherapists) to support performers during their identification and progression.
- Organisations involved in Talent ID work together (e.g. EIS, UK Sport and NGBs).
- Equality of opportunity is ensured by allowing anyone who feels they meet the initial criteria for a programme to apply to be part of it.

4   **Explain how the structure of the World Class Performance Pathway is supporting the development of elite athletes in the UK.**

Three points for an explanation of the structure of the WCPP and one point for recognition of organisation responsible for it:

- World Class Talent: feeds into the pathway to identify those with potential to progress through the pathway and places them on the development programme involving training and competing.
- World Class Podium Potential: this consists of athletes whose performances have suggested realistic medal-winning capabilities 6–8 years from the podium.
- World Class Podium: this is the top end of the pathway which supports athletes with realistic medal-winning chances at the next Olympic/Paralympic Games (i.e. a maximum of four years from the podium).
- UK Sport is responsible for the WCPP.

5   **Identify the advantages and disadvantages of introducing structured Talent ID programmes in the UK to support the development of elite performers.**

Advantages of Talent ID programmes:

- All potential performers are screened/nothing is left to chance.
- Individuals get directed to a suitable sport linked to their talents.
- The programme of development can be accelerated.
- It makes the best use of funding/resources available.
- It increases the chances of winning medals.
- It helps organisations work together/co-operate.

Disadvantages of Talent ID programmes:

- They may miss late developers.
- They require high levels of funding.
- They require large numbers to be tested to be of use.
- There are no guarantees of success.
- Many sports are in competition for the same talent pool; high profile sports may attract more performers or the best performers.

6   **The Gold Events Series is a 10 year programme running from 2013 to 2023 which aims to attract major sporting events to the UK.**
Discuss the suggestion that hosting major championships will benefit the individual performer and the sport.

Agree

- Increase in the number of home spectators
- Increase chance of success via home performers as a result of boost from home crowd/home field advantage

- Increased familiarity with venue/arena; no need to travel; no need for acclimatisation
- Increased motivation/determination to do well
- Increased social facilitation
- Increased success leads to increased chance of funding (e.g. Lottery/sponsorship)
- Increased potential for engagement in sport, e.g. increased success can lead to increased participation/ increased awareness of a sport; higher profile for a performer
- Positive legacy of top class facilities; facilities of a high standard are developed for future use (e.g. positive legacy of facilities following London 2012 including Olympic Stadium and velodrome, etc)

Disagree

- Increased pressure to succeed/win medals/titles
- May lead to increased doping/deviancy/win at all costs attitude; increased gamesmanship
- Social inhibition may occur
- Financial costs if unsuccessful hosts, e.g. lack of attendance at events/poor ticket sales
- Poorly organised events can have a negative influence when bidding to host future international events

Chapter 6.3 Ethics in sport

Answers to Check your understanding questions

(p.140)

Give three ways in which elite level sports performers fail to adopt the sportsmanship ethic; and identify three ways in which sportsmanship is encouraged and maintained in high level/elite sport.

Three ways sports performers fail to adopt the sportsmanship ethic from:

- By time wasting.
- By cheating/playing unfairly, e.g. diving to win a free kick/penalty in football.
- By deliberately trying to injure an opponent through over-aggressive/violent actions.
- By refusing to shake hands with an opponent before/after a sporting contest.
- By arguing with officials.

Three ways to encourage sportsmanship from:

- Use of national governing body campaigns promoting sportsmanship/fair play (e.g. FA Respect).
- Give awards for Fair Play to encourage it in top-level sport, therefore providing positive role models for youngsters to follow. For example, UEFA Fair Play Awards which include a place in Europe awarded on the basis of fair play/sportsmanship.
- Use of technology to help match officials reach the correct decisions and allow performers to be cited after matches for behaviour which goes against the rules, e.g. a dangerous tackle missed by the referee in rugby.
- Introduction of national governing body rules promoting fair play (e.g. banning high tackles/late tackles, etc.).
- Punish foul play/unsporting behaviour within the sporting event, e.g. officials can sin bin, book or send a player off.
- Punish foul play/unsporting behaviour after the event, e.g. fines/bans imposed by national governing bodies of sport.
- Use of positive role models to promote sportsmanship/fair play.
- Use of rigorous drug testing to try to ensure fairness in sporting contests and catch out the drugs cheats.

(p. 141)

Identify two similarities and two differences between gamesmanship and deviance in sport.

Similarities:

- Both are more evident in professional sport where a win-at-all-costs ethic dominates.
- Both conflict with amateur ethics/sportsmanship.
- Both lower the status of sport/give sport a bad name/create negative role models.

Differences:

- Gamesmanship is pushing the rules to the absolute limit, e.g. sledging an opponent/time wasting; deviance is cheating, e.g. taking illegal performance-enhancing drugs/match fixing.
- Gamesmanship is increasingly coached whereas deviance is usually not.

(p.142)

The Lombardian ethic is a dominant sporting ethic in twenty-first century elite sport. How is such a 'win at all costs' ethic displayed in sporting contests?

Three from:

- No drawn games, i.e. there is always a winner in basketball, American football, league cup football in England.
- Managers/coaches are fired if unsuccessful.
- Via high amounts of deviance, e.g. violence/over-aggression/doping.
- Via media praise for winners/positive newspaper headlines.
- Via media negativity for losers.

(p.143)

Using examples, explain the terms positive and negative deviance.

Positive deviance: behaviour which is outside the norms of society but with no intent to harm or break the rules. It involves over-adherence to the norms/expectations of society. For example:

- Competing when injured
- Training when injured
- Unintentionally injuring an opponent when striving to win (within the rules/etiquette of a sport).

Negative deviance: behaviour that goes against the norms and has a detrimental effect on individuals and society in general. For example:

- Taking drugs
- Violent/over-aggressive actions deliberately harming an opponent
- Match fixing
- Diving to win a free kick/penalty.

Answers to Activities

(p.139)

Research further the examples of sports performers breaking or stretching the Olympic oath to the limit, and identify why this might lead some to suggest that such an oath is irrelevant in the modern-day Olympics:

a) **Ben Johnson at the 1988 Seoul Olympics**

b) **Philip Hindes at London 2012.**

The Olympic oath has been stretched to the limit by the following and/or is of less relevance today because:

a) Ben Johnson: positive drugs test therefore against the oath.

b) Philip Hindes: linked to a potential 'cheating scandal' when he claimed that he deliberately fell from his bike to get a restart to improve the chance to win gold.

(p.141)

Identify three different examples of gamesmanship in:

a) Football

b) Cricket.

In football:

- Time wasting, e.g. taking the ball to the corner when winning in last few minutes of a game; taking a restart very slowly when ahead in a game.
- Delaying a restart to get set up defensively.
- Over appealing to officials to pressure them to make decisions in your favour, e.g. give a penalty after a number of appeals.

In cricket:

- Over appealing to pressure an umpire to give a batsman out.
- Sledging an opponent to upset their concentration and play a shot which gets them out.
- Taking a toilet break as a fast bowler to quickly refresh/refuel and return to the field in a better physical state to bowl later in the innings.

(p.143)

Identify two examples of positive deviance and two examples of negative deviance.

Positive deviance examples:

- Competing when injured.
- Training when injured.
- Unintentionally injuring an opponent when striving to win (within the rules/etiquette of a sport).

Negative deviance examples:

- Drug taking
- Violent/over-aggressive actions deliberately harming an opponent
- Match fixing
- Diving to win a free kick/penalty

Answers to Practice questions

(p.143)

1 **Which of the following statements best describes an example of gamesmanship?**

Answer: c) Time wasting at the end of a game.

2 **Using examples, explain the difference between sportsmanship and gamesmanship.**

- *Sportsmanship* = Fair play/playing by the unwritten rules/code of ethics.
- Example, give ball back if opponents kicked ball out of play due to injury to one of your team; shaking hands at start of a game/end of a game.
- *Gamesmanship* = Stretch the rules to the absolute limit
- Example, time wasting/sledging/injury time outs.

3 **The development of professionalism has led to a 'win-at-all-costs attitude' being the dominant ethic in twenty-first century sport.**
Discuss the view that sportsmanship has declined over the last century or so.

- 'Sportsmanship' links to fair play ethics of sports participation.
- In late nineteenth-century Britain, sport was run by middle and upper classes.
- Middle/upper classes were the elite performers of the late nineteenth century.
- Middle/upper classes adhered to the 'amateur code' playing sport 'for the love of it'.
- 'Amateurism' was based on the concept of athleticism.
- Athleticism = physical endeavour with moral integrity.

Agree:

- Sportsmanship has declined over last hundred years or so.
- 'Professionalism' developed in working classes during the twentieth century with participation motivated by 'extrinsic' rewards (i.e. money!).
- The twentieth into the twenty-first centuries have seen increased pressure to win from fans/media (etc.); to gain extrinsic rewards on offer.
- Led to Lombardian ethic more in evidence (win at all costs).
- Led also to increased 'gamesmanship' (i.e., stretching the rules to their absolute limit).
- Examples of evidence of decline in sportsmanship as a result of increased drug taking; performer violence; cheating; abusive language/arguing with officials; match fixing.

Disagree:

- Ethics of sportsmanship are still evident in modern-day twenty-first century sport.
- Sport still operates with officials enforcing rules/decisions being accepted in the main.
- Sportsmanship is still promoted and encouraged (e.g. via the Olympic ideal/Fair Play Awards).
- Positive sporting ethics are still promoted within school PE programmes.
- Modern-day sports performers are 'role models' and understand their responsibilities to act 'responsibly'
- Sports performers are aware of importance of maintaining a positive image to retain commercial deals.

4   **Give reasons why an elite performer may display behaviour which is deemed unacceptable by coaches, managers and officials.**

- Pressures from sponsors to continue succeeding
- Financial rewards
- Fear of losing (e.g. job/contract)
- Retaliation (e.g. performer tackle/crowd jeer)
- Poor decision by official
- Win-at-all-costs ethic.

5   **Outline strategies sporting authorities such as national governing bodies could use to encourage higher standards of individual performer behaviour.**

- Booking/sending off (on field)
- Fine/ban (off field)
- Club fine/points deducted
- Code of conduct for players
- Improve officiating via use of technology
- Cite player after game for foul play
- Fair Play Awards and campaigns.

Chapter 6.4 Violence in sport

Answers to Check your understanding questions

(p.145)

Suggest three possible reasons why a performer becomes violent during a sporting contest.

- Win-at-all-costs ethic/pressure to win/high financial rewards at stake/job at stake.
- Retaliation against an opponent/crowd.

- Frustration with officiating.
- Importance of event, e.g. local derby/local rivalry/pre-match hype/over-psyched.
- Nature of game – violence is part of it, e.g. ice hockey.
- Lack of effective deterrents.

(p.147)

Outline the possible causes of spectator violence such as football hooliganism.

Seven different causes from:

- Emotional intensity/ritual importance of the event, e.g. a local derby; team loyalty taken to extremes.
- Too much alcohol/the 'highs' caused by drug taking.
- Pre-match media hype stirring up tensions between rival fans.
- Poor policing/stewarding/poor crowd control (e.g. this was one of the key reasons identified for the Hillsborough Stadium disaster in 1989).
- Lack of effective deterrents/punishments to deter individuals from involving themselves in violence at football matches.
- Diminished responsibility by individuals in a large group (i.e. a football crowd); organised violence as part of a gang/peer pressure to get involved in violence.
- Reaction of working class to middle class taking over 'their' game.
- Poor officiating or frustration with match officials can heighten tensions between rival fans.
- Violence by players on the pitch is reflected in the crowd.
- Religious discord, e.g. at a Celtic versus Rangers match, tensions are particularly high between rival fans.
- A negative violent reaction may result in chants/taunts by rival fans.
- Frustration at one's own team losing can lead some in the crowd to become violent.
- Violence is sometimes used by young males as a display of their masculinity caused by an adrenaline rush when attending a match.

(p.149)

Identify three negative effects of hooliganism for law-abiding football fans.

- Fan violence can lead to poor treatment of legitimate fans/supporters.
- Fans are 'herded' through the streets to reach the stadium and after the game, to take transport home.
- All fans following a particular team are treated with suspicion and distrust.
- All fans of a particular team are banned from certain matches/for a certain time period as a result of the violent/negative actions of individuals following their club.

Explain the negative implications of hooliganism for the sport of football.

Three from:

- Negative image of sport causes decline in participation rates/smaller foundation base.
- Spectator attendance declines.
- Supporters banned from travelling/attending matches, or matches are played behind closed doors.
- All supporters treated as hooligans.
- Teams banned from competing/loss of points/fined.
- Sponsors/commercial deals withdrawn.
- Additional costs to police events/provide more stewards.
- Relationship with other countries declines/negative impact for hosting future events.

Answers to Activities

(p.146)

Research and identify three ways in which the sport of rugby (i.e. League or Union) has tried to reduce the number of violent acts during matches.

- Use of TMO (i.e. video technology used by additional off-field officials to review decisions and help on-field match officials reach the correct decision).
- Use of 'on-report' system to put violent/aggressive acts under the microscope of video review by a panel of officials after the games.
- Tough punishments for offenders, e.g. long bans/heavy fines for violent acts.
- Promotion of fair play/positive role models to promote fair play.

(p.147)

Try to reduce the number of different causes of football hooliganism outlined above by grouping them into five separate headings, with examples of each. For example, under the heading 'Emotions': these can be stirred up by the importance of the game; heightened by alcohol or drugs; increased by media hype before matches.

Possible groupings as causes of hooliganism:

- **Emotions:** emotional intensity, e.g. derby game
- **Poor security:** poor policing/poor stewarding
- **Frustration:** with officials/team is losing
- **Negative reaction:** to provocative taunts from rival supporters
- **Lack of deterrents:** punishments are minimal and do not necessarily fit the crime

(p.148)

Research the Taylor Report via its summary document and identify three of its recommendations for improving crowd control and decreasing football hooliganism.

- Football grounds in the top leagues to be made all-seater.
- Alcohol: sales to be controlled more (e.g. within football grounds).
- Perimeter fences to be removed.

Answers to Practice questions

(p.149)

1 **Which of the following is a technological aid or innovation that can be used in a sport to help try to decrease performer violence in that sport?**

Answer: c) Use of a television match official (TMO) in Rugby League

2 **Outline strategies sporting authorities such as national governing bodies could use to encourage higher standards of individual performer behaviour.**

Four from:

- Booking/sending off (on field)
- Fine/ban (off field)
- Club fine/points deducted
- Code of conduct for players
- Improve officiating via use of technology
- Cite player after game for foul play
- Fair Play Awards/campaigns
- Use of the law.

3   Identify the possible solutions to violent behaviour among spectators in high level sports such as football.

   Four from:

   ● Kick-off times imposed by police.
   ● Control of alcohol sales; pubs banned from opening prior to kick-off.
   ● Introduction of all-seater stadia.
   ● Tougher deterrents/prosecution of violent individuals.
   ● Specific laws passed, e.g. against trespass on pitch.
   ● Violent individuals banned from grounds/travel abroad.
   ● Increased security at events/increased policing/police 'intelligence'/crowd segregation/family-friendly areas.
   ● Use of CCTV to monitor fan/spectator behaviour.
   ● More responsible media reporting prior to matches.

4   While hooliganism has declined since the 1970s and 1980s, clashes between rival fans at Euro 2016 in France illustrate the fact that it has not been completely eliminated.
   Discuss how football clubs, the community and the players themselves can work together to keep spectator violence at football matches down to a minimum.

   ● Tighter club control of ticket sales/all ticket matches
   ● Increased investment by the club in security measures before/during and after matches, e.g. via CCTV/increased policing/increased stewarding/fan segregation
   ● Club bans alcohol/denies access to drunken fans
   ● Harsher punishments by the club for violent/abusive behavior, e.g. banning orders
   ● Creation of family enclosures/all-seater stadia to decrease potential spectator tensions
   ● Players during matches can display positive behaviour/sportsmanship/not incite crowds (e.g. via inappropriate gestures)
   ● Players and club officials prior to/after games do not make any inflammatory statements which might incite trouble among fans
   ● Players/club/community all condemn any acts of violence among fans
   ● Increase links between clubs and communities to promote social inclusion; increase club activities within the community
   ● Community informs the club of any potential/known troublemakers/report incidents observed
   ● Clubs can educate fans about the negative implications of hooliganism (e.g. potential damage to property/health of an individual; potential fines/bans for clubs, etc.)

Chapter 6.5 Drugs in sport

Answers to Check your understanding questions

(p.151)

Identify three social and three psychological reasons why elite performers continue to take illegal performance-enhancing drugs despite obvious dangers to their health.

Social reasons:

● A win-at-all-costs attitude which dominates modern-day elite sport.
● The fame and fortune attached to success at elite level (i.e. the very high level of extrinsic rewards/money received for sporting success via prize money, sponsorship deals and so on).
● The high levels of pressure to win from a variety of different sources such as coaches, family and media expectations (e.g. coaches might persuade athletes to take drugs illegally because their main competitors already do, and they won't be able to compete with them on a level playing field if they don't).
● The lack of effective deterrents and firm belief that they will get away with it and not get caught.
● Poor role models set a bad example that drug taking in sport or certain sports is viewed in some way as being acceptable (e.g. athletics, cycling etc.).

Psychological reasons:

- To steady nerves/decrease anxiety.
- To increase aggression.
- To increase confidence/self-belief.

(p.152)

Some performers break the rules and use banned substances to enhance their performance. Identify the physiological reasons why a performer may use

a) Beta-blockers, or

b) EPO to aid performance.

Three different reasons for using beta-blockers:

- Due to their ability to counteract adrenaline that interferes with performance by binding to nerve receptors.
- By keeping heart rate low.
- Decreases trembling in the hands.
- Increases blood flow through the arteries.
- Decreases muscle spasms.

Three different reasons for using EPO:

- Stimulates red blood cell production.
- Increases endurance; performer can keep going for longer.
- Delays onset of fatigue.
- Aids recovery from training.

(p.153)

Explain the advantages of all sports in all countries testing for performance-enhancing drugs.

Three advantages from:

- Uphold the traditions of sport/sporting ethics/all competitors are equal.
- Standard list of banned substances/same testing procedures/similar punishments.
- Random tests are more effective.
- Shared costs between all sports.
- Performers are not able to 'pick and choose' sports based on drug testing procedures.

Answers to Activities

(p.153)

Visit https://elb.wada-ama.org and identify three key elements of the World Anti-Doping Code.

- Document aiming to bring consistency/harmonise anti-doping rules/regulations in all sports/in all countries.
- It includes a list of prohibited substances and methods that sports performers are not allowed to take or use.
- It accredits the laboratories which are able to perform the scientific analysis for doping control.

Visit www.ukad.org.uk/athletes and identify three ways in which the 100% Me programme is promoting ethically fair, drug-free sport.

- Helps athletes through their sporting journey throughout their careers by providing anti-doping advice and guidance.
- Encourages athletes to succeed cleanly as a result of their own efforts, hard work, determination and talent.
- Provides a guide to athletes to ensure they are clean and stay clean.
- Provides interactive workshops, webinars and a support helpline to help athletes stay clean.

Answers to Practice questions

(p.155)

1 Which of the following is a key psychological reason why an elite performer takes drugs in order to improve their chances of success?

Answer: b) Increased confidence

2 Elite athletes continue to take performance-enhancing drugs despite obvious risks to their health and the negative implications of being caught. Give reasons why drug taking continues at elite sporting events such as the Olympics.

- Physiological benefits (e.g. increased power/endurance)
- Psychological benefits (e.g. increased aggression/confidence)
- Win-at-all-costs attitude
- Financial rewards/fame
- Pressure from coaches/peers/media – to win
- Levels playing field (others doing it, can't win if don't)
- Belief – won't get caught/effective masking agents)
- Poor punishments/lack of effective deterrents

3 Describe the physiological reasons why an elite performer might use anabolic steroids just like any other training aid.

Three from:

- Aid in the assimilation/storage of protein.
- Decrease in fat in the muscles.
- Increased ability to train for longer and train at a higher intensity.
- Increased ability to train more frequently/have a faster recovery time due to quicker repair of the muscles.
- Increase in muscle size/muscle mass/strength.

4 Outline the strategies being used by sports organisations to try to decrease the use of drugs by elite performers.

Four from:

- **Testing:** random testing/out-of-competition testing/'whereabouts' system.
- **Education/anti-doping culture:** education programmes for athletes/coaches; create a strong anti-doping culture/promote ethically fair, drug-free sport (e.g. 100% Me).
- **Co-ordination:** improve co-ordination between organisations involved in drug detection (e.g. WADA, UKAD, NGBs).
- **Punishment:** harsher punishments (e.g. life bans/return of medals or career earnings/loss of sponsorship deals).
- **Investment in technology:** increased investment/funding into new testing programmes/new technology.
- **Role models:** promote successes of positive role models; name and shame drugs cheats.

5 Explain the problems which are being faced by drug enforcement agencies in the world of sport (e.g. WADA/UK Anti-Doping) in their fight to eliminate performance-enhancing drugs at the elite performer level.

- Difficulty in keeping testing procedures/practices up to date; cheaters always try to keep one step ahead of the testers (e.g. via developing new drugs/masking agents to avoid detection)
- Difficulty sometimes in classifying which drugs are illegal and which are acceptable to use for medical reasons
- Sometimes sponsors continue to support athletes despite positive drugs tests resulting in bans; athletes continue to take drugs as motivated by high financial rewards available for success achieved as a result of taking them
- There is a battle which is hard to win against the illegal support/encouragement to take PEDs, e.g. via coaches/fellow competitor/and even via the state/Government as in the case of Russia

- Different countries/sports have different policies/procedures for testing/punishments linked to PEDs
- Difficulty in issuing an appropriate ban/'clean' athletes may be 'unfairly' banned, e.g. Russian athletes in Rio 2016
- Very high costs are associated with drug testing both financially and time-wise
- Legal challenges sometimes challenge positive results/bans (e.g. appeals of various Russian athletes to Court of Arbitration of Sport to compete in Rio)
- Difficulty in gaining access to athletes to administer tests/out of competition testing is sometimes difficult to administer

Chapter 6.6 Sport and the law

Answers to Check your understanding questions

(p.157)

Identify the reasons why sports performers may need protection from the law during their careers.

Three from:

- Protection vs foul play/violent acts of opponents (leading to compensation claims).
- Protection from fans/violent spectators during a game.
- Protection from contractual issues with employers.
- Protection from contractual issues with sponsors/commercial deals.
- Protection from issues linked to equality of opportunity (e.g. racism from fans/opponents).
- Appeals vs NGB decisions/disciplinary issues.
- Protection vs negligence of poor referees.

(p.158)

Define the term 'negligence' and give an example of how a sporting official might be deemed to be negligent in the execution of their duties.

Negligence is a failure in the duty of care to a player (e.g. enforcing rules properly).

Examples of negligence linked to rugby officials:

- Repeatedly allowing dangerous incidents to occur (e.g. scrum collapses).
- Failure to follow national governing body rules/guidelines in relation to safe procedures/practice.
- Failure in duty of care to a player (e.g. enforcing rules properly).

(p.161)

Identify the three offences banned at football matches included in the Football Offences Act (1991).

The Football Offences Act (1991) created three offences at football grounds, which prevented:

- throwing of missiles
- chanting of racist remarks
- trespassing onto the field of play.

Answers to Activities

(p.156)

Research and identify two examples of professional footballers who have successfully claimed damages for career-ending tackles on the field of play.

- Chris Casper suffered a career-ending double leg fracture when playing for Reading vs Cardiff. Casper secured out-of-court damages for the tackle from the player (Richard Carpenter) and his club, Cardiff. The damages related to past and future loss of earnings and the pain suffered.
- Matt Holmes received £250,000 damages at the High Court for a tackle by Kevin Muscat which ended his career.

(p.159)

Using the information above and using www.bowlschildprotect.co.uk/Duty_of_Care.html, identify four steps a sports coach should consider in order to demonstrate a reasonable standard in terms of a legal duty of care to children and young people.

Four from:

- Keeping up-to-date contact details/medical details/registers of attendance.
- Maintaining appropriate supervision ratios.
- Ensuring that appropriate first aid provision is available at the club.
- Ensuring that individuals regularly involved in coaching children have a current DBS clearance.
- Ensuring an appropriate risk assessment has been undertaken for the activities being coached.

(p.161)

Explain three key ways in which the various pieces of legislation identified have helped control and improve crowd behaviour and safety at football matches.

- Placed a legal responsibility on clubs with a duty of care to provide a safe spectator environment (e.g. prevention of over-crowding).
- Controlled who can attend matches by placing banning orders on certain known trouble makers.
- Controlled rival fans chanting racist remarks at each other/players.
- Controlled alcohol sales/alcohol consumption prior to and at football matches.

Answers to Practice questions

(p.161)

1   Which of the following is an example of a sports coach ensuring they fulfil their 'duty of care'?

Answer: d) Coaching netball on a dry, clean sports hall surface

2   Identify the potential benefits of the law becoming more closely linked to the world of sport.

- Increased protection for those involved; for example:
  - increased spectator safety (e.g. via all-seater stadia)
  - increased performer safety (e.g. via legal actions against players and fans for assault causing actual bodily harm)
  - against officials/coaches failing in their duty of care and being prosecuted for negligence.
- Anti-discriminatory (e.g. on the basis of racial issues).

3   Explain how the law aims to protect spectators from hooliganism at football matches.

- Games played at specified kick-off times imposed by the police (e.g. early kick-offs at local derby matches).
- Control of alcohol consumption/alcohol sales in and around grounds prior to and during matches.
- Removal of perimeter fencing and terraces leading to all-seater stadia which meet health and safety requirements (e.g. of local authorities).
- Tougher deterrents; prosecution of violent/racist individuals; banning orders from grounds at home and abroad.
- It has made trespass onto the field of play illegal.
- Use of CCTV/increased security at matches via increased policing/stewarding.
- Use of shared intelligence between police forces at home and abroad.
- Control of ticket sales/prosecution of ticket touts.

Chapter 6.7 Impact of commercialisation on physical activity and sport and the relationship between sport and the media

Answers to Check your understanding questions

(p.163)

Discuss the relationship between sport, sponsorship and the media.

Four discussion points from:

- The media uses sport to gain viewers/readers.
- The media is itself used by businesses/sponsors for advertising purposes, promoting the company name and the products it sells.
- Businesses/sponsors pay the media for advertising time and space on TV, online, on the radio and in the newspapers.
- They also pay large amounts to sports/sports performers to act for them as an advertising medium to sell more of their goods.
- Sports are aware that they need to appear in the media to attract sponsorship, increase their profile and appeal to a wide audience.
- Sports need to be more professionally managed as a result of the increasingly commercialised nature of sport.

(p.164)

State three reasons why certain sporting events should continue to be 'ring-fenced'.

Three from:

- To access the widest number/widest range of viewers to watch the event.
- To avoid restricting coverage to subscription channels available only to those who can afford them.
- To increase geographical access to all viewers in all parts of the country to major sporting events.
- To enable viewing of certain events which are seen as part of our sporting heritage/sporting culture.
- To enable access to sporting events which should be freely available to all to view (e.g. Olympic Games, Football World Cup, etc.).

(p.165)

Identify three possible disadvantages of media coverage for a sport.

Three from:

- National governing bodies/sports performers lose control to TV sponsors; the traditional nature of a sport is lost; e.g. rule structures/timings of a sport are adapted to suit the demands of TV/sponsors.
- The media controls the location of events, as well as kick-off times and, in some cases, playing seasons (e.g. Super League Rugby switch to a 'summer' game). There is sometimes too much sport on TV which can lead to possible boredom of spectators and/or lower attendance at events which are on TV.
- There are inequalities of coverage – more popular sports (e.g. football) gain at the expense of minority sports (e.g. squash). Certain prestigious events are now available only on satellite TV which requires a subscription payment, e.g. Test cricket, Ryder Cup golf, etc. This means there are fewer viewers for some sports due to the increasing control of SKY/BT Sport.
- Demands of media/sponsors negatively impact on high level performers (e.g. demands for interviews/personal appearances, etc.).
- The media can sometimes over-sensationalise or over-dramatise certain negative events in sport. A win-at-all-costs attitude develops due to high rewards on offer which leads to negative, deviant acts and players becoming negative role models (e.g. in football, arguing with officials, diving to cheat and try to win a penalty, etc.).
- More breaks in play (e.g. for adverts) can disrupt the spectator experience.

(p.166)

Identify three characteristics of commercial sport.

Three from:

- It has extensive media coverage.
- It gains large audiences/viewing figures/high level of ticket sales.

- It links to professional sport.
- Players are contracted to perform/endorse products.
- Extensive advertising/merchandising/sponsorship deals are evident.
- Winning is important as it creates a linkage with success.
- The sport is media friendly/entertaining.

(p.167)

Discuss the impact of sponsorship deals on the behaviour of elite sport performers.

A discussion of the positive and negative impact of sponsorship on elite performer behaviour.

Positive impact:

- Train harder to produce higher quality performances.
- Increased need to maintain discipline to protect the positive image that sponsors require.
- Increased need to display sportsmanship/fair play on the field of play.
- Increased need to develop good image off the field of play (e.g. community/charity work).

Negative impact:

- Increased pressure to win/win-at-all-costs attitude.
- Increased deviancy/temptation to cheat, e.g. drugs/increased use of gamesmanship/over-aggression.
- Negative off-field behaviour, e.g. drinking/gambling.
- Increased pressure to compete when injured/overtraining.
- Increased control of sponsors which negatively impacts on performance.

(p.171)

Explain how the increased level of media coverage of sport and sporting events has positively affected the audience.

Four from:

1 Improved quality of facilities; bigger, higher quality stadiums result from increased investment.
2 Improved viewing experience via innovations such as changes in ball colour, creation of team merchandise to create team loyalty.
3 Increased access to watch sport; more opportunities to watch events live via more competitions/more events/more matches taking place.
4 More variations of a sport format develop which provide alternative viewing experiences.
5 More funding is available to provide entertainment (e.g. cheer leaders/pop stars) at sports events.
6 Rule changes introduced provide extra interest and extra excitement for the spectator (e.g. Twenty20 cricket).
7 Increased funding for improved technology at a ground (e.g. video screens) and at home (e.g. interactive technology/HD coverage of sport/referee link).
8 Increased excitement in the audience while awaiting the decisions of off-field officials (e.g. Hawkeye in tennis).
9 Increased awareness of/knowledge of sport; creation of role models for fans to idolise.
10 Increased elimination of negative aspects of sport (e.g. hooliganism).
11 Increased performance standards; players are of a higher standard and provide a high level of excitement and entertainment.

Answers to Activities

(p.164)

Research and identify three sporting events which are ring-fenced for all to view on free-to-access terrestrial TV.

Three examples of 'listed/ring fenced' events from 2009 including:

- FIFA World Cup football finals
- FA Cup final
- Rugby Union World Cup
- Wimbledon tennis championships
- Summer Olympics (multi-sport event).

(p.165)

Research and identify three different ways in which cricket has changed and adapted to make it more attractive to TV coverage.

Three from:

- Twenty20 cricket format creates lots of exciting/high scoring/wicket-taking action.
- Twenty20 format creates an improved visual spectacle with use of coloured clothing/white ball, etc.
- Twenty20 format is relatively easy to understand.
- Twenty20 format fits into relatively short time periods of 20 overs a side.
- Twenty20 format tends to be played early evenings/weekends to maximise audiences/viewing figures.

(p.167)

Using the examples above, or sports performers known to you, identify key characteristics which make a sports performer marketable in the modern sporting world.

Three from:

- Looks good/attractive to the public
- Appeals to a wide-ranging audience/the sport is popular/belongs to a high status club
- Highly talented/skilled
- Consistent/high level performance
- Offers an image reflecting a product
- Positive role model/good sporting image.

Answers to Practice questions

(p.172)

1 **Which of the following statements is a disadvantage of increased media coverage to an official?**

Answer: c) Increased pressure to get decisions right

2 **Discuss the impact of the 'golden triangle' on elite sport.**

There are a number of *advantages/positives* to elite sport of the golden triangle, including the following:

- Increased income to the sport for allowing events to be televised. This can be spent at all levels of the sport, funding participation initiatives at grassroots level, as well as providing finance to support elite athletes at the top of their profession so they can devote themselves full time to sport.
- Increased promotion of the sport to gain more fans and increase its popularity.
- Increased sponsorship/income from business sources to pay for advertising at grounds/sporting events.
- Sports are organised and funded better to improve the way they are run (i.e. in a more professional manner).
- Improved facilities benefit performer and spectator alike.

However, there are also a number of possible *disadvantages/negatives* to elite sport resulting from their links to the media and sponsorship. These include the following:

- Possibility of sensationalist media reporting which focuses too much on negative aspects of a sport.
- The media/sponsors can dictate kick-off times/scheduling of sports events to the detriment of performers/fans.
- The media/sponsors can change the nature of a sporting activity (e.g. introducing more/longer breaks in play to allow for advertising).

- The media/sponsors only televise/focus on already popular, high-profile sports.
- Sponsors/the media can be too demanding on elite performer/coaches (e.g. in relation to personal appearances and giving interviews).
- Sponsorship deals can increase the pressure to win to maintain lucrative contracts with companies willing to pay for an association with successful sports/sports performers.

3 **Define the term 'sponsorship' and identify how companies benefit from their involvement in sport.**

Sponsorship: The provision of funds, money, support for a commercial return.

- Via increased sales/promotion of a product.
- Increased brand awareness and improved company image linked to the healthy image of sport.
- By providing the opportunity for corporate hospitality.
- By decreasing the amount of tax a company pays as sponsorship is tax deductible.

4 **Discuss whether an elite performer should consider the nature of a sponsor before accepting a sponsorship deal.**

There are a number of possible reasons why an elite performer *should* consider the nature of a potential sponsor before deciding whether or not to accept a deal.

- As elite performers, they are role models and strongly influence the behaviour of others, so sponsorship from a junk food company or product association with alcohol might not be considered as appropriate.
- Such products do not reflect the nature of sport which is more about health and fitness.
- Performers have a social duty to others and need to carefully consider the ethical nature of any sponsorship deal.
- To ensure it does not negatively affect their reputation and potentially endanger future commercial support (e.g. sportswear companies who are accused of the unethical manufacturing of goods might require careful consideration before a decision is reached on a potential deal).
- Elite performers need to look at the level of control a sponsor is potentially exerting on them before deciding whether or not to accept a sponsorship deal (e.g. what are their demands for personal appearances, filming of commercials and so on?).

Possible counter-arguments which can be used to explain why elite performers *should not* have to consider the nature of a potential sponsor before deciding whether or not to accept a deal:

- If a product is legal, elite performers have a right to accept a sponsorship deal if they so wish.
- It is unfair to expect elite performers to engage in a protest or statement when there are financial considerations at stake and their livelihood is at risk.
- Performers do not ask to be role models so they should be able to accept a sponsorship deal if they choose to do so.
- Indeed, they could argue that if they do not accept the sponsorship deal on offer, someone else will!

Chapter 6.8 The role of technology in physical activity and sport

Answers to Check your understanding questions

(p.174)

Define what is meant by sports analytics.

The analysis of sports data using analytical tools and methods; data to be subjected to analytical procedures in order to try to improve results.

(p.177)

Identify three potential problems a sports coach might have if they choose not to use video analysis programs, but rely instead on their own observation and analysis skills.

- Issues with memory retention of the performance observed.
- May lead to incorrect decisions during matches/competitions, e.g. when making substitutions.
- May lead to incorrect training programmes being implemented.

(p.178)

Imagine you are a basketball coach and you have the following shooting data available on your main two offensive players. This information can be used to help feed back to the players concerned, as well as inform future shooting strategies.

1   Use the data below to explain which player (i.e. Player 1 or Player 2) has been the most successful at shooting.

2   What other additional information would you need to consider when making your judgement on the relative shooting capabilities of Player 1 and Player 2?

3   How could you use the data to inform your offensive players' shooting strategies in their next match?

Basketball shooting data

	No. of lay-ups attempted	No. of lay-ups scored	No. of set shots in key attempted	No. of set shots in key scored	No. of 3-point shooting attempts	No. of successful 3-point shots
Player 1	5	5	4	3	4	1
Player 2	5	4	5	3	4	1

1   Player 1 has been the most successful at shooting with lay-ups (100 per cent success rate compared to 80 per cent for Player 2), set shots in the key (75 per cent success rate compared to 60 per cent for Player 2). But they were both the same at 25 per cent for 3-point shots.

2   Considerations would include the amount of pressure from opponents when executing the shot; the angle/actual relative distances of shots; the game situation when shots were attempted – did this add to the pressure when taking the shot?

3   Strategies would include trying to feed Player 1 into the basket for lay-ups and into the key way for set shots whenever possible; also try to avoid taking 3-point shots unless game context requires it and the team is a long way behind, as the relative success of 3-pointers was very low, at 25 per cent for both players.

(p.179)

Identify different reasons for individual variations in an individual's REE over a period of time.

- Due to overall weight/obesity.
- Due to height; height/weight ratio.
- Due to chemistry of body in response to various drugs.
- Due to illnesses.

(p.180)

Identify four different ways in which GPS data can help to improve player performance.

- It helps to monitor player performance overall (e.g. is it 'as expected'?).
- It can measure impact, e.g. G-forces.
- It can help make objective decisions about substitutions.
- It can decrease injury risk by gauging levels of fatigue.
- It can help manage workload during rehabilitation, and ultimately get the player through it successfully at a faster rate.
- It can help make better use of training time and ensure training meets game demands.
- It improves tactical analysis.
- It enables player comparisons.

(p.181)

Identify three ways to ensure data integrity is maintained.

Three from:

- Regularly backing up data.
- Controlling access to data and protecting against malicious intent via security mechanisms.
- Designing interfaces which prevent the input of invalid data; taking care when entering data.
- Using error detection and correction software when transmitting data.
- Not switching on, logging on to and then leaving a computer unattended for anyone to access.

(p.182)

Identify three possible benefits to health of using vibration therapy technology.

Three from:

- Improving bone density.
- Increasing muscle mass/increased muscle power.
- Improving circulation.
- Reducing joint pain.
- Reducing back pain.
- Alleviating stress.
- Boosting metabolism.
- An overall reduction in pain/delayed onset of muscle soreness (DOMS).
- Maintenance of cartilage integrity where weight-bearing activities are difficult to undertake.

(p.186)

Discuss the benefits to sport of technological developments in artificial surfaces.

- They can be played on more frequently (e.g. matches/training).
- They give consistent conditions.
- They enable fixtures to be played without disruption.
- They have had a very positive impact on certain sports, e.g. hockey.

Negatives of artificial surfaces include:

- They have an unnatural bounce which is difficult for performers to judge (e.g. footballers).
- Their rigidity can lead to injuries (e.g. to joints/ligaments and tendons).

(p.188)

Identify three benefits of wearing compression clothing for athletes.

Three from:

- Optimised muscle temperature decreases the risk of injury.
- Decreased pain from muscle stiffness/soreness/decreased muscle vibration/decreased DOMS.
- Decreased time for muscle repair.
- Potential for increased venous return and oxygen delivery to working muscles/it enhances recovery.

(p.189)

Identify three potential negative impacts of technology for sports performers.

There are a number of potential negative effects of technology for the sports performer including the following.

Three from:

- It can lead to injury or over-aggression; e.g. from bladed boots; or due to the use of protective equipment which makes some performers feel 'invincible'/less inhibited.
- It can lead to cheating as drugs are taken by athletes who believe they will get away with it (e.g. via taking effective masking agents or taking a newly developed performance-enhancing substance for which there is no test).
- It can be expensive and unaffordable to some, which leads to potential inequalities and unfair advantages if the technology is not available to all.
- The availability of technological advancements aiding performance might be dependent on an individual/team sponsor which might positively/negatively impact on the chances of success.

(p.190)

Identify three ways in which broadcasting technology has positively impacted on the audience in sport.

Three from:

- Developments in high quality sound and picture technology which gives users an impressive view of the sport.
- The introduction of digital TV allows for highly individualised experiences. Viewers can choose the way they experience sport, e.g. by selecting camera angles, watching more than one match at a time on a split screen.
- In many ways the inclusion of expert commentary and close-up visuals can be said to give the TV audience a heightened experience of sport.
- Action replays and freeze-frames allow increasingly detailed analysis of key incidents to take place which informs and educates the viewing public.

Answers to Activities

(p.175)

A netball coach tries out two different players in the position of Centre in pre-season matches, with a view to selecting one of them to start the first competitive league game of the season. They both play two out of the four pre-season games against similar levels of opposition. Give examples of valid, objective data which is quantitative in nature that you would advise the netball coach to collect to help inform them when making their decision.

- Number of passes attempted; number of successful passes completed (i.e. ratio/percentage success rate).
- Number of successful centre passes at game restarts.
- Number of passes to team-mate in the circle; number of successful passes into the circle (i.e. ratio/percentage success rate).
- Number of pass interceptions achieved.
- Total distance covered (in km).

(p.176)

To help understand the basis of reliability of information received, think about standing on a set of weighing scales which should be well maintained to ensure meaningful data is obtained.

When would the scales be considered

a) **reliable**

b) **unreliable?**

a) *Reliable*: when the same/similar weight readings are received every time you step on the scales (when weight levels are stable!).

b) *Unreliable*: when very different weight readings are received every time the scales are used, regardless of whether or not weight has been gained/lost!

(p.177)

Visit one of the following links to find out more about PA/motion analysis software used in sport.

- Dartfish: www.dartfish.com
- Upmygame: www.upmygame.com
- Prozone: www.prozonesports.com

No solutions: visit analysis software internet references.

(p.178)

Choose an invasion game where opponents are in direct competition with one another (e.g. hockey, netball, rugby, football, basketball, etc.) and attempt to design and complete your own simple player analysis. Focus on one player involved in the match and gather data on one aspect of skill or technique (e.g. passing) used in the activity selected.

You can look the number of passes made in a set time period. This can then be expressed as a ratio or percentage of successful passes during the time observed.

No solutions – use own design/solutions.

(p.180)

Think about and write down three pieces of information a rugby coach might receive from a GPS tracking system during training or matches.

- Metres being covered (i.e. overall distances).
- Level of fatigue/amount of effort being made/ effort in attack and defence.
- Technical success rates; monitor performance levels.
- Force being applied into tackles (i.e. G-forces).
- Speed of performers/dynamic acceleration.
- Player heart rate.
- Recovery time of a player.

(p.181)

Research how a smart wearable fitness/sport device can help in performance monitoring and improvement (e.g. Adidas MiCoach; Adidas MiCoach Smart Run or via www.wareable.com/fitness-trackers/the-best-fitness-tracker).

Points on Adidas MiCoach:

Use via players attaching a wearable device to their jerseys, which leads to coaches receiving data on who the top performers are, and who needs rest, via real time individual player stats (e.g. speed/heart rate/acceleration).

Points on Adidas MiCoach Smart Run:

Information from training workouts (e.g. average pace; distance covered; calories burned; steps per minute; height climbed).

It can be set to enable virtual coaches to remind the athlete to speed up/slow down during a run as appropriate to reach their 'ideal' Heart rate.

(p.185)

Research and identify three key differences between wheelchair designs for wheelchair rugby players compared to wheelchair tennis players.

Adaptive equipment examples:

- Wheelchair tennis: highly manoeuvrable/lightweight to enable very fast changes of direction.
- Wheelchair rugby: strong frames; foot protection; wheel covers; increased stability and to protect against injury.

(p.188)

Visit www.pgatour.com/changing-game/2014/09/02/wearable-technology.html and describe a wearable technology which is being used to help golfers monitor and improve performance:

i) **technologically**

ii) **psychologically**

iii) **physically**

i) *Technologically:* e.g. Game Golf or Zepp Golf.
Game Golf is a lightweight GPS and tracking device; it captures accurate shot locations; calculates club performance during a round of golf.
Zepp Golf is a lightweight sensor which attaches to a golf glove and captures, measures and analyses a golfer's swing in three dimensions which they can replay and analyse via side-by-side comparisons.

ii) *Psychologically:* e.g. iFocusBand, a wearable brain training device with three sensors that determine brain activities and help golfers self-regulate emotional stress levels/nerves during a round of golf.

iii) *Physically:* e.g. Fitbit, a wearable device which measures calories burnt, steps completed, and sleep quality. It can also be used to help an individual to sleep better.

Answers to Practice questions

(p.191)

1   **Which of the following is a negative aspect of technology when used to aid officials in their decision making?**

Answer: b) Increased disruption to a sporting event as a result of lots of referee referrals.

2   **Identify two types of adaptive equipment used in the sport of athletics.**

- Wheelchairs for track racing
- Throwing frames for discus/shot put

3   **State the disadvantages to the sporting event of the increased use of technology to help officials in their decision making.**

- Officials using technology can be wrong/over-reliance on technology/loss of respect for official's decision being final.
- Specific technology used must be accurate/have a high level of reliability.
- It changes the nature of the sport.
- Costs limit technology to certain events.
- Breaks in play can be disruptive for performers and fans if they take too long.

4   **Modern technological products are becoming an increasingly important part of modern-day twenty-first century sport.**
Outline the advantages on performance in sport of using such technology.

- Technological developments for officials lead to a correct outcome which leads to fewer disputes/increased player confidence in the right decision being reached.
- Increased performer safety (e.g. cricket helmets).
- Increased performer comfort (e.g. clothing/footwear improvements).
- Increased performer ability/skill/technique development (e.g. body suits in athletics; modern-day footballs/golf club design, etc.).
- Increased analysis of performance (e.g. Dartfish).
- Improvements in training/recovery from training (e.g. compression wear).
- Improved sports surfaces which allow better/more consistent performance/increased usage.
- Improved drug detection.

5   **How have sports spectators benefited from advancements in technology?**

- Increased sense of crowd excitement/involvement (e.g. awaiting decisions via big screen, e.g. Hawkeye).
- Improved experience of watching sport at home (e.g. 3D/HD/split-screen coverage).
- Increased excitement from watching top level performances resulting from technological advancements.
- A wider range of sports are more accessible as a result of media advancements/satellite technologies.

Glossary

3G surfaces: Third-generation artificial synthetic grass pitches.

Acceleration: Measured in m/s² and is the rate of change of velocity.

Achievement motivation: The tendency to approach or avoid competitive situations. Summed up as the Drive to Succeed *minus* the Fear of Failure.

Active stretch: When a stretched position is held by the contraction of an agonist muscle.

Actual behaviour: What the leader decides to do in relation to leadership style.

Acute injury: A sudden injury caused by a specific impact or traumatic event where a sharp pain is felt immediately.

Adenosine triphosphate (ATP): The only usable form of energy in the body.

Altitude training: Usually done at 2500 m+ above sea level where the partial pressure of oxygen is lower.

Amateurism: Participation in sport for the love of it, receiving no financial gain; it is based on the concept of athleticism (i.e. physical endeavour with moral integrity).

Anaerobic: A reaction that can occur without the presence of oxygen.

Angle of attack: The tilt of a projectile relative to the air flow.

Angular acceleration: The rate of change of angular velocity.

Angular displacement: The smallest change in angle between the start and finish point of a rotation.

Angular momentum: Spin.

Angular motion: Movement around a fixed point.

Angular velocity: The rate of change of angular displacement.

Anticipation: Pre-judging a stimulus.

Association: Linking the stored actions of a skill to a stored emotion or other action.

Athleticism: A fanatical devotion to sport involving high levels of physical endeavour and moral integrity.

Attributing success internally: Giving a reason for success that is due to the responsibility of the player.

Attribution retraining: Changing the reasons given for success and failure.

Attribution: A perception of the reason for an outcome of an event.

Autocratic approach: Leader makes the decisions.

BALCO: The 'Bay Area Laboratory Cooperative' which was behind one of the biggest scandals in drugs history as the source of THG, with several athletes implicated and subsequently banned from sport, including sprinters Dwain Chambers and Marion Jones.

Ballistic stretching: Uses swinging and bouncing movements.

Bernoulli principle: Where air molecules exert less pressure the faster they travel and more pressure when they travel slower.

Bosman Ruling: A ruling by the European Court of Justice which gave a professional football player the right to a free transfer at the end of their contract.

Buffering: A process which aids the removal of lactate and maintains acidity levels in the blood and muscle.

Calorimetry: The calculation of heat in physical changes and chemical reactions.

Calorimetry: The measurement of the heat and energy eliminated or stored in any system.

Central executive: The control centre of the working memory model, it uses three other 'systems' to control all the information moving in and out of the memory system.

Characteristics: Key features used to identify a particular concept (e.g. enjoyment in physical recreation or serious about sport).

Chronic injuries: Often referred to as over-use injuries.

Chunking: Breaking the skilled action into parts or sub-routines.

Citing: Players can be cited (i.e. reported and investigated) for dangerous play, whether they are seen by the referee or not.

Cognitive effects of stress: These are psychological.

Commercialisation: The treating of sport as a commodity, involving the buying and selling of assets, with the market as the driving force behind sport.

Competitive orientation: The degree to which a performer is drawn to challenging situations.

Compression clothing: Items such as elasticated leggings, socks or shirts worn to promote recovery by improving circulation. They can decrease the pain suffered from muscle soreness/stiffness and decrease the time for muscle repair.

Confidence: A belief in the ability to master a task.

Continuum: A scale representing gradual change.

Cori cycle: The process where lactic acid is transported in the blood to the liver where it is converted to blood glucose and glycogen.

Coupled reaction: When energy required by one process is supplied by another process.

Cryotherapy: The use of cold temperatures to treat an injury.

Cue utilisation: The ability to process information is directly linked to the level of arousal.

Cycle ergometer: A stationary bike that measures how much work is being performed.

Damages: Individuals seeking legal redress and compensation for loss of earnings must prove that they have suffered an actual injury as the result of the deliberate harmful, reckless actions of an opponent.

Data integrity: Maintaining and ensuring the accuracy and consistency of stored data over its entire lifetime.

Deep vein thrombosis (DVT): A blood clot in one of the deep veins in the body.

Democratic: Decisions are made by group consultation.

Direct gas analysis: Measures the concentration of oxygen that is inspired and the concentration of carbon dioxide that is expired.

Displacement: Measured in metres and is the shortest route in a straight line between the starting and finishing position.

Display: The sporting environment.

Distance: Measured in metres and is the path a body takes as it moves from the starting to the finishing position.

Doping: In competitive sports, doping refers to the use of banned performance-enhancing drugs by athletic competitors.

Drag force: A force that acts in opposition to motion.

Duty of care applied to coaches: This requires coaches to take such measures as are 'reasonable' in the circumstances to ensure that individuals will be safe to participate in an activity.

Duty of care: A legal obligation imposed on someone if they are responsible for a group of people.

ECG: Stands for an electrocardiogram machine where electrodes are placed onto the player's chest and the wires connect to an ECG machine and a printout is produced of the heart's electrical activity.

Effector mechanism: The network of nerves that sends coded impulses to the muscles.

Electron transport chain: Involves a series of chemical reactions in the cristae of the mitochondria where hydrogen is oxidised to water and 34 ATP are produced.

Electrostimulation: The production of muscle contraction using electrical impulses.

Elite: The best, highest level sports performers at 'excellence' level.

Emergent leader: Appointed from within the group.

Emotional arousal: A perception of the effects of anxiety on performance.

Energy continuum: A term which describes the type of respiration used by physical activities. Whether it is aerobic or anaerobic respiration depends on the intensity and duration of the exercise.

Episode buffer: Co-ordinates the sight, hearing and movement information from the working memory into sequences to be sent to the long-term memory.

EPOC (post-exercise oxygen consumption): The amount of oxygen consumed during recovery above that which would have been consumed at rest during the same time.

Erythropoietin (EPO): A hormone which is naturally produced by the kidneys but can also be artificially produced to increase performance in endurance athletes such as long-distance cyclists.

Eustress: A positive response of the body to a threat.

External attribute: Outside the performer's control.

Fascia: A layer of fibrous connective tissue which surrounds the muscle or group of muscles.

Football hooliganism: Unruly, violent and destructive behaviour by over-zealous supporters of association football clubs.

'G' forces: Forces acting on the body as a result of acceleration or gravity (e.g. the G-load/force of an American football 'hit' on an opponent).

Game Golf: A lightweight GPS tracking device which captures accurate shot locations and calculates club performance during a round of golf.

Gamesmanship: Bending the rules and stretching them to their absolute limit without getting caught; using whatever dubious methods possible to achieve the desired result.

Glycolysis: A process in which glucose is converted to pyruvate to produce energy.

GPS (Global Positioning System): A space-based navigation system that provides location and time information.

Hick's law: Reaction time increases as the number of choices increases.

High socio-economic demographic: A sport played or watched by individuals with high levels of disposable income.

Hooliganism: Acts of vandalism and violence in public places committed especially by youths.

Horizontal component: The horizontal motion of an object.

Horizontal displacement: The shortest distance from the starting point to the finishing point in a line parallel to the ground.

Impulse: Impulse equals force *times* time.

In loco parentis: A Latin phrase which means 'in the place of a parent'. It is the authority parents assign to another responsible adult who will be taking care of their child (e.g. a sports coach at a sports club).

Indirect calorimetry: Measures the production of CO_2 and/or the consumption of O_2.

Indirect calorimetry: The measurement of the amount of heat and energy generated in an oxidation reaction.

Information processing: The methods by which data from the environment are collected and utilised.

Initial conditions: Information from the environment.

Input stage: Information picked up by the senses.

Interaction: The combination of the situational and personality factors that decide the level of achievement motivation.

Internal attribute: Within the performer's control.

Kinesthesis: The inner sense that gives information about body position and muscular tension.

Krebs cycle: A series of cyclical chemical reactions that take place using oxygen in the matrix of the mitochondrion.

Lactate threshold: The point during exercise at which lactic acid quickly accumulates in the blood.

Lateral epicondylitis: The medical term for tennis elbow.

Leader: Someone who has influence in helping others to achieve their goals.

Learned helplessness: Using internal stable reasons for losing.

Leisure: Free time during which individuals can choose what to do.

Lift force: Causes a body to move perpendicular to the direction of travel.

Long-term memory (LTM): Receives information from the working memory and has an unlimited capacity for the storage of motor programmes.

Mass: The quantity of matter the body possesses.

Media: An organised means of communication by which large numbers of people can be reached quickly.

Mental practice: Going over the action in the mind without physical movement.

Mentor: An individual who helps and guides another person's development (e.g. Olympic silver medal-winning diver Leon Taylor acted as a mentor to Tom Daley in the run-up to London 2012 and Rio 2016.)

Merchandising: The practice in which the brand or image from one 'product' is used to sell another (e.g. professional sports performers/teams promote various products including mobile phones, betting companies, etc.).

Metabolic cart: A device which works by attaching headgear to a subject while the person breathes a specific amount of oxygen over a period of time.

Movement time: The time taken to complete the task.

NACH: The need to achieve; approach behaviour. The player welcomes competition.

NAF: The need to avoid failure; avoidance behaviour. The player avoids risk.

National governing body (NGB): An organisation which has responsibility for managing its own particular sport (e.g. England Netball).

Negative deviance: Behaviour that goes against the norms and has a detrimental effect on individuals and society in general.

Negligence: Conduct that falls below a 'reasonable person standard' and leads to a breach of the duty of care, which results in foreseeable harm to another.

Net impulse: A combination of positive and negative impulses.

Non-REM sleep (NREM): Means there is no rapid eye movement. It consists of three stages of sleep which get progressively deeper.

Objective data: Fact-based information which is measurable and usable (e.g. the level achieved on the multi-stage fitness test which links to a VO_2 max score).

Objective sporting situation: The performance takes into account the situation in which the task is being undertaken.

OBLA (onset blood lactate accumulation): The point when lactate levels go above 4 millimoles per litre.

Oedema: A build-up of fluid which causes swelling.

OFCOM: The communications regulator in the UK (e.g. they regulate the television sector).

Outdoor education: Activities which take place in the natural environment and utilise nature/geographical resources such as mountains, rivers, lakes, etc.

Oxygen consumption: The amount of oxygen we use to produce ATP.

Parabola: A curve with matching left- and right-hand sides.

Participation level: An emphasis on taking part recreationally with enjoyment as a key motivator to participate.

Passive stretch: Uses an external force to help the stretched position.

Perceived risk: A challenge that stimulates a sense of danger and adventure for beginners or inexperienced performers in a safe environment, with danger minimised via stringent safety measures (e.g. wearing a safety harness when climbing).

Perception: The process of coding and interpreting sensory information.

Performance accomplishments: What you have achieved already.

Performance analysis (PA): The provision of objective feedback to performers trying to get a positive change in performance. (Feedback can be gained on a variety of performance indicators including the number of passes made; distance run in kilometres; number of shots attempted, etc.)

Performance Pathway Team: A combination of EIS and UK Sport expertise used to identify and develop world-class talent.

Personal qualities: The attributes and personality characteristics of an individual person.

Person-orientated leadership: Concerned with interpersonal relationships.

Phonological loop: Deals with auditory information from the senses and helps produce the memory trace.

Phosphocreatine (PC): An energy-rich phosphate compound found in the sarcoplasm of the muscles.

Plyometrics: Involves repeated rapid stretching and contracting of muscles to increase muscle power.

Positive deviance: Behaviour which is outside the norms of society but with no intent to harm or break the rules. It involves over-adherence to the norms or expectations of society.

Preferred behaviour: What the group wants.

Prescribed leader: Appointed from outside the group.

Proprioceptors: The senses that provide internal information from within the body.

Psychological refractory period: A delay when a second stimulus is presented before the first has been processed.

Qualitative data: Data that is descriptive and looks at the way people think or feel.

Quantitative data: Data that can be written down or measured precisely and numerically.

Radian: The unit of measurement for angles.

Reaction force: This occurs when two bodies are in contact with one another.

Reaction time: The time taken from the onset of a stimulus to the onset of a response.

Recall schema: Initiates movement, comes before the action.

Receptor systems: The senses that pick up information from the display.

Recognition schema: Controls movement, happens during the action.

Reliability: Refers to the degree to which data collection is consistent and stable over time.

Required behaviour: What the situation demands.

Research: A systematic process of investigation and study carried out with the aim of advancing knowledge.

Respiratory exchange ratio (RER): The ratio of carbon dioxide produced compared to oxygen consumed.

Response outcome: Feedback about the result.

Response specifications: Information about what to do.

Response time: The time taken from the onset of a stimulus to the completion of a task. Response time = Reaction time + Movement time.

Resting energy expenditure (REE): The amount of energy, usually expressed in Kcal, required for a 24-hour period by the body during rest.

Restraint of trade: Action that interferes with free competition in a market. In sport, this might involve a clause in a contract which restricts a person's right to carry out their profession.

RICE: Stands for **R**est, **I**ce, **C**ompression, **E**levation.

Ring-fenced: A number of sporting events at national and international level must be available for viewing on terrestrial or free-to-access TV rather than on satellite and subscription channels.

Sarcoplasm: The fluid that surrounds the nucleus of a muscle fibre and is the site where anaerobic respiration takes place.

Scalar quantities: Quantities that just have size.

School Games: Initiative to increase participation in school sport from intra/inter-school level through to county and national levels.

School Sport Partnerships: The creation of increased opportunities for school sport via junior/primary schools working together with secondary schools and further education providers.

Selective attention: Filtering relevant information from irrelevant information.

Self-efficacy: A belief in the ability to master a specific sporting situation.

Self-serving bias: Using external and/or unstable reasons for losing.

Sensory consequences: Information about the feel of the movement.

Sexism: Discrimination on the basis of sex/gender (i.e. whether an individual is male or female).

Simulation: Trying to deceive an official by over-acting, for example, diving to win a free kick.

Smart wearable fitness and sports device: Device that is worn or attached to a performer's body while in use to provide instant feedback on aspects of performance such as distance covered, heart rate, etc.

Socio-economic status: An individual's position in the social structure, which depends on their job, level of income and area they live in.

Soft tissue: Includes tendons, ligaments, muscles, nerves and blood vessels.

Software and hardware: Computer **software** is any set of machine-readable instructions which direct a computer's processor to perform specific operations. Computer **hardware** is the physical component of computers.

Somatic effects of stress: These are physiological.

Spatial anticipation: Where and what is going to happen.

Speed: A measurement in metres/second of the body's movement per unit of time with no reference to direction.

Sponsorship: Provision of funds, money and/or support for a commercial return.

Sporting development continuum: Participation in various forms of physical activity at various stages of development. For example, grass roots 'foundation stage' in primary school PE or 'participation stage' involvement as an adult in physical recreation.

Sports analytics: Studying data from sports performances to try to improve performance.

Sports equity: Fairness in sport; equality of access for all; recognising inequalities in sport and taking steps to address them.

Sports law: The laws, regulations and judicial decisions that govern sports and athletes who perform in them.

Sportsmanship: Conforming to the rules, spirit and etiquette of a sport.

Stable attribute: Unlikely to change in the short-term.

State confidence: A belief in the ability to master a specific sporting moment.

Static stretching: When the muscle is held in a stationary position for ten seconds or more.

Stimulants: Drugs that induce a temporary improvement in mental and physical function (e.g. increase alertness and awareness).

Stimuli: The important and relevant items of information from the display such as the flight of the ball.

Streamlining: Involves shaping a body so it can move as effectively and quickly through a fluid as possible.

Stress: A negative response of the body to a threat causing anxiety.

Subjective data: Based on personal opinion, which is less measurable and often less usable!

Sub-maximal oxygen deficit: When there is not enough oxygen available at the start of exercise to provide all the energy (ATP) aerobically.

Talent identification: The multi-disciplinary screening of athletes in order to identify those with the potential for world-class success.

Task leadership: Concerned with getting results.

Television match official (TMO): Rugby League use a television match official who is a referee who can review plays by looking at TV footage as and when asked to by the on-field referee.

Temporal anticipation: When is it going to happen?

Tetrahydrogestrinone (THG): A banned steroid used to increase power which was tweaked by chemists to make it undetectable by 'normal tests'.

Torque: The rotational consequence of a force.

Trait confidence: A belief in the ability to do well in a range of sports.

Translatory mechanisms: Adapting and comparing coded information to memory so that decisions can be made.

Unstable attribute: Can change in a short amount of time.

Validity: An indication of whether the data collected actually measures what it claims to measure.

Varied practice: Changing the type and content of the practice session.

Vector quantities: Quantities that have size and direction.

Velocity: Measured in metres/second and is the rate of change of displacement.

Verbal persuasion: Encouragement from others.

Vertical component: The upward motion of an object.

Vibration technology: Vibration training/therapy is also known as whole body vibration (WBV) and an example of its usage involves the use of vibration plates to induce exercise effects in the body.

Vicarious experience: Seeing others do the task.

Video motion analysis: A technique used to get information about moving objects from video.

Violence in sport: Physical acts committed to harm others in sports such as American football, rugby, football and ice hockey.

Visuospatial sketchpad: Used to temporarily store visual and spatial information.

VO$_2$ max: The maximum volume of oxygen that can be taken up by the muscles per minute.

WADA (the World Anti-Doping Agency): A foundation created in 1999 through a collective initiative led by the IOC to promote, co-ordinate and monitor the fight against drugs in sport.

Weight: The gravitational force exerted on an object.

Weight: Weight equals mass *times* acceleration due to gravity and is measured in newtons (N).

Whereabouts system: A system designed to support out of competition testing which requires athletes to supply the details of their whereabouts so that they can be located at anytime and anywhere for testing, without advance notice.

Whole Sport Plan: A business plan/document submitted to Sport England outlining national governing body strategies to increase participation and enhance talent in the sport(s) they are responsible for. For the four-year period the Whole Sport Plan is in operation, i.e. 2013–17, £83 million has been allocated to develop talented young athletes.

Working memory: So named since it performs a number of functions.

Index